Horror after 9/11

Horror after 9/11
World of Fear, Cinema of Terror

EDITED BY AVIVA BRIEFEL
AND SAM J. MILLER

University of Texas Press ⟪⟫ *Austin*

Requests for permission to reproduce material from this work should be sent to:
    Permissions
    University of Texas Press
    P.O. Box 7819
    Austin, TX 78713-7819
    www.utexas.edu/utpress/about/bpermission.html

∞ The paper used in this book meets the minimum requirements of ANSI/NISO
Z39.48-1992 (R1997) (Permanence of Paper).

Library of Congress Cataloging-in-Publication Data

Horror after 9/11 : world of fear, cinema of terror / edited by Aviva Briefel and
Sam J. Miller. — 1st ed.
        p.   cm.
Includes bibliographical references and index.
Includes filmography.
ISBN 978-0-292-72662-8 (cloth : alk. paper) — ISBN 978-0-292-73533-0 (e-book)
1. Horror films—History and criticism.   2. Terror in motion pictures.
3. September 11 Terrorist Attacks, 2001—Influence.   I. Briefel, Aviva.
II. Miller, Sam J.   III. Title: Horror after September eleven.
PN1995.9.H6H64   2011
791.43′616409—dc23   2011019055

Contents

Acknowledgments

We are extremely grateful to our contributors and to our editors at University of Texas Press, Jim Burr and Victoria Davis. Aviva would like to give special thanks to her colleagues in the Bowdoin English Department; to her parents; as well as to her friends and inspirations Elisabeth Ford, Monica Miller, Sianne Ngai, and Marilyn Reizbaum. She sends loving thanks to Jonah and Leah, whom she hopes will one day become horror fans, and to David, whom she forgives for disliking the genre. Sam would like to thank his comrades at Picture the Homeless, who provide an object lesson in understanding and resisting real terror every single day—in particular, DeBoRah Dickerson, Lynn Lewis, Nikita Price, Jean Rice, and Tyletha Samuels. And he also thanks his mom, whose own obsession with horror movies got him started early on when she watched *Alien* and *Halloween* while pregnant with him. Finally, to Juancy, whose love for horror movies is just one of the many things that makes him The One.

Introduction

AVIVA BRIEFEL AND SAM J. MILLER

This collection of essays examines the thriving afterlife of horror, a genre whose obituary many critics composed following the events of September 11, 2001. In the darkened-tower issue of the *New Yorker*, Anthony Lane wrote that the day presented "circumstances that Hollywood should no longer try to match."[1] How could American audiences, after tasting real horror, want to consume images of violence on-screen? The omnipresent posttraumatic response of "It was like a movie" seemed to herald the death of a genre that would either remind viewers of catastrophes they wanted to forget or pale in comparison to the terrors of the real thing. Some critics, on the other hand, viewed horror as the perfect medium for re-presenting 9/11 and its aftermath. An October 23, 2001, article from the *New York Times* tried to imagine the forms that horror films would take to adapt to the new global context: "The horror movie is just sitting there waiting to deal with this. . . . It is one of the most versatile genres out there, a universal solvent of virtually any news issue. And it is now perfectly positioned to cop some serious attitude, to play a role where it's not simply a date movie but going further back, to the 1950's, where you have the horror movie as metaphor."[2] Indeed, the horror genre has experienced a dramatic resurgence over the last decade, both from major and independent studios. These films now pervade the box office, attracting A-list talent and earning award nods, while at the same time becoming darker, more disturbing, and increasingly apocalyptic. It is significant that many of them retell stories of 9/11 through visual narratives of horror.

The essays in *Horror after 9/11* examine the allegorical role that the horror film has played in the last ten years. They analyze metaphorical representations of concrete events like the destruction of the World Trade Center, the Iraq War, and the tortures perpetuated at Abu Ghraib and other detention centers; the rise of new subgenres such as "torture porn"; big-budget remakes of classic horror films, as well as the reinvention of traditional monsters (e.g., vampires, B-movie creatures, and zombies); and the new awareness of visual technologies as sites of horror in themselves. Through these various perspectives, we hope to provide new models for interpreting the horror film as an allegorical genre, a "meaning machine"—to borrow Judith Halberstam's term for gothic monsters[3]—that transfigures the "real" into the representational.

In the Clinton years, our national atrocities and military interventions (Somalia, Kosovo) were far away and easy for Americans to overlook, resulting in a lack of urgency in the public debate. The horror genre during this period partook of this national apathy. In fact, in the late 1990s, horror films had largely fallen off the cultural map. The ones that reached theaters were characterized by disengagement and psychological introversion, retreading the fundamental tropes of the genre (imperiled overprivileged teens, predictable monsters, and even more predictable situations). Prime examples are *I Know What You Did Last Summer* (Jim Gillespie, 1997) and its sequels, *Urban Legend* (Jamie Blanks, 1998) and its sequels, *Dracula 2000* (Patrick Lussier, 2000), *Jason X* (James Isaac, 2001), and so on. One of the biggest horror successes of the period, *Scream* (Wes Craven, 1996), was a parody, self-reflexively calling out the clichés of the genre to subvert and then reaffirm them, and its popularity was largely due to just how stagnant and predictable the genre had become. Perhaps in response to *Scream*, other horror examples from this period steered clear of generic conventions. *The Sixth Sense* (M. Night Shyamalan, 1999), for example, went for a distinctly introspective personal-crisis narrative that had more in common with the suburban drama *American Beauty* (Sam Mendes, 1999) than with other horror films of the period. *The Blair Witch Project* (Daniel Myrick and Eduardo Sánchez, 1999) followed a cinema verité aesthetic, rejecting the pyrotechnics that had defined much of the genre. Both of these films shifted their attention from broad political questions to the domain of personal psychology.

If in the late 1990s there seemed to be little at stake in public discourse—one of our greatest concerns was the president's marital fidelity—9/11 ushered in a period that would be framed by the government and the media as one in which the fundamentals of our society and our very existence were threatened ("They hate our freedom"), and in which every government and individual would have to pick a side ("You're either with us or with the terrorists"). Whereas before September 11 it was acceptable to refer to the president as a dim-witted draft dodger whose wealth and connections helped him steal an election (this was the entire premise of the Comedy Central sitcom *That's My Bush!* [Trey Parker and Matt Stone, 2001]), afterward critique and reflexivity were suddenly unacceptable. Susan Sarandon was pilloried for making a peace sign at the 2003 Oscars. Right-wing smear campaigns were launched against Danny Glover for stating that the United States was in no moral position to judge the terrorists because it was the greatest "purveyor of violence" around the world.[4] Pop-country singers the Dixie Chicks were demonized for making mildly critical remarks about the president, with radio stations refusing to play their music and concert attendance dropping dramatically. Two separate wars were being waged; the Patriot Act had granted the executive branch the power to tap our phones and restrict our speech, and immigrants of color were subject to new discriminatory policies. Yet to criticize any of this while in the public eye became career suicide, due in large part to the echo chamber of cable news.

In a context where we could not openly process the horror we were experiencing, the horror genre emerged as a rare protected space in which to critique the tone and content of public discourse. Because they take place in universes where the fundamental rules of our own reality no longer apply—the dead do not stay dead, skyscraper-sized monsters crawl out of the Hudson River, vampires fall in love with humans—these products of popular culture allow us to examine the consequences not only of specific oppressive acts funded by our tax dollars, but also of the entire Western way of life. To list only a few, Danny Boyle's *28 Days Later* (2002) features critiques of vivisection, Bong Joon-ho's *The Host* (2006) takes on environmental practices, and the *Saw* franchise (2004–2010) addresses American apathy and self-satisfaction. Under the mask afforded by their genre, these and other films often generate narratives that are frighteningly timely. As Stephen Prince predicts, "The most significant long-term influence of the terrorist attacks of 9/11, and of the Iraq War that followed, is likely to be found in the provision of new templates for genre filmmaking. The influence here is potentially long-term because the imprinting can be relatively subliminal in ways that do not conflict with or compromise genre appeal and therefore posing less of a threat to box office returns."[5]

In the past few years, a number of books—three of which were written or edited by contributors to this volume—have focused on the horror film's ability to represent national trauma, even though the genre is "rarely considered 'serious' enough to portray traumatic history."[6] Among these is Adam Lowenstein's influential *Shocking Representation*, which examines horror's engagement with trauma in contexts ranging from the Holocaust, to Hiroshima, to 9/11.[7] Linnie Blake's *The Wounds of Nations* begins with the compelling premises that "horror cinema exists at the conjunction of cultural analysis and cultural policy," and that it can "actively discourage an easy acceptance of cohesive, homogenising narratives of identity, national or otherwise, promoting instead a form of encoded/decoded engagement with traumatic events,"[8] which Blake explores in a spectrum of global horror films. Although they do not focus on trauma per se, Steffen Hantke's *American Horror Film* and Ian Conrich's *Horror Zone* both feature essays that address the genre's depiction of recent terrors. Hantke's anthology takes up the scholarly assumption that the horror film has undergone an identity crisis in the last several years; the various pieces examine the implications of this crisis in the new millennium, while "taking inventory of the American horror film at a time of great political turmoil."[9] Despite this American focus, many of the essays examine the horror genre in a transnational context. For its part, Conrich's collection sets plot aside to look at structures that complement the horror genre: amusement park rides, DVD commentaries, websites, costume and set design, and so forth. A number of the essays in his anthology also discuss the various forms of trauma that the horror film has had to address in its many permutations.[10]

Horror after 9/11 takes these scholarly works—and many others—as starting points for its analysis of the genre in a post-9/11 context. Although we recognize that ours is a work in progress, as horror continues to be produced at a dynamic rate, we believe that the decade that has passed since 9/11 offers a useful point of retrospection. Our objective is not to create a homogenous narrative about the genre, suggesting that "post-9/11 horror" is a cohesive category, but rather to appreciate the multiplicity of forms it has taken, and the complexity of stories it has generated about a date that has become coterminous with terror itself. Perhaps not surprisingly, most of the essays do not focus specifically on *the* day itself; instead, they focus on the events' aftershocks, both at home and abroad.

One of the main objectives of this anthology is to challenge and dissect the concept of allegory as it applies to the horror film. We have come to expect that a monster is never just a monster, but rather a metaphor that translates real anxieties into more or less palatable forms. According to a 2005 article from the *Nation*, "Every generation gets the movie monster it deserves. The Depression spawned Frankenstein and Dracula—a victim of modernity and a figment of predatory, shape-shifting capitalism. The nuclear age begat mammoth mutants; the chaotic 1970s produced super psycho-killers; the feminist era inspired hyper-macho crazies and the ultimate patriarchal cannibal, Hannibal Lecter. For reasons that have much to do with the rise of Fortress America, our current creature of choice is the invader from space."[11] While this is a seductive model for understanding the horror film's relationship to the real, its direct-ratio approach to the genre is overly formulaic. The article goes on to examine the rise of science fiction and zombie films—such as

Steven Spielberg's remake of *War of the Worlds* and George Romero's *Land of the Dead*, both released in 2005—as indicative of a growing fear of invasion, but it does not question what it means to create such associations. Must we interpret every zombie, vampire, or alien from a specific era in the same way? Moreover, how can we reconcile the tangible presence of the monster with its often-spectral allegorical meaning? In his instrumental essay on the gothic genre "The Dialectic of Fear," Franco Moretti argues that monsters such as Dracula and Frankenstein's creature must be seen in concrete as well as metaphorical forms: "In the literature of terror . . . the metaphor is no longer a metaphor: it is a character as real as the others. . . . The monster *lives*. Frankenstein's first moment of terror arises precisely in the face of this fact: a metaphor gets up and walks."[12] Treating the monster as a sign that transparently gives way to an ulterior meaning is to overlook the monster's material presence, which is as crucial to the horror film as it is to gothic literature. The essays in this volume consciously seek to address the allegorical *and* concrete manifestations of the monsters that have taken over film screens since 9/11.

It is particularly crucial to consider the dual nature of the monster given that 9/11 has itself been described as an "event" that encompasses both the literal and the symbolic. It represents the very real deaths and destruction that took place on that day and in its aftermath, as well as the day's resounding symbolic import. As Marc Redfield writes, "The event called September 11 or 9/11 was as real as death, but its traumatic force seems nonetheless inseparable from a certain ghostliness, not just because the attacks did more than merely literal damage (that would be true of any event causing cultural trauma) but because the symbolic damage done seems spectral—not unreal by any means, but not simply 'real' either."[13] His reference to the ghostly (informed, perhaps, by the Tribute in Light that towered over Manhattan in the months following 9/11) evokes the relationship between the concreteness of undeniable events and their metaphorical import. The tension inherent in this duality is apparent in the frequency with which critics acknowledge—even if only parenthetically—the unmistakable impact that 9/11 had on real individuals, before going on to explore its symbolic significance. While this tendency can be read as the product of guilty impulses, acknowledgment that suffering and abstraction do not always mix, it also confirms the insistent duality (it's never just a death, or a symbol, but always both) of the events. The horror film monster reminds us of this duality through its own doubled nature as killing and meaning machine.

The particular context of 9/11 also demands a critical rethinking of allegory because it scrambles the relationship between the real and the imaginary. The cinematic resonance of the destruction of the towers provides a bleak version of life imitating art; in Slavoj Žižek's words, "That is the rationale of the often-mentioned association of the attacks with Hollywood disaster movies: the unthinkable which happened was the object of fantasy, so that, in a way, America got what it fantasized about, and that was the biggest surprise."[14] Žižek goes on to discuss the ever-dizzying aspects of this reversal in terms of Hollywood's growing role in shaping reality: after 9/11, the Pentagon commissioned film directors to imagine "possible scenarios for terrorist attacks and how to fight them," while the White House encouraged the film industry to create products that would get "the right ideological message across not only to Americans, but also to the Hollywood public around the globe."[15] The faith that cinematic representation could rewrite the real was also apparent in the smaller-scale operations of filmmakers who edited the towers out of films such as *Serendipity* (Peter Chelsom, 2001), *Zoolander* (Ben Stiller, 2001), and *Spider-Man* (Sam Raimi, 2002), all of which, produced before 9/11, included the World Trade Center in the New York skyline. This strange impulse to alleviate trauma through a technological repetition compulsion conveys the fantasy or nightmare that the towers "were never there to begin with."[16] Under these new circumstances, it becomes difficult—perhaps even impossible—to treat allegory as a one-way representational process.

We thus need new models through which to reconsider the complex relationship between the real and the allegorical in a post-9/11 context. Lowenstein offers one effective strategy in *Shocking Representation*, when he asks us to think of the relationship between horror and real trauma in terms of an "allegorical moment," "a shocking collision of film, spectator, and history where registers of bodily space and historical time are disrupted, confronted, and intertwined."[17] Lowenstein adds to this paradigm in a recent essay, emphasizing the importance of spectatorship in understanding allegory: "The allegorical moment, like any theorized act of spectatorship, can only represent a horizon of possibilities for potential viewer reactions. No physiological sensors or strategic interviews or questionnaire results can ever tell the whole story about a matter as complicated and idiosyncratic as how exactly spectators interact with a film."[18] This model, with its attention to a multiplicity of intersections both on- and off-screen, allows for a more nuanced interpretation of the factors that contribute to political allegory, going beyond a unidirectional transformation of the real into its metaphorical counterpart. Each of the essays in *Horror after 9/11* devises its own strategy for addressing the many valences of allegory.

We borrow the title for the first part of the anthology—"Why Horror?"—from Noël Carroll's oft-cited question about why individuals would "find pleasure in what by nature is distressful and unpleasant."[19] In this case, we use the same question to examine why the genre seems particularly suited to address global, national, and personal trauma after 9/11. Chapter 1, Laura Frost's "Black Screens, Lost Bodies," takes up the issue of visibility as it applies to media and cinematic representations of the terrorist attacks. Frost contrasts the elision of images of death and violence effected in realistic films such as Michael Moore's *Fahrenheit 9/11* (2004) and Paul Greengrass's *United 93* (2006) to the visually graphic reimagining of the events found in the horror films *Mulberry Street* (Jim Mickle, 2006) and *Cloverfield* (Matt Reeves, 2008). By juxtaposing these two representational strategies, she argues for horror's status as a "genre that thrives on what is repressed elsewhere." In the next chapter, "Let's Roll," Elisabeth Ford also examines Greengrass's film, arguing that its "aesthetics of cinematic dispassion" are enabled by conventions drawn from the "body genres" of horror, pornography, and melodrama. Ford contends that the over-the-top Samuel L. Jackson vehicle *Snakes on a Plane* (David R. Ellis and Lex Halaby, 2006) exposes the fictionality of films that seek to establish a transparent relationship to the real. The section concludes with Adam Lowenstein's "Transforming Horror," which discusses David Cronenberg's post-9/11 thrillers, *A History of Violence* (2005) and *Eastern Promises* (2007). According to Lowenstein, these films deploy tropes from the director's earlier horror films, including *Shivers* (1975) and *The Brood* (1979), to develop a new visual vocabulary for representing the "conjuncture of violence and globalized geopolitics."

The second part of the volume closes in on moments in which "Horror Looks at Itself" and reflects on its own themes, technologies, and cultural statuses. Catherine Zimmer's "Caught on Tape?" examines the role of surveillance in torture porn, a subgenre that flourished after September 11 and in the wake of Abu Ghraib. Zimmer discusses the methods through which the *Saw* films (and others in this category) deploy torture and surveillance as mutually reinforcing mechanisms of power. By juxtaposing this popular franchise with Michael Haneke's art-house films—most notably *Caché* (2005)—Zimmer contends that surveillance can also destabilize relations based on visuality and violence. Matt Hills revisits the *Saw* films in his "Cutting into Concepts of 'Reflectionist' Cinema?," focusing on the relationship they claim to the real. He makes the compelling case that these films subvert the one-to-one ratio we often expect of allegory; through their use of "traps," the *Saw* movies "circle thematically around contemporary political controversies, without quite being 'about' them." Homay King's succinctly titled "*The Host* versus *Cloverfield*" also posits that horror conventions often avoid a straightforwardly referential relationship to "true" events. She analyzes these creature features through their condensation of "multiple historical traumas into aggregate, globally resonant visual forms," a strategy that informs us about the representational politics of the horror film more generally. Finally, Aviva Briefel's "Shop 'Til You Drop!" traces the intertextual flashbacks to George Romero's *Dawn of the Dead* (1979) performed by horror films seeking to establish an adversarial relationship to post-9/11 politics. A number of films from the last decade, including *28 Days Later, Dawn of the Dead* (Zack Snyder, 2004), *Land of the Dead* (Romero, 2005), and *The Mist* (Frank Darabont, 2007), reference the blissful scenes of "free shopping" from Romero's 1979 film to try to reconcile their dual status as popular commodities and agents of cultural critique.

"Horror in Action," the last section of the volume, features four case studies of how horror films negotiate the growing conservatism of post-9/11 America. Steffen Hantke analyzes Francis Lawrence's *I Am Legend* (2007) as a "key text of the final period of the Bush years," one whose plot and visual aesthetics herald a return to Cold War–style suspicion and values. The next chapter, Linnie Blake's "'I Am the Devil and I'm Here to Do the Devil's Work," reads Rob Zombie's "hillbilly horror" as a cinematic response to the stifling patriotism of the American War on Terror. The films *House of 1000 Corpses* (2003) and *The Devil's Rejects* (2005) reference 1970s backwoods horror to challenge xenophobic modes of nationalism. In their "'Forever Family' Values," Travis Sutton and Harry M. Benshoff take on the conservative reinvention of the vampire in the novel and film versions of *Twilight* (2005 and 2008, respectively). Drawing from Mormonism, the extremely popular franchise transforms the sexually polymorphous figure of the vampire into a heteronormative icon of monogamy and chastity. The section and volume end with a manifesto of sorts: Sam J. Miller's "Assimilation and the Queer Monster." Miller explores the disappearance of the queer monster (à la Norman Bates from *Psycho* [Alfred Hitchcock, 1960] or Buffalo Bill from *The Silence of the Lambs* [Jonathan Demme, 1991]) in a conservative political climate marked by the normalization of the gay and lesbian movement. He mourns and calls for the return of a monster that, historically, has provided a site of identification for radical queer audiences and that has the potential to radicalize horror cinema itself.

Susan Willis describes post-9/11 America as being "in a popular genre hyperdrive, churning out formulaic fictions in a frenzied attempt to determine who we are and what we're doing. Our historical moment is like a cineplex where every genre is playing simultaneously."[20] This collection is interested in the crucial role that the popular genre of horror has played in this climate of self-evaluation and—in many cases—self-deception. In the process, *Horror after 9/11* attempts to tease out the relationship between horror (as a set of generic conventions) and terror (as the catalyst and response to 9/11); the first tends to be associated with the fictional realm and the other with the real. And yet, as Geoffrey Galt Harpham reminds us, "Terror is a feature of the symbolic order, the vast mesh of representations and narratives both official and unofficial, public and private, in which a culture works out its sense of itself. . . . Terror may or may not be itself symbolic, but its effects are registered in the symbolic domain."[21] For the past decade, the horror film has been translating and reinterpreting the discourses and images of terror into its own cinematic language. These translations are multifarious, unpredictable, and constantly developing, as the open-ended title of our collection suggests. In the coming years, artists, audiences, and critics will continue to rely on horror films as we struggle to put a shape and a face on our most existential fears, so we can drag them out into the sunlight.

NOTES

1. Anthony Lane, "This Is Not a Movie," *New Yorker*, September 24, 2001, http://www.newyorker.com/archive/2001/09/24/010924crci_cinema.

2. Robert J. Thompson quoted in Rick Lyman, "Horrors! Time for an Attack of the Metaphors?; From Bug Movies to Bioterrorism," *New York Times*, October 23, 2001, http://www.nytimes.com/2001/10/23/movies/horrors-time-for-an-attack-of-the-metaphors-from-bug-movies-to-bioterrorism.html.

3. Judith Halberstam, *Skin Shows: Gothic Horror and the Technology of Monsters* (Durham, NC: Duke University Press, 1995), 21.

4. Stacy Jenel Smith and Erick Johnson, "Top 10 Most Outspoken Stars in Hollywood," Netscape, accessed September 8, 2010, http://webcenters.netscape.compuserve.com/celebrity/becksmith.jsp?p=bsf_celebbigmouths.

5. Stephen Prince, *Firestorm: American Film in the Age of Terrorism* (New York: Columbia University Press, 2009), 286.

6. Adam Lowenstein, "Living Dead: Fearful Attractions of Film," *Representations* 110 (Spring 2010): 109.

7. Adam Lowenstein, *Shocking Representation: Historical Trauma, National Cinema, and the Modern Horror Film* (New York: Columbia University Press, 2005).

8. Linnie Blake, *The Wounds of Nations: Horror Cinema, Historical Trauma and National Identity* (Manchester, UK: Manchester University Press, 2008), 3, 14.

9. Steffen Hantke, "Introduction: They Don't Make 'Em Like They Used To: On the Rhetoric of Crisis and the Current State of American Horror Cinema," in *American Horror Film: The Genre at the Turn of the Millennium*, ed. Steffen Hantke (Jackson: University Press of Mississippi, 2010), xxv.

10. Ian Conrich, ed., *Horror Zone: The Cultural Experience of Contemporary Horror Cinema* (London: I. B. Tauris, 2010).

11. Richard Goldstein, "The Naked and the Undead," *Nation*, August 11, 2005, http://krogers-dev.thenation.com/doc/20050829/goldstein.

12. Franco Moretti, *Signs Taken for Wonders: Essays in the Sociology of Literary Forms*, trans. Susan Fischer, David Forgacs, and David Miller (London: Verso, 1983), 105–106.

13. Marc Redfield, "Virtual Trauma: The Idiom of 9/11," *diacritics* 37 (Spring 2007): 56.

14. Slavoj Žižek, *Welcome to the Desert of the Real! Five Essays on September 11 and Related Dates* (London: Verso, 2002), 15–16.

15. Ibid., 16. And, in turn, tapes of the "real" events themselves were "marketed as public entertainment," both in the endless repetition of the falling of the towers on television screens and in the selling of videotapes depicting this destruction. In Yueqing, China, for instance, these tapes were distributed starting on September 14 and, as Peter Hessler describes, were often stocked "on the same racks as the Hollywood movies." Quoted in Richard Schechner, "9/11 as Avant-Garde Art?" *PMLA* 124 (October 2009): 1822.

16. Steven Jay Schneider, "Architectural Nostalgia and the New York City Skyline on Film," in *Film and Television after 9/11*, ed. Wheeler Winston Dixon (Carbondale: Southern Illinois University Press, 2004), 40.

17. Lowenstein, *Shocking Representation*, 2.

18. Lowenstein, "Living Dead," 120.

19. Noël Carroll, *The Philosophy of Horror; or, Paradoxes of the Heart* (New York: Routledge, 1990), 159.

20. Susan Willis, *Portents of the Real: A Primer for Post-9/11 America* (London: Verso, 2005), 7.

21. Geoffrey Galt Harpham, "Symbolic Terror," *Critical Inquiry* 28 (Winter 2002): 573.

PART 1

WHY HORROR?

CHAPTER ONE

Black Screens, Lost Bodies

The Cinematic Apparatus of 9/11 Horror

LAURA FROST

If, reader, you are slow now to believe
what I shall tell, that is no cause for wonder,
for I who saw it hardly can accept it.
DANTE, *INFERNO*

Here, as emergency services groped through the black-and-white fallout
of the vanished towers, and as color drained from the scene, the horror
was new. We couldn't bear to look, and all we did was look.
ANTHONY LANE, "THIS IS NOT A MOVIE"

The medieval Florentine poet Dante Alighieri may seem an odd starting point for a discussion of the representation of 9/11. But to understand the power of visual horror, we can do no better than to consider his *Inferno*, which influenced the artistic depiction of horror for centuries to follow.[1] The audacious premise of Dante's *Divine Comedy* is that the poet is also the poem's main character, who finds himself middle-aged and lost in a dark wood and proceeds to give an eyewitness description of the geography of damnation. In the seventh circle of *Inferno*, the poet and his guide, Virgil, pass through a forest of blackened, gnarled trees. "Look carefully," Virgil instructs Dante, "you'll see such things / as would deprive my speech of all belief," sure that his own reasoned, logical words will fail to convince Dante. Yet seeing fails, too. Dante writes:

> From every side I heard the sound of cries,
> but I could not see any source for them,
> so that, in my bewilderment, I stopped.
> I think that he was thinking that I thought

so many voices moaned among those trunks
from people who had been concealed from us.[2]

Before Dante is able to understand that, according to the ruthless law of *contrapasso* (by which people are given a punishment in hell that fits their particular crime in life), the barren trees were once violent against themselves—suicides—he needs to hear, see, and feel the suffering souls' stories. Seeing here is not necessarily believing or understanding, and visual experience is closely related to problems of cognition.

Dante's imagery is startlingly dramatic and vivid—even anachronistically "cinematic"—and it sets forth some of the most basic principles of horror fiction. *Inferno* demonstrates how gruesome spectacles can operate on many levels at once, as both grippingly literal tales and complex allegories of political, moral, and theological dramas. The body—tortured, transformed—is always at the center of this imagery, both in Dante's elaborate descriptions of the damned and in his own visceral responses (he weeps, faints, and shakes with terror as he is threatened and heckled by the sinners).[3] The sequence of initially failing to see or understand heightens the suspense around discovering the actual scope of the horror. Similarly, the horror film, in its classic forms, is structured around withholding, as the monster or fiend initially leaves spectators gaping and wondering, in epistemic confusion. The horror film pays particular attention to the dread and disbelief of the viewer, which precedes the revelation of the beast, maniac, or whatever the menace may be. J. P. Telotte, adopting a phenomenological approach to horror film, alerts us to how the genre highlights the very process of seeing: it "calls our attention to the way in which we perceive its horrors and underscores that manner of seeing with specific imagery of a failed or improper vision."[4] Dennis Giles also proposes that "delayed, blocked, or partial vision" is "central to the strategy of horror cinema,"[5] and that it is essential to the genre's means of building suspense, which is typically resolved, like Dante's narrative, with the revelation of the shocking spectacle that has produced such fear and confusion.

This drama of the discrepancy between the spectacle and its meaning, seeing and believing, vision and cognition, underpins fictions of horror. But the dynamic is not limited to the realm of fiction. It was a constitutive part of the way the events of 9/11 were seen, understood, and experienced, and how they were represented in mainstream media. As I will explain here, images from that day were disseminated through a combination of repetitive spectacle and obfuscation that created epistemic confusion. Mainstream representations of 9/11 constructed a particular relationship between spectacle and viewer, presenting selected elements of the events while withholding others. Although this mode was meant to protect people from the most upsetting images of 9/11 devastation, the strategy resulted in representations that remain stalled in the preliminary stage of suspense and confusion.

"I can't believe what I'm seeing."

This utterance appeared to be a reasonable response to what happened in Manhattan on the morning of September 11, 2001. As one plane and then another crashed into buildings so high that the sky itself seemed to hang from them, and as people jumped from these burning buildings to their deaths shortly before one edifice and then the other crumbled to the ground, all 220 floors, disbelief was an entirely appropriate reaction.

In the face of such shocking scenes, the impulse to analogize was almost immediate. For most people, 9/11 was so out of the range of typical experience that there was no clear framework in which it could be assimilated. These analogies were a cognitive effort to integrate 9/11 into the order of things by establishing a collective, public understanding of the events and bringing it out of its seeming singularity into a larger frame of reference and historical precedent.[6] For those who were watching 9/11 unfold on television, as well as those who were in downtown Manhattan that morning, the most common comparison made was to action movies, such as *Die Hard* (John McTiernan, 1988), *Independence Day* (Roland Emmerich, 1996), *Escape from New York* (John Carpenter, 1981), *Armageddon* (Michael Bay, 1998), and *The Towering Inferno* (John Guillermin, 1974).[7]

The action film analogy, however, did not have lasting traction. While the events themselves—crashing planes and collapsing buildings—were reminiscent of action films, the mood in New York and in the nation became much more psychological and internal, shifting to the more insidious and subtle dynamics of paranoia and dread. This change was embodied by the difference between planes colliding with buildings and mysterious anthrax terrorism. This new psychological landscape was less appropriate to action films and more to horror films, which center on the drama of the unknown and the unreal.

If September 11 looked like cinema, it was then ironic that cinema started to look like September 11. Films of many different genres began to explore the disaster, explicitly or indirectly, including drama (*World Trade Center* [Oliver Stone, 2006], *The Great New Wonderful* [Danny Leiner, 2005], *25th Hour* [Spike Lee, 2002]); the buddy movie (*Reign over Me* [Mike Binder, 2007]); and even comedy (*Postal* [Uwe Boll, 2007] and *Sarah Silverman: Jesus Is Magic* [Liam Lynch, 2005]) and romantic comedy (*Love Actually* [Richard Curtis, 2003]). 9/11 imagery was quickly absorbed into the lexicon of horror and suspense. Many horror films of the past five years allude to 9/11 with varying degrees of complexity, including *The Omen* (John Moore, 2006), which uses images of 9/11 in its opening sequence to set a particular tone, and M. Night Shyamalan's *The Happening* (2008), which shows construction workers committing suicide by throwing themselves off a building near Central Park. Critics were skeptical of any film using 9/11 imagery, and even more critical of horror films that did so.[8]

As others have noted, there has been a recent proliferation of horror films about zombies, killer viruses, and urban apocalypses since 2001, and these films can be read as metaphorical commentaries on the political climate in the United States following 9/11.[9] Given horror film's history of engaging—however perversely—contemporary sources of fear, anxiety, and political strife, it is not surprising to see this genre responding to 9/11. It has become routine to read horror as an allegorical response to political anxieties (e.g., the Cold War, Vietnam, the Reagan Era),[10] and critics have paid increasing attention to horror films responding to national trauma.[11] We expect horror to play the role of provocateur: the genre that will go where no genre has gone before, however taboo.

What interests me is not so much the story of horror films behaving as we would expect, but rather in pointing out a specific contrast between the manner in which the events of 9/11 were disseminated and represented in mainstream media and horror film's way of approaching the spectacle. Carol Clover asserts that horror film is "not only the form that most obviously trades in the repressed, but [is] itself the repressed of mainstream filmmaking."[12] Insofar as the treatment of 9/11 in horror films is grounded in mainstream representations of the events, my exploration of horror films hinges on a detailed analysis of how news sources as well as documentary and "art" films narrate 9/11. I will argue that horror films point to the strategies of mainstream representation of 9/11 that are meant to protect the audience but which, in fact, present cognitive problems that have not yet been solved.

While many of the other essays in this anthology are interested in exploring the tendency of horror film to eschew literal in favor of metaphorical means of representation, I will primarily investigate films that take a literal approach to September 11—that is, films that directly address the events in New York, including Paul Greengrass's *United 93* (2006), Oliver Stone's *World Trade Center*, Michael Moore's *Fahrenheit 9/11* (2004), and Gédéon and Jules Naudet's *9/11* (2002).

Though radically different in their style and approach, all these films share common visual strategies in their representation of the events in Manhattan on September 11. I will consider how certain elements of their cinematic apparatus—audio tracks, POV shots, handheld camerawork, and, most strikingly, black screens—are deployed to figure particular aspects of September 11 as unrepresentable, and how the films offer common thematic substitutions (heroic firefighters, wondering witnesses, and burning buildings) for human casualties. Subsequently, I will examine two horror films, *Cloverfield* (Matt Reeves, 2008) and *Mulberry Street* (Jim Mickle, 2006), which, while offering very different approaches to narrating 9/11, both point to what is elided in mainstream representations of that day and suggest what is at stake in such elision.

FADE TO BLACK: TRAUMATIC NARRATIVE

What's immediately noticeable about most 9/11 representation to date—both fiction and nonfiction—is its emphasis on narratives of redemption, bravery, noble sacrifice, dignified human connection, and, above all, heroism. Films such as *Flight 93* (Peter Markle, 2006), *United 93*, *Saint of 9/11* (Glenn Holsten, 2006), and *World Trade Center* participate in narrating the events of loss and destruction as stories of human courage, community, and dignity. Of course, the heroic acts of 9/11 should be applauded, but the disproportionate emphasis on those stories should give one pause. In his *Village Voice* review of *World Trade Center*, J. Hoberman addressed this tendency: "The key to converting disaster into entertainment is uplift. . . . By focusing on two of the 20 people pulled alive from the pile that crushed some 2,700, . . . spectators can invest their emotions in the handful of individuals miraculously chosen to survive the disaster rather than the overwhelming anonymous multitude who perished."[13] What do we lose if "uplift" is the requisite slant of 9/11 representation—that is, if the lens is trained on the heroic exception rather than more upsetting but perhaps more representative events? Even a film such as Michael Moore's documentary *Fahrenheit 9/11*, which positions itself as staunchly critical of the status quo, averts its eyes from significant parts of 9/11.

The memorable opening credit sequence of *Fahrenheit 9/11* shows Bush, Cheney, Rice, Powell, and Wolfowitz getting made up for television appearances. The screen goes black for one minute, during which, after a few seconds of silence, we hear the roar of a plane engine, a crash, screams, and sirens. The first image that follows the darkness is a shot of panicked, weeping pedestrians. As bells toll, a sequence of images shows people looking up, reacting, and crying, interspliced with brief shots of debris flying through the air. The Trade Center ruins appear only briefly in the background of a couple of shots.

Three minutes in, Moore's narration begins with the following voice-over: "On September 11, 2001, nearly 3,000 people, including a colleague of mine, Bill Weems, were killed in the largest foreign attack ever on American soil."

Some critics found the black screen admirable for its restraint; some thought it was all the more powerful for requiring the viewer to imagine the accompanying spectacle. Others saw the gesture as manipulative.[14] Moore's abandonment of direct representation is particularly striking given his personal approach to documentary: didactic, polemical, and strongly dependent on voice-overs. Whatever we think of Moore's black screen, it must be read in relation to the unique circumstances of the dissemination of 9/11 imagery.

Most people experienced September 11 as a visual event. The planes crashing, the buildings collapsing, the blanket of gray ash that cast the city into darkness, and the smoking wreckage afterward were the dominant images through which the events were witnessed. At the same time that the media inundated viewers with certain images, primarily the towers burning and crumpling and the rescue and cleanup efforts of firefighters and police officers, some of the most striking and upsetting images of the day were quickly censored. It could be argued that the parts of 9/11 that could not be seen—could not be witnessed—are equally important and more haunting. There is almost no visual record of the loss of human life during 9/11. "Images of corpses, body parts, and human gore were absent from the coverage following the events," Barbie Zelizer notes in her article on 9/11 reportage.[15] Those who died on the hijacked planes could not be seen. Those who died in the collapsing towers were only glimpsed in photographs taken with a telephoto lens. The human remains that did survive intact did not appear in newspapers or on television. Zelizer notes a single example of a photograph in the *Daily News* of a severed hand. This absence of damaged bodies and death was echoed in the "Missing" posters throughout Manhattan, frequently shown by the media, which gesture toward absence rather than death.[16]

One striking example of the erasure of bodily damage from 9/11 is the people falling from the WTC, who were the most visible victims of the disaster in New York City. Their very public deaths registered as especially dreadful. Two weeks after September 11, Anthony Lane wrote in the *New Yorker* that "the most important, if distressing, images to emerge from those hours are not of the raging towers, or of the vacuum where they once stood; it is the shots of people falling from the ledges."[17] Psychological studies after 9/11 singled out the witnessing of falling people—live or on TV (some people were traumatized by images they did not witness firsthand)—as a major predictor of PTSD. This, of the many upsetting images from the day, had a lasting traumatic effect on some viewers.[18] Arguably, the traumatic impact of these images was exacerbated by the way they were presented in the media. Live video footage and photographs appeared briefly on TV and in newspapers, but the images were then immediately taken out of circulation and continued to be carefully edited from most retrospective coverage of 9/11 in the United States.[19] In his *Esquire* essay on "The Falling Man," Tom Junod discusses how footage of the falling bodies was driven from mainstream American news sources into more obscure channels, such as Internet sites that traffic in sensational and pornographic material: "In a nation of voyeurs, the desire to face the most disturbing aspects of our most disturbing day was somehow ascribed to voyeurism, as though the jumpers' experience, instead of being central to the horror, was tangential to it, a sideshow best forgotten."[20] Casting the desire to see as a pathology (i.e., voyeurism) not only insinuates that there is something shameful and disrespectful about the impulse, but also that the desire itself can only—and should only—be addressed in "low" forms.

"Low" or "disreputable" is exactly how the American horror film has historically been characterized, and Robin Wood suggests that it is precisely this debased cultural position that allows the genre to respond "in the most clear-cut and direct way" to content that is otherwise repressed.[21] One major category of repressed imagery that Wood does not account for in his anatomy of the American horror film is death. The furor around the beheading videos of Daniel Pearl and others, and photographs that show American soldiers' bodies in unheroic postures, for example, demonstrate that such imagery is subject to repression both for civilians and for the military.[22] Given the conditions of representation, we can read this migration of images of 9/11 death to "fringe" or "alternative" media as something of an invitation to genres such as horror.

The media offered a number of visual substitutions for death imagery. One of the most prominent was the heroic firefighter. Many witnesses and oral histories of 9/11 insist that the images that "haunted" them, as Art Spiegelman puts it in his graphic memoir *In the Shadow of No Towers*, were those of falling bodies: these became psychologically iconic.[23] But the images that became culturally iconic were those of the rescue workers, and most principally, Thomas E. Franklin's photograph of three firefighters raising the American flag in the wreckage of Ground Zero, which became a U.S. postage stamp. In other historical traumas, the physical traces of bodies (shoes and hair, for example) have been an important part of mourning, as they invoke individual people instead of symbolic, abstract entities. The point is not that the gruesome details of the deaths should be dwelled on, but rather that there is a need to see the more concrete, bodily dimension of the disaster acknowledged and reflected in representation. The memento mori that we have for 9/11 do not address human death.

When devastation is shown, it is usually expressed as architectural obliteration. The burning towers, as Zelizer notes, "displaced the bodies that might have been visualized instead."[24] Another strategy of substitution is demonstrated by Moore's film. In the days after the falling people were removed from American newspapers and television, there was a notable shift to footage of bystanders responding to the carnage, which was not itself shown.[25] Images of thunderstruck, wondering spectators were enlisted, like the images of brave firefighters and falling buildings, to shift the collective gaze away from the awful facts of bodies torn apart, disintegrated, and destroyed: signs of a vulnerable nation.

The phenomenon of the "disappearing" falling bodies—shockingly present one day and conjured away the next—and the ensuing confusion around their meaning echo the structure of trauma: an event not fully cognized in the moment, so that it must be returned to later. In PTSD, Cathy Caruth writes, "the pathology consists . . . solely in the *structure of its experience* or reception: the event is not assimilated or experienced fully at the time, but only belatedly, in its repeated *possession* of the one who experiences it. To be traumatized is precisely to be possessed by an image or event."[26] The suppression or censorship of particularly awful images, which was intended to protect viewers from being traumatized, in fact reinforced the traumatic structure of the events. This is illustrated by the production of so many narratives about 9/11 that are formally structured as a traumatic event, circling around a representational absence. Characterized by aporia, disavowal, and fragmentation, traumatic narratives compulsively return to whatever has not been understood or assimilated, and either represent it in a distorted, evasive way, or elide it entirely.[27]

Just so, the black screen in *Fahrenheit 9/11* represents September 11 as a bodiless trauma. The imaginative reenactments in A&E's drama *Flight 93* and Paul Greengrass's *United 93* both show some elements of the passengers' drama, but they are reticent about depicting real human casualties. At the moment that *United 93* is about to show the crash that actually killed the passengers and the hijackers, a scene that would undermine the film's heroic thrust, the screen goes black.[28]

Heroic firefighters, collapsing buildings, gaping spectators, and black screens were the main tropes of mainstream representations of 9/11, and specifically the images that were substituted for human devastation. The film that epitomizes this strategy—and which proved curiously influential for one horror film's response to 9/11—is Gédéon and Jules Naudet's *9/11*. The Naudets' original mandate was to make a documentary about a rookie fireman at Engine 7, Ladder 1, on Duane Street in New York, placing the film exactly at the center of the heroic 9/11 narrative (the firefighters' story). The filmmakers are busy capturing the life of men in the firehouse when they are blindsided by 9/11. In a scene that could have been scripted in Hollywood, there is a nighttime sequence just before September 11 showing the fire chief talking to the new recruit, with the WTC glittering menacingly behind them: "Tunnel vision," he instructs his apprentice. "That's what's gonna keep you alive and give you the opportunity to help anybody else."

The brothers are separated early in the day, and each shoots his own video. Jules, by astounding chance, happened to train his camera on the first plane colliding with the North Tower; he races downtown with the company to the scene. The film has a substantial amount of footage of the burning and collapsing buildings; its preface highlights this feature, declaring that it includes "THE ONLY KNOWN FOOTAGE FROM INSIDE TOWER I—AN EYEWITNESS ACCOUNT OF ONE OF THE MOST DEFINING MOMENTS OF OUR TIME." The camera work is foregrounded throughout the film, and particularly in two of its most dramatic moments: two black screen sequences. The first occurs when Jules is in the lobby of Tower 1 with members of the fire company as the tower collapses. He runs in the concourse with the firefighters, his camera still recording, and debris starts to fall as the lens goes black. The story resumes as the light comes up and the camera, through a lens covered in dust, captures moving figures in the dark space. Jules uses his camera floodlight to help the firefighters navigate in the gloom. Here the POV shot, which typically reflects the perspective of a protagonist or a sympathetic character (except, markedly, in horror, where films such as *Halloween* [John Carpenter, 1978], *Friday the 13th* [Sean Cunningham, 1980], and *The Silence of the Lambs* [Jonathan Demme, 1991] exploit the POV of the psychopath), becomes a technical part of the rescue effort. This turn of events only makes more explicit the assumption behind the Naudets' approach to 9/11. Not only is the camera, by aligning itself with the firefighters' POV, a vehicle for their heroic story, but it is also literally a beacon of light.

Meanwhile, the other Naudet, Gédéon, is standing with a group of stunned firefighters "in the shadow of Tower One" when it falls. Running with his camera, as it records his bumpy trajectory, suddenly Gédéon and the camera fall to the ground. The air gets progressively darker and grittier, and we hear whistling air. Papers blow up against the camera lens, rustling, as feathery bits of debris alight on the camera. After a period of darkness, outlines of objects start to emerge through the sepia lens: a car, a tree, ground covered in a heavy, gray blanket of debris. Both scenes of dropped cameras are moments in which the image reasserts itself out of the darkness as a miraculous assertion of life against all odds.[29]

The neat way in which the black screen scenes are incorporated into the film's heroic narrative raises the question of what does not fit so neatly or, as Susan Sontag urges us to ask of all photography, what is not being shown.[30] The dropped Handycam scenes—accidental moments—imply that the filmmakers are delivering raw footage and showing us everything, but this makes all the more striking what the Naudets do not show: bodies. We see large expanses of rubble-strewn streets but no signs of fatalities, with one notable exception: a scene of firefighters carrying the body of the FDNY chaplain Mychal Judge (the "Saint of 9/11"), the composition of which strongly resembles Christ being carried from the Cross.

Thirty-nine minutes into the film, Jules Naudet is in the lobby of one of the towers with the fire chiefs and there is a loud thudding sound. As in Moore's film, the falling bodies are heard but not seen. Instead, we see reaction shots of the firefighters and pedestrians and formal interviews with the firefighters and Jules himself explaining how terrible the noise was: "Every thirty seconds that same crashing sound would resonate throughout the lobby. It is probably the thing that will stay with me always, the realization that every time I heard this sound, it was a life that was gone."[31] The representation of the scene in the lobby does accurately reflect Jules's dominant impression, which was aural; but even the sound of bodies striking the ground was later edited to decrease its impact and imply that there were fewer "jumpers" than there actually were.[32]

It must have taken a true feat of editing to remove most visual signs of death from the film, even as otherwise the Naudets are at pains to reflect a gritty realism. The omission of damaged bodies is not presented as a deliberate, stylized effect; rather, it operates according to the same kind of discretionary censorship that characterized mainstream news reportage. *Time* magazine praised the Naudets for their restraint: "Jules recalls that as soon as he entered the lobby, he saw two people fleeing the building, engulfed in flames, but he chose not to tape them. 'I saw that horrible image,' he remembers, 'and I thought, "Well, maybe this is censorship, but I don't think anyone should see this."'"[33]

What does it mean for a film to show nothing?[34] While the black screen is often used in documentaries to reflect footage of an event that was not filmed or to allow the audience to imagine a scene rather than see it, the consistent black screens in 9/11 films are paradoxical, given what otherwise seems like a bombardment of prescribed imagery. Although the black screens in *Fahrenheit 9/11*, *United 93*, and *9/11* function differently, they all imply that the bodily, human destruction of 9/11 at the center of the events must not be shown.

"WHERE WERE *YOU* WHEN THE *CLOVERFIELD* MONSTER HIT?"

If we think of horror film as a genre that thrives on what is repressed elsewhere, mainstream representations of 9/11, which were so openly constructed to protect the viewer from upsetting imagery and, less openly, to maintain a heroic narrative tone, seem like obvious candidates for the "horror treatment." The Naudet documentary, hailed as a masterful representation of 9/11, has the curious distinction of having appeared to be a key influence on one of the more direct responses to 9/11 in horror film: Matt Reeves's *Cloverfield*. Upon its release, Anthony Lane decreed that the film marked a shift in the treatment of 9/11, arguing that the "real story of 'Cloverfield' is that of a major studio biding its time—more than six years—before breaking cover and forging a blockbuster from the fear that was born on 9/11."[35] Roger Ebert agreed that *Cloverfield* demonstrates that "the statute has run out on the theory that after 9/11 it would be in bad taste to show Manhattan being destroyed. So explicit are the 9/11 references in *Cloverfield* that the monster is seen knocking over skyscrapers, and one high-rise is seen leaning against another."[36]

Bad taste is what *Cloverfield* is all about. The film's poster shows a decapitated Statue of Liberty pointing toward an ominous path cut through both the water and smoking, torn buildings in lower Manhattan. "Some Thing Has Found Us," the poster warns. An homage to John Carpenter's *Escape from New York*, with Lady Liberty's head lodged in a Manhattan street, the image also reads like a parody of a *United 93* poster, which features a similar shot of the statue and Manhattan on the verge of invasion by plane. Within the initial twenty minutes, *Cloverfield*'s first major special effect is the Statue of Liberty's head careening into the street like a bowling ball, making a sight gag out of the common post-9/11 anxiety that the statue would be attacked (it was closed to tourists and heavily guarded for months after September 11). The spectacle, so excessive in its literalization of symbolism and its spoof on the discretion with which other 9/11 films avoid showing human dismemberment, signals that *Cloverfield* is "horror satire": this is *Attack of the Killer Tomatoes!* (John De Bello, 1978) territory.[37]

Like the immediate drama of September 11, *Cloverfield*'s action is short and compressed, set primarily in the streets of New York over the course of one night. Its main conceit is its cinema verité style, ostensibly shot by a

FIGURE 1.1. Cloverfield *poster (Paramount, 2008).*

FIGURE 1.2. United 93 *poster (Universal, 2006).*

Handycam in real time. (As Carol Clover observes, "Horror movies rub our noses in camerawork.")[38] The film begins with a leader from a digital video found by U.S. Department of Defense: "Camera retrieved at incident site 'US-447.' Area formerly known as Central Park." The Handycam is held by several characters at various times, including the main character, Rob, who used the camera a month before to shoot a trip to Coney Island with his one-time lover, Beth. Snippets of this footage appear whenever there is a pause in the monster story, which is palimpsestically recorded over the romantic tryst. These camera techniques—and their studied artlessness—are meant to establish narrative authenticity. Sontag observes that "pictures of hellish events seem more authentic when they don't have the look that comes from being 'properly' lighted and composed, because the photographer either is an amateur or—just as serviceable—has adopted one of several familiar anti-art styles. By flying low, artistically speaking, such pictures are thought to be less manipulative."[39] *Flight 93* also adopts this style of camera work to show the drama of its heroic passengers' revolt.

While *Cloverfield* is heavily indebted to *The Blair Witch Project* (Daniel Myrick and Eduardo Sánchez, 1999), it is also strikingly close in many ways to the Naudet documentary, both in its imagery and, above all, its style. Scenes of groups of people panicking, streets filling with rolling clouds of dust, buildings collapsing, and people running for their lives and taking refuge in stores and under cars, are all shot in the same bumpy, out-of-focus style as *9/11*. There even seems to be a couple of direct quotes of the Naudets' film in this flippant monster movie.[40]

Cloverfield begins with a going-away party in downtown Manhattan for Rob, a twenty-something who is about to leave for a job in Japan. Out on the fire escape, Rob's brother is giving him a "deep" lecture about how to treat people: "It's about moments, man, that's all that matters. You gotta learn to say forget the world and hang onto the people you care about the most." Uncannily close to the "tunnel vision" speech in the Naudets' film, which immediately precedes September 11, no sooner is the soppy sentiment spoken than there is a tremendous jolt and the lights in the surrounding buildings flicker and go out. The cameraman, Hud, races to join the screaming people at the party. When the chaos outside continues, the group hurtles into the street.

This early sequence (before Lady Liberty loses her head) conjures up many elements of the 9/11 experience: confusion, panic, the search for a working cell phone, and groups of people moving uptown or across the Brooklyn Bridge, debating where to go and what was happening. Shots of smoke clouds that darken the air are, as Roger Ebert notes, "unmistakable evocations of 9/11." TV reports broadcast "Panic in Manhattan," "Lower Manhattan is in an absolute state of siege," and "Military mobilized as thousands flee city." There is a "lockdown," and the tunnels leading out of the city are sealed. Here, *Cloverfield* touches very closely on the claustrophobia and escalation of the real 9/11 experience in Manhattan. The seemingly illogical premise of *Cloverfield*—that the characters keep the camera recording through life-threatening danger—was made more plausible by the copious amount of photography and film footage from September 11 shot in the middle of the attack, and the ubiquitous image of people wielding their camera phones in that footage. *Cloverfield* also captures the vertigo of characters watching news programs reporting the events that are unfolding around them. At one point, the characters retreat to an electronics store, where looters are stopped in their tracks by the images on the televisions there. The sensation of being caught up in events that are already news, but which are no more comprehensible for it, was a disorienting effect of experiencing September 11 from downtown Manhattan. Even Stephanie Zacharek, who otherwise panned the film at Salon.com, observes, "*Cloverfield* harnesses the horror of 9/11—specifically as it was felt in New York."[41] The effect is achieved both through the imagery and the camera work, which cannot be thought about apart from the amateur films of 9/11, the amateur photographs that were featured in nationwide exhibitions such as *Here Is New York: A Democracy of Photographs* (2001), and the Naudets' documentary.

Unlike *Blair Witch*, where the tension never lets up precisely because we never see the threat itself, the claustrophobic tension of *Cloverfield* dissipates as soon as the morphologically perplexing monster and its crayfish-like babies show up. It's frankly a relief to be delivered from a simulation of 9/11 into the fake terror of a monster movie. We see, in fact, too much of the monster, in ways that make it excessively concrete. There's no real tension about when the monster will appear; like a bull in the china shop of Manhattan, it seems to be bumbling everywhere at once. Somehow, the film manages to make the monster both completely unexplained ("If you're watching this film, you know more about it than I do," Rob says in his last recorded statement) and un-mysterious. The monster is, in a way, beside the point. The film's real interest is in its own camera work.

Its most "authentic" moments—shot from the POV of the terrorized characters—include two scenes in which the Handycam falls to the ground and goes black. The first occurs early in the film, when Hud, *Cloverfield*'s main cinematographer, fumbles the camera in a bodega while hiding from the monster. The second, more significant scene, is at the end of the film, when Rob and Beth huddle under a Central Park bridge after the monster has killed Hud. In the face of their friend's death and their own terror, they have the presence of mind to recover his camera. They quiveringly record their last words, à la *Blair Witch*: "I don't know why this is happening," Beth cries. There is an explosion and the camera falls to the ground, boulders and debris occlude the lens, and the screen goes black, giving way to a final scene of the lovers at Coney Island recorded a month earlier. For a film that is, if anything, excessively demonstrative, the black screen here seems to serve a more calculated purpose. Perhaps it spares us seeing the deaths of Rob and Beth as boulders crush them, but it also leaves Reeves room to reprise them in a possible sequel. Indeed, at the very end of the film, following the credits, a voice breathes, "It's still alive."

Cynically humorous and cheekily derivative, *Cloverfield* turns the conventional representation of 9/11 inside out through parody. The original Naudet POV, aligned with those of the firefighters, is rendered irrelevant in *Cloverfield*: police and military authorities have set up headquarters in Bloomingdale's, where their main task seems to be exploding people who have been bitten by the monster's babies. Otherwise, they are peripheral to the action. The black screen of reticence seems pretentious and meaningless in a film that operates through visual excess.

The parody continues, inadvertently or not, in the publicity apparatus around *Cloverfield*. Its producer J. J. Abrams released a statement about the film's purpose: "We live in a time of great fear. Having a movie that is about something as outlandish as a massive creature attacking your city allows people to process and experience that fear in a way that is incredibly entertaining and incredibly safe."[42] The notion of *Cloverfield* as a kind of prophylactic to fear is preposterous. The terms Abrams uses — "process" and "experience" — are strikingly psychological, offering up the film as a therapeutic device. While some film critics credit horror films with a similarly cathartic, productive, or constructive purpose, this line of argument domesticates — or defangs — the unsettling power of horror.[43] Closer to the spirit of horror film, critics such as Steven Shaviro, Carol Clover, and Linda Williams maintain that the pleasure of horror, as Judith Halberstam puts it, "often resides in abjection, loss, revulsion, dread, and violence."[44] Shaviro reminds us that "fearfulness is itself a thrill and a powerful turn-on, as any devotee of horror films knows."[45]

While *Cloverfield* does initially imitate the fearful conditions of 9/11, catharsis is not its goal. Indeed, the film's website continues to play 9/11 as a gag. Paramount initiated a competition inviting viewers to send in footage in response to the question "Where Were *YOU* When the *Cloverfield* Monster Hit?" Taking up the refrain that became popular after JFK's death, and which subsequently became a much-asked question about people's 9/11 experiences, *Cloverfield* manages to conflate two historical traumas and make both equivalent to a monster movie. The film renders the idea of trauma itself as a game. Far from reinscribing 9/11 as unrepresentable, *Cloverfield* simulates disastrous conditions quite elaborately, but in the very excess of spectacle it renders trauma irrelevant and eschews the psychological depth that trauma requires. Too literal to be repressed, too glib to be traumatic, *Cloverfield* does derail the typical way of representing 9/11. The film inadvertently demonstrates how mainstream representation's consistent devices—its focus on heroism and its respectful black screens—are so dislocated from the real trauma of human devastation that they function as well for a *Godzilla* revival as they do for the real deaths of thousands of people.

THE "AL-A-GORY" OF *MULBERRY STREET*

If *Cloverfield* represents one tradition of horror filmmaking—horror satire—then I want to conclude by discussing a different tradition in which horror involves a more serious cultural reckoning. *Mulberry Street* is an independent "rat-zombie" film directed by Jim Mickle that brings 9/11 imagery into the tradition of classic horror films such as *Night of the Living Dead* (George Romero, 1968). Of all of the films considered here—including *Fahrenheit 9/11*, *9/11*, and *Cloverfield*—*Mulberry Street* is the most conventional in its filmmaking, and yet it stands most clearly in contradiction to mainstream representation of 9/11.

The film's first frames show urban rooftops at dawn, followed by a shot of the Staten Island Ferry moving toward Manhattan and then one of the Statue of Liberty, vividly green in the morning sun, seen from the perspective of the protagonist, Clutch, who is fishing in the river. As in *Cloverfield*, the Statue of Liberty alludes to a host of earlier horror, action, and suspense films shot before September 11, and it also invokes the national and political narratives associated with that quintessentially American landmark after September 11. Here, given the film's attention to class, it also echoes the opening of *Working Girl* (Mike Nichols, 1988), with its sweeping shots of Ellis Island, the World Trade Center, and Manhattan, as symbols of promise for individual freedom and class advancement—all the better to show the gruesome collapse of those promises. *Mulberry Street*'s point of view could be said to be that of a hypothetical working-class, Lower East Side Manhattan pedestrian; scenes are shot in a naturalistic fashion, through windows, framed and occasionally blocked by signposts, cars, people, and other urban obstacles to vision. The

FIGURE 1.3. *Clutch and Lady Liberty (* Mulberry Street, *After Dark Films, 2006).*

opening shot of the Statue of Liberty, for example, is occluded by a blurry dark form, which turns out to be Clutch's arm on the railing of the Battery Park City esplanade.

The film follows Clutch as he jogs through lower Manhattan, the area most affected by September 11. He passes the fenced-in site of Ground Zero, which is covered with signs describing the plans for the area's rebuilding. As he runs north through SoHo, the camera cuts to the cover of *NY News Daily*: "Crome Wins Bid to Develop Lower Manhattan: Hundreds Face Eviction." The slogan of Crome Development, we read on a billboard, is "The Neighborhood Is Changing," flanked by a tall, gleaming, multistory office building. A quick shot of the giant inflatable rats that unions set up around the city in front of picket lines is a visual joke, which is then followed by a shot of menacing, greenish rats congregating under the street. Crome or the critters: who is the real rat? Over the course of a day and night, these vermin spread their evil contagion throughout the city, turning people into aggressive, flesh-eating killers. The film focuses on the inhabitants of a Lower East Side building on Mulberry Street that has just been bought by Crome Development. This narrative frame references the real-estate battle that followed the destruction of the World Trade Center, as developers such as Larry Silverstein forged ahead with plans for commercial space while residential advocacy groups clamored for more affordable housing in a city that was (and is) edging out working-class people like those who live on Mulberry Street, including Clutch.

While *Cloverfield*'s downtown Manhattan is essentially a "green screen" set for special effects, *Mulberry Street* features shots of local bars, streets, and intimate scenes of daily life in the city. Amid this quotidian calm, however, there are cues that allude to PTSD. At a loud rumbling of a plane engine, characters freeze; the camera lingers on low-flying helicopters and the clear blue sky that has become a trope in 9/11 representation (and a sight that many people in Manhattan associated with 9/11 long after the events of that day). The contagion, spreading southward from Harlem, is tracked by media updates that strike familiar 9/11 notes: first one subway shuts down after a rat attack, and then all subway service ceases, stranding people and forcing them to walk home; as the alert code is "raised to red," the FDR Drive is closed, tunnels are sealed, and Manhattan is put "under official quarantine" as the National Guard gathers in New Jersey and Staten Island. Television stations eventually lose their signals, and a voice on the radio asks, "At this point, the big question coming from state and local officials is, where is the emergency response and why has it taken so long for information to trickle down?"

Most of the characters in *Mulberry Street* have been through not only 9/11 but also other historical and personal traumas. One elderly man is a World War II vet; another character is a Vietnam vet in a wheelchair. Clutch's daughter, Casey, is on her way home from fighting in Iraq. Her face is deeply scarred, but her experience is never explained. Other characters include a single mother and her teenage son, and Clutch's black, gay roommate. These layered stories produce a complex narrative in which real historical trauma intersects with fictional trauma (the rat-zombie plague)—or, as Halberstam describes *The Silence of the Lambs*, "the horror of the extraordinary and the horror of the ordinary side by side."[46]

The apartment building becomes that classic setting in horror film, a "terrible house,"[47] as the rat plague makes its way downtown, a process the film follows through Casey battling her way south through the city, from Harlem, through Central Park, and home to her father's Mulberry Street building, which is swarming with bloodthirsty rat-zombies. A particularly unsettling sequence centers on rat-zombies attacking and devouring people in a local bar; the film lingers both on the rat-zombies' movements as they tug against resistant human flesh, and on the sounds of this cannibalistic feast.

After a long, brutal night, the survivors of the rat attacks are winnowed down to Clutch, Casey, and the teenage boy who lives in the building. They make their way to the building's roof, battling the rat-zombies in an energizing fight scene. Clutch's roommate, who has been zombified, confronts Clutch and bites his neck, thereby infecting him. Grappling, Clutch throws

FIGURE 1.4. *Fallen men (*Mulberry Street, *After Dark Films, 2006).*

himself and his friend over the side of the building. The camera focuses on their bodies on the pavement. At that point, a mysterious but presumably government-directed troop in hazmat suits bursts onto the roof, grabbing the boy and shooting Casey in the chest with a hypodermic needle, which is another homage to *Night of the Living Dead*, deemed by Charles Derry to be "the bleakest horror film, devoid of even an iota of hope."[48] Unlike the traditional valorization of firefighters and police officers in most 9/11 narratives, *Mulberry Street* treats its authorities as useless and evil, just as the posse of white men that murders the remaining black character in *Night of the Living Dead* behaves more brutally than any zombies. In *Mulberry Street*'s last minutes, Casey staggers and finally collapses over the side of the building. A scarf falls from her hand and settles on top of the bodies of the two men. The last shot of the film shows the men, dead on the pavement, surrounded by blood.

Of course, this is not a literal treatment of the bodies that fell from the World Trade Center, but the final scene can be read as what Adam Lowenstein calls an "allegorical moment": "a shocking collision of film, spectator, and history where registers of bodily space and historical time are disrupted, confronted, and intertwined."[49] *Mulberry Street* is not "about" 9/11; rather, it places the events in a climate of cultural violence ranging from wars to rent hikes to rat-zombies. If we consider how explicitly the film signals the drama of 9/11 in its opening scenes, the last scene completes the frame and makes the spectacle of bodily violence part of that narrative. We see that damage in the veterans of three wars—World War II, Vietnam, and Iraq—in the bodies of the people ravaged by the rat-zombies, and finally, in the men who fall from the building.

Mulberry Street's press kit declares that the film is

> our allegory (pronounced "al-a-GORY") on post 9/11 New York City. . . .
> The rats in this movie aren't just about infestation. They stand for urban de-
> cay. They're about encroachment, gentrification, and an inevitable sense of
> change and modernization for better or worse. . . . As much as *Mulberry
> Street* is a rat-zombie film, it's also meant to show how everyday people deal
> with problems in this city. It's about scaling down the zombie genre. It's
> about the struggles of the middle class. It's about the unstoppable force of
> change and power. It's about the supposedly imminent threat of terrorism
> (and everything else).[50]

As convincingly as the film pursues its "al-a-GORY" of capitalism and gen-
trification, these lofty ideological ambitions fade into harrowing scenes of
rabid rat-people tearing into human flesh and rat-zombies pushing their way
up through the insulation of the Mulberry Street building. The film proves
Tom Gunning's point in the 2000 documentary *The American Nightmare*
(Adam Simon) that "the horror film, in many ways, even though it may respond to social traumas . . . , ultimately hits someplace else. In many ways, the
social trauma opens the door, but then you plummet into some of the most
primal elements . . . really psychological themes." *Mulberry Street* is neither
cathartic nor redemptive—as its nihilistic ending makes clear—but its sensational visceral effects can be read productively against the absence of such
representation in other 9/11 narration.

In evaluating horror films responding to historical trauma, it is helpful, as
Lowenstein suggests, to move away from a moral reading of them as redemptive or negligent, and to instead focus on the ways they are "culturally specific
[and] historically contextualized."[51] I have been arguing that horror films responding to 9/11 are integrally related to more mainstream representations,
but not in any simple way. That is, they are not the antidote or the solution to
"better" 9/11 representation. Rather, they make visible the ways other media
tell the story of 9/11. In contrast to the strict moral universe of Dante's Italian Catholic *Inferno*, where spectacles of human violence were displayed to
serve a clear theological purpose, the contemporary effort to promote a heroic
narrative of 9/11 relies on the suppression of explicitly violent bodily imagery.
Our current representations of 9/11 attempt to protect us from being wounded
by history.

The expectation is that 9/11 will be treated with sensitivity and reverence toward the events and the survivors: no bodies, no blood, no dishonorable behavior. What films such as *Mulberry Street* introduce to the American narrative of September 11 is a more bodily and antiheroic response. It cannot be absorbed or taken up in any "useful" way, but rather it expands the narrative possibilities for thinking about 9/11. Horror's antiheroic articulations are not the solution to representing 9/11, but they call attention to the limits of how 9/11 is currently represented, the way in which narrative possibilities have been strategically narrowed. History has taught us that early representation of violent and traumatic events usually serves an ideological purpose, and that subsequent narratives begin to free themselves from this necessity and address aspects of the story that had not been admissible before. (The classic model of this in literature is Tim O'Brien's 1990 Vietnam story collection, *The Things They Carried*.)[52] Horror films do not offer a picture of 9/11 that many of us want to adopt, but in explicitly rendering what is not shown elsewhere, they draw our attention to the mechanisms by which heroic exceptions have been substituted for the human, bodily devastation of that day.

In his elegant 2006 critique of the representation of September 11 in films such as *United 93* and *World Trade Center*, Daniel Mendelsohn remarks, "However much they seek to illumine the events of September 11, the films of Greengrass and Stone are, in the end, more like curtains than windows. For the present, at least, we still can't bring ourselves to look."[53] The increasing appearance of horror films and other narratives that represent 9/11 unconventionally suggests that the impulse to look is becoming more urgent.[54] These counter-narratives make visible how difficult it is to relinquish the heroic narrative and imagine one marked by vulnerability and dignity as well as complicity. They point to the resistance to representing the events of 9/11 as a national wound that was in some ways enabled both by the nation's political activities and—perhaps the most frightening story of all—by the vast systematic failures of internal measures that were supposed to protect the nation. These new counter-narratives are appearing, slowly and steadily, even if we can only watch them in that time-honored way of taking in a particularly scary horror movie, holding our hands over our faces and peering through our fingers, but watching nonetheless.

NOTES

1. Most studies of horror place its genesis much later, in the eighteenth century. See Noël Carroll, *The Philosophy of Horror; or, Paradoxes of the Heart* (New York: Routledge, 1990); Ken Gelder, "Introduction: The Field of Horror," in *The Horror Reader*,

ed. Ken Gelder (London: Routledge, 2000), 1–7; and James B. Twitchell, *Dreadful Pleasures: An Anatomy of Modern Horror* (New York: Oxford University Press, 1985).

2. Dante Alighieri, *Inferno*, trans. Allen Mandelbaum (New York: Bantam, 1982), 13.16–27.

3. Dante's portrait of himself in the *Divine Comedy* might well remind horror film aficionados of a gender-bending version of Carol Clover's "Final Girl": the "one who encounters the mutilated bodies . . . and perceives the full extent of the preceding horror and of her own peril; who is chased, cornered, wounded; whom we see scream, stagger, fall, rise, and scream again." She, like Dante, is the one who survives. Carol Clover, *Men, Women, and Chain Saws: Gender in the Modern Horror Film* (Princeton, NJ: Princeton University Press, 1992), 35.

4. J. P. Telotte, "Faith and Idolatry in the Horror Film," in *Planks of Reason: Essays on the Horror Film*, rev. ed., ed. Barry Keith Grant and Christopher Sharrett (Lanham, MD: Scarecrow Press, 2004), 25.

5. Dennis Giles, "Conditions of Pleasure in Horror Cinema," in Grant and Sharrett, *Planks of Reason*, 39.

6. Telotte argues that the basis of cinematic horror is also essentially cognitive: "some unbelievable terror, something which stubbornly refuses to be accounted for by our normal perceptual patterns." "Faith and Idolatry in the Horror Film," 24–25.

7. Jules and Gédéon Naudet's *9/11* shows the formation of these analogies in real time when a flabbergasted pedestrian on the scene remarks that it is like "something out of *The Towering Inferno*, like a movie." See also Anthony Lane's "This Is Not a Movie," and Susan Sontag's suggestion that "It felt like a movie" may have "displaced the way survivors of a catastrophe used to express the short-term unassimilability of what they had gone through: 'It felt like a dream.'" Lane, "This Is Not a Movie," *New Yorker*, September 24, 2001, http://www.newyorker.com/archive/2001/09/24/010924crci_cinema; and Sontag, *Regarding the Pain of Others* (New York: Picador, 2003), 22.

8. For example, in her review of *The Happening*, Elizabeth Weitzman writes, "The film never builds past its initial idea, the references to 9/11 feel cheap." *New York Daily News*, June 12, 2008, http://www.nydailynews.com/entertainment/movies/2008/06/13/2008-06-13_m_night_shyamalan_is_toxin_our_patience_.html. In the *New York Press*, Armond White pronounces Shyamalan's movie to be "sheer exploitation." Considering the critical response to other films that allude to 9/11, White contrasts "reviews that trashed Spielberg's *War of the Worlds* [2005], resenting its metaphoric/cathartic use of the 9/11 experience," to critics who "fall for the cheap disaster-movie device of *United 93*. They'd rather profound experience be depicted lightly. It's a form of moral, political, and artistic retardation." "Shock and Denial," *New York Press*, June 18, 2008, http://www.nypress.com/article-18417-shock-and-denial.html.

9. Linnie Blake proposes that there is a particular subgenre of horror film, the "new hillbilly horror," that responds to September 11 and is "concerned with the complex relation between knowing and not knowing the truth, seeing and not seeing the wounds inflicted on the national psyche by recent events." *The Wounds of Nations: Horror Cinema, Historical Trauma and National Identity* (Manchester, UK: Manchester University Press, 2008), 126.

10. Gregory A. Waller proposes a specific year at which American horror cinema began explicitly addressing political issues: "Horror film has engaged in a sort of ex-

tended dramatization of and response to the major public events and newsworthy topics in American history since 1968." "Introduction to *American Horrors*," in Gelder, *Horror Reader*, 263. Others suggest a much longer history of allegorical horror. See, for example, Charles Derry, *Dark Dreams 2.0: A Psychological History of the Modern Horror Film from the 1950s to the 21st Century* (Jefferson, NC: McFarland, 2009); and Adam Lowenstein, *Shocking Representation: Historical Trauma, National Cinema, and the Modern Horror Film* (New York: Columbia University Press, 2005).

11. For example, see Blake, *Wounds of Nations*; Lowenstein, *Shocking Representation*; and Janet Walker, *Trauma Cinema: Documenting Incest and the Holocaust* (Berkeley: University of California Press, 2005).

12. Clover, *Men, Women, and Chain Saws*, 20.

13. J. Hoberman, "Good Soldiers," *Village Voice*, August 1, 2006, http://www.villagevoice.com/2006-08-01/film/good-soldiers/.

14. A sympathetic review in the *Washington Post* describes the black screen as a confrontation with "the unspeakable. . . . We hear the impact and, a second later, the agonized cries and gasps of the witnesses. . . . We don't see the jumpers. But we feel we do." Desson Thomson, "'Fahrenheit 9/11': Connecting with a Hard Left," *Washington Post*, May 18, 2004, http://www.washingtonpost.com/ac2/wp-dyn/A34917-2004May17. The *National Review* was equally favorable. "There was one scene where I felt Moore had reached high art," James S. Robbins writes. "He passed up using the most compelling visuals of recent decades, appealing instead to the viewer's imagination and memory, with an auditory prompt. It was disorienting and frightening, and in my opinion the best moment of the movie qua movie." "The Left's Masterwork: Michael Moore's *9/11*," *National Review*, June 29, 2004, http://old.nationalreview.com/robbins/robbins200406290935.asp. Peter Bradshaw, reviewing the film in the *Guardian*, however, called the sequence a "showman flourish," "a nightmare recalled with eyes tight shut." *Guardian* (London), July 9, 2004, http://www.guardian.co.uk/theguardian/2004/jul/09/1.

15. Barbie Zelizer, "Photography, Journalism, and Trauma," in *Journalism after September 11*, ed. Barbie Zelizer and Stuart Allan (London: Routledge, 2002), 64.

16. See also Nancy K. Miller, "'Portraits of Grief': Telling Details and the Testimony of Trauma," *differences* 14 (Fall 2003): 112–135.

17. Lane, "This Is Not a Movie."

18. See Sandro Galea, Heidi Resnick, Jennifer Ahern, Joel Gold, Michael Bucuvalas, Dean Kilpatrick, Jennifer Stuber, and David Vlahov, "Posttraumatic Stress Disorder in Manhattan, New York City, after the September 11th Terrorist Attacks," *Journal of Urban Health* 79 (September 2002): 340–353.

19. CBS News's *What We Saw: The Events of September 11, 2001, in Words, Pictures, and Video* (New York: Simon & Schuster, 2002), includes several accounts of witnessing the bodies, but the accompanying DVD does not show any footage of them. *In Memoriam: New York City, 9/11/01* (Brad Grey, 2002) does show jumping people, as does Ric Burns's PBS documentary *American Experience: New York: Center of the World* (2003).

20. Tom Junod, "The Falling Man," *Esquire*, September 2003, http://www.esquire.com/features/ESQ0903-SEP_FALLINGMAN.

21. Robin Wood, "An Introduction to the American Horror Film," in Grant and Sharrett, *Planks of Reason*, 113.

22. Sontag provocatively argues that the brutal Pearl beheading video, which was briefly posted online by the *Boston Phoenix* until the paper was criticized and forced to take it down, actually contained footage of "a montage of stock accusations . . . and a list of specific demands—all of which might suggest that it was worth suffering through (if you could bear it) to confront better the particular viciousness and intransigence of the forces that murdered Pearl." *Regarding the Pain of Others*, 69–70.

23. Art Spiegelman, *In the Shadow of No Towers* (New York: Pantheon, 2004). See also Lane, "This Is Not a Movie," and the Naudet documentary *9/11*.

24. Zelizer, "Photography, Journalism, and Trauma," 65.

25. Zelizer argues that the emphasis on reaction shots in 9/11 coverage invoked the "earlier visual template" of the liberation of German concentration camps in 1945, in which photographs of people bearing witness to the camps' atrocities were widely employed to "move collective sentiment from shock and horror into a post-traumatic space demanding responsiveness and action." Ibid., 49, 51.

26. Cathy Caruth, "Introduction," in *Trauma: Explorations in Memory*, ed. Cathy Caruth (Baltimore: Johns Hopkins University Press, 1995), 4–5.

27. See my article "Still Life: 9/11's Falling Bodies" for a discussion of literature and art depicting the events of 9/11. In *Literature after 9/11*, ed. Ann Keniston and Jeanne Follansbee Quinn (New York: Routledge, 2008), 180–207.

28. A formally similar but more thoughtful treatment of this choreography of spectatorship is reflected in Alejandro González Iñárritu's "Mexico," his contribution to *11'09"01: September 11* (2002), a collection of short films by directors from different countries. Like Moore's depiction of the events of September 11, Iñárritu's film highlights *not* seeing; however, Iñárritu addresses the problems of vision and cognition by constructing his film around brief flashes of footage of people tumbling from the WTC. While audio in *Fahrenheit 9/11* is a transparent medium, Iñárritu's film layers many different languages, and hence sound works in tandem with the indeterminate images. Iñárritu's editing of the footage of the falling people calls attention to the edges of the frame and the parts of the story that are excluded. It makes the elements of 9/11 we can't see, can't know, can't understand, seem more urgent than ever as we strain to see them in the dark voids between the images.

29. Janet Walker reads the Naudets' *9/11* as an example of what she calls "trauma cinema." For Walker, the dropped Handycam scene and the subsequently occluded and black screen "is what nobody saw but what the lens captured when circumstances forced its operator to turn away from the crumbling tower and run for his life. Its denotative meaning is vague, but, partly because of this, it connotes a sensory shock that could barely be grasped at the time." *Trauma Cinema*, 193.

30. In looking at pictures such as the November 13, 2001, *New York Times* triptych of a Taliban soldier being killed by Northern Alliance forces, Sontag asks, "What pictures, whose cruelties, whose deaths are *not* being shown." *Regarding the Pain of Others*, 14.

31. The statement is also quoted in CBS News, *What We Saw*, 23–24.

32. See Ken Tucker, "Truth Be Told," *Entertainment Weekly*, March 12, 2002, http://www.ew.com/ew/article/0,,216458,00.html: "I was startled to read various reports that the CBS producers who helped shape the Naudets' work actually edited out the sound of some of the bodies that fell with loud crashes as the filmmakers recorded the firefighters' rescue missions. To presume what might be in good taste—in this case,

to decide that we could hear a few bodies falling to their death, but not the 'rain' of them, as one firefighter told us—is the umpteenth example of the way network news condescends to and insults both the victims and the viewers. Why must TV always act like a national grief counselor? Why do we always need to be lulled into comfort, rather than left deeply shaken, enlivened, or furious, when a tragedy occurs?"

33. James Poniewozik, "Television: Within Crumbling Walls," *Time*, March 11, 2002, http://www.time.com/time/magazine/article/0,9171,1001982,00.html.

34. Filmmakers have used black screens for many different purposes. For example, Godard often exploited the black screen, perhaps most memorably in *Le Gai savoir* (1969), in which a voice-over meditates on the technique's purpose.

35. Anthony Lane, "Monstrous Times," *New Yorker*, January 28, 2008, http://www .newyorker.com/arts/critics/cinema/2008/01/28/080128crci_cinema_lane.

36. Roger Ebert, review of *Cloverfield*, RogerEbert.com, January 17, 2008, http:// rogerebert.suntimes.com/apps/pbcs.dll/article?AID=/20080117/REVIEWS/ 801170302.

37. William K. Everson, "Horror Films (1954)," in *Horror Film Reader*, ed. Alain Silver and James Ursini (New York: Limelight, 2000), 29. The opening scene of Uwe Boll's *Postal* shows a similarly crude decapitation, as the wing of one of the hijacked planes chops off the head of a man who is washing windows at the World Trade Center.

38. Clover, *Men, Women, and Chain Saws*, 10.

39. Sontag, *Regarding the Pain of Others*, 26–27.

40. Several critics have speculated that *Cloverfield* was influenced by the Naudets' *9/11*. See, for example, William Wiles, review of *Cloverfield*, *Icon*, http://www.iconeye .com/index.php?option=com_content&view=article&id=2918:review-cloverfield.

41. Stephanie Zacharek, review of *Cloverfield*, Salon.com, January 18, 2008, http:// www.salon.com/entertainment/movies/review/2008/01/18/cloverfield/.

42. Quoted in Dana Stevens, "When Monsters Attack Pretty People," *Slate Magazine*, January 17, 2008, http://www.slate.com/id/2182344.

43. Isabel Pinedo, for example, calls "the dialectic in recreational terror between seeing and not-seeing," which she compares to the dynamic of the *fort/da* game described in Freud's "Beyond the Pleasure Principle," a rehearsal of "the loss of control through a controlled loss." *Recreational Terror: Women and the Pleasures of Horror Film Viewing* (Albany: State University of New York Press, 1997), 141, 142.

44. Judith Halberstam, *Skin Shows: Gothic Horror and the Technology of Monsters* (Durham, NC: Duke University Press, 1995), 154.

45. Steven Shaviro, *The Cinematic Body* (Minneapolis: University of Minnesota Press, 1993), 55.

46. Halberstam, *Skin Shows*, 26.

47. See Clover, *Men, Women, and Chain Saws*, and Wood, "Introduction to the American Horror Film."

48. Derry, *Dark Dreams 2.0*, 68.

49. Lowenstein, *Shocking Representation*, 2.

50. Murphy PR and Belladonna Productions, "*Mulberry Street* Press Notes," n.d., http://mulberrystreetmovie.com/Media/MSPressKit.pdf.

51. Lowenstein, *Shocking Representation*, 8.

52. Tim O'Brien, *The Things They Carried: A Work of Fiction* (New York: Houghton Mifflin, 1990).

53. Daniel Mendelsohn, "September 11 at the Movies," *New York Review of Books*, September 21, 2006, http://www.nybooks.com/articles/archives/2006/sep/21/september-11-at-the-movies/.

54. There is a small but growing body of fiction that articulates counter-narratives of 9/11: for example, Neil LaBute's play *The Mercy Seat* (New York: Faber and Faber, 2003); Claire Tristram's *After* (New York: Farrar, Straus and Giroux, 2004); Jess Walter's *The Zero* (New York: Regan Books, 2006); and Ken Kalfus's *A Disorder Peculiar to the Country* (New York: Ecco, 2006). All these works elicited some scathing reviews cast on explicitly moral grounds. See also Salon.com's feature, on the first anniversary of 9/11, inviting its readers to send in "forbidden thoughts" about 9/11 that departed from the standard, heroic themes. Damien Cave, "Forbidden Thoughts about 9/11," Salon.com, September 7, 2002, http://dir.salon.com/mwt/feature/2002/09/07/forbidden/index.html.

CHAPTER TWO

Let's Roll

Hollywood Takes on 9/11

ELISABETH FORD

The appalling images of death, destruction, and daring that invaded our homes on September 11 left us with no doubt that these unimaginable scenes belonged to a moral universe alien to ours, acts perpetrated by people foreign to the very fiber of our being.

But CNN had a sobering tale to tell. While the headline news staggered from one towering inferno to another, the ticker tape at the bottom of the screen interspersed its roll call of the brave and the dead with lists of Hollywood movies—films that had told a similar story many times before, and new, unreleased movies that were about to tell it again. What was only an action movie last month had turned, this month, into acts of war. Same mise en scene, different movie.

HOMI BHABHA, "A NARRATIVE OF DIVIDED CIVILIZATIONS"

As eyewitnesses, TV anchors, and home viewers have been saying since the day they occurred, the terrorist attacks of September 11, 2001, were always already "just like a movie." In an essay written just days later, Homi Bhabha describes the realization that we've seen this film before as "sobering," as if our conviction that such attacks must emanate from "a moral universe alien to ours" is undercut by the recognition that we've long imagined such "unimaginable scenes." As if the "images of death, destruction, and daring that invaded our homes on September 11" are "appalling" and invasive exactly because they use the language of Hollywood, *our* language, to tell a story narrated by "people foreign to the very fiber of our being."[1] One of the primary functions of the films to which Bhabha refers has always been to define who "we" are by dwelling on those others, the aliens and foreigners who illuminate the boundaries of our moral universe by violating them. In this essay, I will examine the efforts of two films released five years after September 11 to take the story back from those others, to narrate "our" experience of that day. The first of these films is Paul Greengrass's "docudrama" about one of the planes hijacked in the attacks, April 2006's *United 93*, but the second is not Oliver Stone's *World Trade Center*; rather, it is *Snakes on a Plane* (David R. Ellis and Lex Halaby), the Samuel L. Jackson vehicle released days after Stone's film in August 2006. *Snakes on a Plane* is, I will argue, the only film of the three to really challenge its audience to consider not just what the attacks themselves might mean to us, but also what it means that we recognized them immediately as cinema; while *United 93* seeks to downplay its status as fiction, *Snakes on a Plane* makes the implicit claim that any film about the events of 9/11 is, by definition, already a sequel.

IT'S TIME: THE TEMPORAL FANTASIES OF *UNITED 93*

When trailers for *United 93* began playing in theaters in the spring of 2006, some audiences reportedly shouted, "Too soon!" at the screen.[2] The audiences' response seemed to answer a question that public commentators had been asking of representations of September 11 ever since the documentary *9/11* (Gédéon Naudet and Jules Naudet, 2002) was first aired on CBS six months after the attacks.[3] In their overwhelmingly positive response to *United 93* upon its release, many reviewers seemed satisfied that the answer to the familiar question "Is it too soon?" was an emphatic "No," referring readers to the film itself as proof. The temporal anxiety surrounding the film's reception, proceeding from an apprehensive "Too soon?" to a cathartic "Right on time," maps cleanly onto Linda Williams's influential account of the temporal structures of two popular film genres, horror and pornography. Williams argues that the horror film tends to dramatize "the anxiety of not being ready," with the symbolic castration of its violence catapulting us into an awareness of sexual difference, "offering a knowledge for which we are never prepared." The porn film, of course, "posit[s] the utopian fantasy of perfect temporal coincidence: a subject and object (or seducer and seduced) who meet one another 'on time!' and 'now!' in shared moments of mutual pleasure that it is the special challenge of the genre to portray."[4] Kendall Phillips describes the successful horror film as achieving what he calls "resonant violation"; that is, its narrative resonates with the audience's collective cultural anxieties, but it also shocks us "through an almost systematic violation of the rules of the game. The truly shocking—and, thus, successful—horror films are those that make us start in our seats and want to cry out, 'Hey, you can't do that!'"[5] Of course, "the anxiety of not being ready" and an attendant sense of "violation" are already hallmarks of the American public's experience of 9/11; the images broadcast by the news media that day are in their own way the perfect horror film. And so, American audiences watching the trailer for Greengrass's film seemed to be reliving the helpless sense of innocence surprised that the initial attacks awakened. In the *Village Voice*, J. Hoberman describes the experience of the trailer's first spectators as such a reenactment: "Just as the now notorious trailer distilled the movie's narrative arc (albeit without offering the final catharsis), audiences mimicked the action: Having paid to see *Inside Man* [Spike Lee, 2006], unsuspecting viewers had their attention 'hijacked.' According to some descriptions, the angry patrons at AMC Loews Lincoln Square banded together to yank the trailer."[6]

Not surprisingly, the "final catharsis" makes all the difference, and reviews of the complete film tend to identify its success with its ability to synchronize the experience of viewers perfectly with that of its characters. Roger Ebert, for instance, wrote: "It is not too soon for *United 93*, because it is not a film that knows any time has passed since 9/11. The entire story, every detail, is told in the present tense. We know what they know when they know it, and nothing else. . . . Even as these brave passengers charge up the aisle, we know nothing in particular about them—none of the details we later learned. We could be on the plane, terrified, watching them."[7] Ebert's account is typical in suggesting that it is *United 93*'s "present tense" narration that causes the spectator to identify so completely with the characters on-screen. Of the film's near-perfect allegiance to "real time," the *New Yorker*'s David Denby writes, "This is true existential filmmaking: there is only the next instant, and the one after that, and what are you going to do?"[8] Hoberman labels the film a "ritual ordeal" whose effect is "experiential and communal," maintaining that its use of real time is "designed for audience participation."[9] Hoberman describes a near-religious communion between spectators and characters, while Denby conflates them into a single "you." While not exactly the "shared moments of mutual pleasure" Williams describes as the ambition of the porn film, the reactions of Ebert, Hoberman, and Denby all emphasize the "perfect coincidence" of the spectator's experience with that of the characters. Not atypically, their reviews evince a real sense of relief that instead of the feared cinematic assault ("Too soon!"), the film invites (seduces?) its spectators into a fantasy of mutuality ("We could be on the plane").

United 93 is neither horror nor porn, of course, but the commonly voiced fear that it would be "exploitative" or traumatizing[10] suggests a link between Greengrass's film and those genres that Williams argues are deemed "excessive" and "low," specifically because of "the perception that the body of the spectator is caught up in an almost involuntary mimicry of the emotion or sensation of the body on the screen."[11] Williams notes that the success of films in the "low body genres" is often measured by the intensity of the bodily mimicry they coerce from audiences; the successful porn film must actually produce orgasms and the horror film screams, and she cites the "long-standing tradition" of measuring the efficacy of the third of these genres, the "women's film," "in terms of one-, two-, or three-handkerchief movies."[12] The reviews of *United 93* are likewise preoccupied with its effect on the bodies of its spectators. The *New York Times'* Manohla Dargis describes the experience of seeing the film as an "emotional pummeling," while Salon.com's Stephanie Zacharek calls *United 93* a film that "sucks the life out of you," and the *Los Angeles Times'* Kenneth Turan agrees that "this is a film that wrings you out completely, makes you feel you have lived the story along with the participants."[13] Williams argues that the genres she discusses engage in a "cultural form of problem solving," in which fantasies of seduction, castration, and family romance are played out via "the spectacle of a 'sexually saturated' female body."[14] While *United 93* doesn't share those genres' fascination with sexual difference or feminine victimization, the critics imply that it leaves its spectators similarly spent; perhaps it engages in a form of problem solving that tries to resolve the boundaries between "self" and "other" in the context of *cultural* difference and *American* victimization.

In fact, it seems an important order of business for *United 93* to posit a definition of "selfhood" and "otherness" for an audience eager to determine its precise relationship to the events of 9/11. Commentators with diametrically opposed ideas about who is "united" by the narrative of that day see their own opinions confirmed by the film, which is one clue that despite its aesthetics of documentary dispassion, *United 93* is passionately engaged in an attempt to delineate the community of victims; further, the offer the film makes to its viewers of membership in that community is so compelling as to forestall petty demands to be more precise about its boundaries. The right-wing pundit Rush Limbaugh, for instance, lauds the film for its clarity about the heroism of the flight's passengers, who "didn't take a vote on that plane," and among whom "there weren't any detractors. . . . They just gathered together." In addition, enthusiastic for an image of an embattled American public unencumbered by dissent or the democratic process, Limbaugh marvels, "There is no sympathy whatsoever for the bad guys in this movie, and I applauded Greengrass for that. You end up coming away without any question who's responsible for all this. There's no political pontificating in this movie."[15] In a rare moment of agreement with Limbaugh, the liberal *New York Times* columnist Frank Rich concedes that "whatever the movie's other failings, that message is clear and essential: the identity of the enemy. The film opens with the four hijackers praying to Allah and, in keeping with the cockpit voice recording played at the Zacarias Moussaoui trial, portrays them as prayerful right until they murder 40 innocent people. Such are the Islamic radicals who struck us on 9/11 and whose brethren have only multiplied since."[16] But while Limbaugh seems happily surprised that Greengrass, whom he calls "admittedly . . . very liberal," doesn't apologize for the hijackers as the Limbaugh caricature of a "liberal" surely would, Rich locates the film within a culture of "denial" about the real nature of the threat exposed on 9/11 and the failure so far of our attempts to confront it. In other words, while Limbaugh sees the film's message about "difference" as a clear taking of sides, heroes against villains, Rich sees the same message about the "difference" of the hijackers as being subordinated to a fantasy about "our" heroism that ultimately prevents us from acknowledging complexity or the possibility of failure.[17]

At any rate, it is evident that the "us" and "them" of *United 93* are divided not by sexual difference but by ideological opposition. I say "ideological" rather than "national," "religious," or "racial" because the film itself seems at pains to minimize the latter distinctions, intercutting the final scenes, for instance, between lines of prayer delivered by the hijackers and their victims, framed identically as if to equate the two; and casting the hijackers with actors whose ethnicity is less visibly distinct than that of their real-world counterparts, even though the casting of the other characters prioritizes realism (indeed, many are played "by themselves" or by nonactors with experience in the jobs their characters perform on-screen). And it's not just "they," the hijackers, who are defined by bonds of choice rather than of inheritance; the narrative trajectory of the film highlights as its climax the moment at which the other passengers' process of intense and furtive discussion leads to their mutual decision to storm the cockpit.[18] In fact, in one of its few embellishments to the plot, *United 93* shows the passengers overcoming and beating to death two of the hijackers before the plane goes down; it's as if the film wants to insist that in their final moments, the passengers have become a constituency capable of the commitment required to perform the kind of blood sacrifice the hijackers have already demonstrated.

"Become" is the key word in the previous sentence. While some have criticized Greengrass's film for insufficiently individualizing United Airlines Flight 93's passengers,[19] and others for excessively individualizing its hijackers,[20] both of these critiques miss the point. The hijackers' narrative role is defined from the opening scene and remains static, while the passengers' evolution into effective agents is dramatized as a rational and even humane response to their circumstances. *United 93* opens with the sound of Arabic prayers unaccompanied by any image; after a few seconds, an extreme close-up of a book, presumably the Koran, appears on-screen. In subsequent shots, the book is located in the lap of the lead hijacker, Ziad Jarrah, and he is placed in the anonymous motel room in which the hijackers are preparing for their mission. The first dialogue we hear is another hijacker, Ahmed al-Haznawi, saying in subtitled Arabic to Jarrah, "It's time." The dynamic between the hijackers never changes after this point: Jarrah is depicted as hesitant and preoccupied, needing to be prodded into action by the others, whose determination to carry out their plans and conviction of their own righteousness never falter (or deepen, for that matter). The incomprehensible (for non-Arabic speakers) prayer that opens the film frames the hijackers' motives as unknowable, belonging to an alien realm; while their motives are evidently religious, their beliefs are without meaningful content, without application in the world inhabited by the rest of the passengers (and, by extension, us, the audience). Once their fates have been determined for them by whatever authority they appeal to in their prayers, they have no autonomy; they seem to operate in their own temporality, in which for the entire course of the film "it's time." Their temporal structure is like the "now!" of pornography robbed of anticipation, of individual will, of release; they are not the seducer, but rather something more like the ejaculate. Jarrah's repeated moments of hesitation—to go through security, to initiate the hijacking once in flight, to crash the plane—serve only as opportunities for the other hijackers to remind him that his fears or compunctions have no bearing on what they must and will do. Opening with a prayer and the conviction that "it's time," the hijackers' narrative ends exactly where it started, with Jarrah, as the passengers storm the cockpit, shouting, "Allahu Akbar!," and pointing the plane toward the ground.

If Jarrah's individual hesitation is depicted as pointless in the face of the sacred (though untranslatable) contract he's entered into, the air traffic control and military personnel depicted in the film suffer the opposite problem: individuals among them want to act (as when military commanders unclear on the rules of engagement repeatedly seek authorization to attempt to shoot down the hijacked planes before they reach their targets) but encounter a structural hesitation in the delay in gathering the necessary information and authorization from disparate sources. The moment for action arrives "too soon!" for a centralized command structure to process and respond to it. Only the resisting passengers hesitate in a productive way; the time they take to gather information from one another and from the cell phone calls they make to witnesses on the ground, to draw conclusions about their situation and their options, to pray and say good-bye, and to marshal their resources for an attack on the cockpit, allows them to act, when they finally do, in a coordinated and strategically sound way. Their own "it's time" moment, manifested in the immortal "Let's roll!" with which the passenger Todd Beamer reportedly initiated their assault on the cockpit, is thus framed as a meaningful narrative climax, validating the process by which they've arrived at this moment and, as Kenneth Turan writes, "mak[ing] you feel you have lived the story along with the participants." The function of the narrative, then, is not just to celebrate the heroes of Flight 93, but also to imagine a group identity created by the events of 9/11 in which we in the audience are also "participants."

But while I've described *United 93* as engaging in "a form of cultural problem solving" concerning the makeup and nature of the community to whom the 9/11 attacks "happened," it's important to remember that this "problem solving," as Williams describes it, is a function of *fantasy*. That is to say, *United 93* is only superficially concerned with the real-world questions "Who is the enemy, and what are they like?," "Who are we, and why are we superior?," and "How can we defeat them?" Williams notes that "fantasies are not, as is sometimes thought, wish-fulfilling linear narratives of mastery and control leading to closure and the attainment of desire. They are marked, rather, by the prolongation of desire, and by the lack of fixed position with respect to the objects and events fantasized."[21] Ultimately, *United 93*'s invitation to the spectator to immerse herself in a fantasized "real time" of unfolding events is countered both by its vexing of the notion of the "real" and by its sophisticated awareness of the simultaneous presence of multiple registers of time in the audience's experience of the film. I have already discussed the contrast between the static time ("now!") of the hijackers and the evolutionary time (culminating in "Let's roll!") of the passengers within the frame of the narrative, but I would argue that *United 93* is also haunted by a "too late!" (the temporality Williams associates with melodrama) lurking in the experience of the spectator herself.

Williams refers to Franco Moretti's claim that "literature that makes us cry operates via a special manipulation of temporality: what triggers our crying is not just the sadness or suffering of the character in the story but a very precise moment when characters in the story catch up with and realize what the audience already knows." Further, there is a "subversive" quality to such tears because they are "based on the utopian desire that it not be too late to remerge with the other who was once part of the self."[22] But *United 93* disavows exactly that "precise moment" of "catching up": the crash of Flight 93 that ends its narrative is represented in the film by a stark cut to black. The visual gesture at once reminds the audience that we don't need to see this conclusion—we've known all along what was coming—and refuses to grant us our tears. It's an outrageous narrative move, the equivalent of a porn film terminating just before the "money shot." But it serves to demonstrate how desperate the film is to avoid being taken for a melodrama by explicitly denying us the genre's traditional climax (you can cry—and you will—at the moment that these characters "catch up" with your knowledge, the black frame seems to say, but I will dramatize no motive or excuse for your doing so). The jolt, almost the violence, of this closing cinematic gesture hints that *United 93*'s disavowal of melodramatic closure is more than a question of good taste: it has an air of protesting too much.

This rejection of the moment in which the passengers' knowledge catches up is a logical extension of *United 93*'s efforts to convince its audience that, as Roger Ebert says, "it is not a film that knows any time has passed since 9/11." But in an obvious way, the film requires its audience at once to immerse itself in a pre-9/11 state of unpreparedness *and* to recognize that unpreparedness from a position of retrospective knowledge, of our awareness that it's "too late!" to avert the inevitable. When the film ruptures its fictional frame to recall us to our post-9/11 consciousness, as when it withholds the final shot (whose content we must supply from our own memories), its melodramatic urges find their expression *outside* the narrative frame, in the perspective we bring as characters in the original drama now being represented before us.

Another important moment of rupture occurs earlier in the film, as personnel at the New York and national air traffic control centers try to figure out the disappearance of American Airlines Flight 11 from their instruments and United Airlines Flight 175 suddenly drops out of electronic sight as well. A flight controller at Newark Airport, who had cleared Flight 93 for takeoff minutes before, is following Flight 175's signal on a screen and dictating what he sees to the New York center when suddenly other personnel begin to point out the window; they've spotted the plane itself descending rapidly over New York City toward the already-smoking North Tower of the World Trade Center. Elsewhere, regional and national air traffic officials are tuning into scenes of the wreckage on CNN and realizing that previous reports of a "small plane" having hit the Trade Center are grossly understated; they begin to make the connection between the televised images of the devastated building and the disappearance of Flight 11. As the Newark witnesses stare out their windows, transfixed, Flight 175 flies directly into the building's South Tower. Though the editing demands a point-of-view shot reflecting what the Newark flight controllers see from their tower, the actual moment of impact is shown on CNN footage of the event (the station's logo is briefly visible before the camera zooms in tighter on the image). The CNN footage of the plane striking the building is shocking, and at first that seems a simple proposition; we have, of course, all been shocked by it many times already, and we experience here an echo of what we felt when we first saw it.

But in this sequence, the film takes great pains to produce a particular *type* of shock at the moment of impact, one that has a very particular place in the film's construction of the relationship between its own narrative and the reality it's portraying. Vivian Sobchack argues that the sudden recognition of "real" or "documentary" cinematic material inserted into the body of a fictional film doesn't just change our perception of film's relationship to reality, it also changes our own relationship to the film: "The designations *fiction* and *documentary* name not merely objective and abstracted cinematic *things* distinguished and characterized historically by particular textual features but name also—and perhaps more significantly—distinctive *subjective relations* to a variety of cinematic objects, whatever their textual features."[23] In particular, Sobchack is interested in the way the fictional film can call forth the kind of conscious "existential and ethical investment" demanded of the spectator by the documentary when it appropriates material belonging to that register. To illustrate such a call, she points to the contrast between the ways in which the spectator experiences the two on-screen deaths in Jean Renoir's *Rules of the Game* (1939)—that of Jurieu, a human character, and that of the rabbit whose actual filmed death ends the hunting sequence:

> As the event occurs before us, we know the rabbit dies not only *in* but also *for* the fiction—in *excess* and *outside* of the irreal fictional world, in the space of the real, where death counts because it is irreversible. At the moment of its death, then, the rabbit loses its ambiguous status as a quasi character and becomes a real—and now definitively dead—once-living creature. Conversely, the human character Jurieu dies *only in* the irreal space of the fiction. . . . Unlike Jurieu's death, the experiential moment of the rabbit's death gains its specific axiological charge of affects and values from an existential and cultural knowledge that exceeds—and contextualizes—the homogenizing devices of both cinematic and narrative representation. Indeed, the rabbit's death *challenges* these devices, not only pointing to but also opening into a perceived domain of the real, a documentary space where, in this instance, aesthetic values are suddenly diminished and ethical ones are greatly heightened.[24]

Sobchack names the "ethical charge" of such moments as "ever-present possibilities in *every* film experience,"[25] though only exceptional moments such as the rabbit's death bring the "existential and cultural knowledge" that undergirds our experience of film fiction into our consciousness. It's implicit in her argument that "the homogenizing devices of both cinematic and narrative representation" normally exist to *enforce* the boundary between the "irreal space of the fiction" and the "documentary space" contiguous with the real. When the boundary between those spaces is already as vexed as it is in the case of a "docudrama" like *United 93*, whose "aesthetic values" evoke the ethically charged space of the documentary, it is perhaps no surprise that there should be moments of eruption of one into the other, as when the "documentary" CNN footage of Flight 175's end represents the fictional reoccurrence of the same event within the narrative of *United 93*.

It is another question, however, why the footage should appear *out of place* within that narrative frame: after all, we've seen CNN's footage from that morning on various TV screens before this scene, and it continues to appear throughout the film, "playing itself." But at the moment of impact, we see grainy video footage appear as if to represent the visual object of an eye-line match following the Newark air controllers' gathering at a window to point at the World Trade Center in the distance. While the controllers gaze into the distance and see a close-up image mediated by cable news cameras, for the film's viewers the medium seems to thin into transparency as we recognize this fictional event as an *actual* one, one that's happened to *us*, as our memories of the disbelief we felt upon seeing the plane collide with the building are confirmed by the exclamations of the characters on-screen. It's a moment of profound confusion for the audience, as the image simultaneously recalls the real events beyond the fictional frame of the film, while the film's characters seem to be experiencing a rupture in their own perceptual framework every bit as unsettling as our own. It's as if *they* are receiving an "ethical charge" from *our* world as our documented memory erupts into their fictional reality. It's also another moment in which the film's characters "catch up" to a knowledge already possessed by the spectators, except the knowledge concerns not their world but rather our own.

Flight 175's disappearance into the South Tower signals a loss of innocence for the film's characters, marking their collective realization that first Flight 11, and now Flight 175, were *meant* to crash where they did, that terrorism can no longer be separated into the categories of "domestic" or "abroad," that a hijacked plane can no longer be presumed to be headed for the nearest safe place to land. These possibilities have become familiar stuff to the audience, but in Moretti's reading of tear-jerking literature, this moment works by evoking our desire for the time *before* we've had to absorb them, despite the film's explicit goal of honoring the collective heroism that can only occur *after* that awakening, as a response to it. Sobchack's goal in highlighting the

FIGURES 2.1 AND 2.2. United 93: *fiction or reality? (Universal, 2006).*

cinema's reliance on the "embodied and extratextual knowledge" that gives it access to its viewers' ethical selves—"even when that experience begins and ends as a designated fiction"[26]—is to remind us that we bring our full selves to our experience as filmgoers, and that cinema in turn counts on our responses being informed by "embodied and extratextual knowledge." In *United 93*, both points seem self-evident. On a purely practical level, it's hard to imagine how one would make sense of the detail-obsessed first half of the film if one didn't know what was going to happen in the second, and when the passengers on Flight 175 suffer the fate awaiting those on *United 93*, we hardly need to be reminded that in both cases, real planes and real passengers are at issue. When the fiction that is already masquerading as a documentary inserts a "real" documentary moment belonging to our own memory of 9/11, our own "embodied and extratextual knowledge" is in the next moment subsumed within the world of the film whose characters are acquiring the exact same knowledge at this moment. As the CNN footage of the smoking towers, and later of the Pentagon, continues to crop up, in these instances properly framed within the diegetic logic of the film, we relinquish our temporal position "ahead" of the characters and for a brief time are able to live as if we, like the film, don't know that any time has passed since 9/11. Rather than being recalled to it, we are encouraged to *forego* the "existential and ethical investment" that has thus far marked our retrospective relationship to the material on-screen.

But why, as an audience, would we *want* to regress into the confusion that marked the brief hours that morning between innocence and knowledge? Tzvetan Todorov describes the hero of the fantastic as defined by just such a confusion; his journey begins when, "in a world which is indeed our world, the one we know, . . . there occurs an event which cannot be explained by the laws of this same familiar world." Eventually, a hero whom such an event has befallen must determine whether it is "an illusion of the senses . . . and laws of the world then remain what they are," or whether the event "is an integral part of reality—but then this reality is controlled by laws unknown to us." When that determination is made, Todorov says, "we leave the fantastic for a neighboring genre, the uncanny or the marvelous," since the fantastic itself comprises only the period of uncertainty marked by "that hesitation experienced by a person who knows only the laws of nature, confronting an apparently supernatural event."[27] As I have noted, in its first shots *United 93* presents the plans of the hijackers as completely incomprehensible to anyone unfamiliar with the language, the religion, and the culture that frame them; afterward, we are faced with the question of whether there is a "rational" explanation for what the hijackers have decided to do, or whether they are the agents of an ideology that violates our "laws of nature." Each possibility is unsettling in its way. The first would require us to empathize with the uncanny proposition that the towers symbolizing American economic power can also be seen as the emblem of a globally corrosive evil, while the second would open up the marvelous possibility that there walk among us people who wear polo shirts, buy airplane tickets, shave, rent cars, speak English, are generally indistinguishable from us, and yet harbor a monstrous and implacable hatred for the lifestyle they can adopt so convincingly. Either the people who have done this are different from us only in circumstance and not in kind, or they're different in a way that shakes the foundations of our reality. While a post-9/11 world is one in which both possibilities must, at least in part, be admitted, the world of that morning is one in which the decision is put off, the uncertainty prolonged as *United 93*'s characters struggle to confront *what* is happening before anyone has had time to consider *why* or *how*. If the hijackers inhabit a millenarian "now," the air traffic controllers and military commanders are surprised "too soon," and the audience's perspective is a jaded "too late," only the passengers in the film can take possession of a present tense in which action is still possible and analysis is as-yet impossible. By offering its audience an experience of a defining national event in which (in Denby's words) "there is only the next instant, and the one after that," *United 93* guides its audience toward a catharsis that in the real world has yet to arrive; at the same time, the film engages our unspoken desire for an imagined past in which we had not yet been asked to attempt to understand what gave rise to the occasion in the first place.

NO BOAT TO HEAVEN: EMBRACING THE LITERAL IN *SNAKES ON A PLANE*

In my reading of *United 93*, it's equally important to understand that the film asks its audience to experience its narrative from multiple temporal perspectives and that it asks its audience to disavow all but one of those perspectives, that of the "real time" in which "we could be on the plane." In doing so, the film inevitably downplays the extent to which its own version of the day's narrative has been mediated by any understandings or opinions that its director has developed about the day's events since they took place. Greengrass seems to concede that since so many political and ideological meanings have been claimed for 9/11 by so many different constituencies, his film must appear to claim none if it is to avoid producing conflicts within an audience it wants to identify as a voluntary collective. While until now I've attempted to draw out some of the ways in which his film shapes the material and directs the audience's relationship to it, I want to turn to another film that seems to make a higher-level critique of enterprises like Greengrass's. That, at least, is the argument I will make about the Samuel L. Jackson vehicle *Snakes on a Plane*. *Snakes on a Plane* is not an admitted 9/11 allegory; in fact, plans for the film, underway already in the fall of 2001, stalled for some time after the attacks, as did those for many films that, appearing to echo aspects of the real events, might have seemed "insensitive" by association.[28] The film's title itself seems to reject the very possibility of allegory, and its unabashed literalness is what attracted fans and, reportedly, its lead actor to it in the first place.[29] Jackson described his reaction on hearing that New Line Cinema was planning to change the film's original title to *Pacific Flight 121*: "The thing they said to me was, 'We really don't want to give too much away about the movie.' I was like, 'ARE YOU OUT OF YOUR F—-ING MINDS? That's EXACTLY what you want to do!' How else are you going to get people into the movie? Nobody wants to see *Pacific Flight 121*. That's like saying 'Boat To Heaven.' Bulls—-! C'mon! People know what they want to see. People either want to see this movie, or they don't."[30]

Tzvetan Todorov, making the point that a fantastic narrative must demand that its seemingly supernatural aspects be read literally, not allegorically, writes, "Allegory implies the existence of at least two meanings for the same words; according to some critics, the first meaning must disappear, while others require that the two be present together."[31] Regardless of whether its first, or literal, meaning disappears entirely, the allegorical narrative explicitly calls for the discovery of a second one, and therefore dissipates the urgency inherent in the literal problem of reconciling a supernatural event to the laws of nature. "Boat to Heaven," no matter how real a boat it takes place on, asks its audience to search for a second, transcendent meaning in the journey it narrates. Jackson's defense of the (ultimately restored) title makes clear that the problem in *Snakes on a Plane* is not one of interpretation; it is that there are snakes on a plane.

But this is not to say that *Snakes on a Plane*, rejecting allegory, fits neatly into the category of the fantastic. To begin with, snakes are not in conflict with the laws of nature, and we know before they appear why they are on the plane: they've been planted there at the command of a gangster, Eddie Kim, who hopes that they will bring down the plane and kill a witness who's being brought by the FBI from Hawaii to LA to testify against him in a murder trial. In fact, whenever a question is raised about the plausibility of any particular plot point, the film seems anxious to explain away any inconsistencies. For instance, we've seen that Eddie Kim is a gleefully vicious murderer (the opening of the film features the witness, a surf rat named Sean, stumbling across the scene of Kim beating a prosecutor to death with a baseball bat), but his plan to kill scores of innocents seems to exceed his demonstrated penchant for violence directed toward a practical end. A henchman raises the point when he asks, "Are you sure about this?" Eddie Kim explains impatiently, "Accidents happen. You think I didn't exhaust every option? He saw me!" What seems like a plot so elaborate that it must be designed to satisfy the aesthetic whims of a madman is actually just an unfortunate necessity. Even the plausibility of the snakes' behavior is a concern. The average audience member may not balk at the idea that hundreds of snakes catapulted explosively out of a nest of leis might go on to bite people, but nonetheless the film scrupulously provides us with a snake expert, back on the ground speaking on the phone with FBI Agent Flynn (Jackson), to object to this scenario: "Snakes don't attack unless they're provoked, right? Something up there is making them crazy." Moments later, he solves the problem he's posed: "It could possibly be a pheromone. That's what female animals release to trigger mating behavior. It could also provoke serious hyper-aggression like—some kind of drug." Only at this point can the spectator make full use of what she's heard earlier from an airline technician who was soaking the leis in which the snakes are nested with an unknown liquid as he loads them onto the plane: "Yes, sir, I'm soaking the leis with it. The pheromone'll make these guys go fuckin' crazy." Not only is the snakes' behavior explained, but we are given to understand that our prior inability to explain it, and indeed our ignorance that it even required special explanation, is due entirely to our unfamiliarity with snakes, and not to any textual uncertainty about its cause.

Given that *Snakes on a Plane* is, by design, a B movie, its preoccupation with slipping plausible explanations into scenes of gratuitously gruesome violence and cartoonish action seems overly conscientious. But if the film's title can be read as a disavowal of allegory, then this relentless rationalism might be a disavowal of its own: of the inexplicability that characterizes the fantastic. *Snakes on a Plane* seems to want to insist that even if it doesn't happen all the time in our world, its narrative is entirely in keeping with our world's "natural laws." Read against the mystification of the terrorists' motives in *United 93*—in which the origins of a perfectly plausible deed are located outside the boundaries of our world, our language, our imaginations—this insistence on locating the implausible *within* the boundaries of what we can know and understand begins to seem like a rebuke. When it explains, however perfunctorily or even unnecessarily, the logic behind its own narrative, *Snakes on a Plane* implies that it is *responsible for* making such explanations, and that any narrative that omits them is using the fantastic's uncertainty to escape its own obligations to make sense of its own narrative world.

Snakes on a Plane's narrative commitment to rationalizing its world is further elaborated in how it presents and visualizes its characters and their environment; the film emphasizes continuities and connections between characters' initial appearances and their later behavior, for instance, so that human behavior seems stripped of its ability to surprise. This is, perhaps, just a fancy way of saying that the cast is a collection of hoary genre stereotypes, such as the gay male flight attendant[32] or the rapt newlyweds. We know the moment we see a preening diva with a yapping Chihuahua board the plane that the dog will end up as snake bait, just as we know that the snobby British businessman will get his comeuppance in some appropriately reptilian fashion. We know that the unaccompanied minors and the infant will be saved from peril, and that the death of the overweight, over-made-up middle-aged woman in a muumuu will be more humorous than horrifying. While the careful explanation of various plot points may seem like a pathetic reach for realism on the part of a film that ought to have relinquished any such effort after the title card, *Snakes on a Plane*'s candor about its reliance on conventional narrative tropes requires us to find another explanation that can make sense of both its realistic and its genre-bound gestures. I have already described the film as distancing itself from the fantastic by claiming membership in one of the genres that Todorov locates at its borders; what initially seemed implausible is actually subject to rational explanation and is therefore merely "uncanny." The fantastic is bounded on the other side by the genre of the "marvelous," in which our knowledge of the laws of nature has been incomplete and therefore must be expanded to allow for that material. While not exactly supernatural, the formulaic and exaggerated caricatures composing the cast of *Snakes on a Plane* certainly don't behave according to our world's "natural laws." But by highlighting the coherence and predictability of the conventions that govern these characters, the film reassures us that they obey their own narrative laws; we can explain them by looking beyond the "natural laws" of realism to the "marvelous" laws of the genre narrative. *Snakes on a Plane*, then, manages to embrace not one but *both* of the genres that border the fantastic, despite the contradiction between the uncanny and the marvelous. A disaster narrative can survive contradiction, the film implies, but not the inability to decipher causes and explanations that defines the fantastic.

I've called *Snakes on a Plane* a "rebuke" to fantastic narratives of airborne terror, and I'd like to focus on one visual element in the film to unpack the ways we might think about it as a critique of the fantastic tropes within the supposedly "documentary" impulse of a film like *United 93*. Like the latter film, *Snakes on a Plane* pauses after the pilots and the passengers board the plane, everyone is seated, and the flight begins normally. We in the audience wait for something to happen but, for the moment, nothing does. The moment is oddly similar to the corresponding one in *United 93*; in both cases, we know what's going to happen, so the suspense we feel derives only from the question of how it will begin. In the case of *United 93*, we see from the exchange of glances and hurried whispers among the hijackers that Jarrah is hesitating, and we recognize that when he recovers his resolve the hijacking will commence; like the motives for the attack, the timing is related to his invisible and unknowable interior life. In the case of *Snakes on a Plane*, a shot of the plane cutting through clouds cuts to one of an altimeter registering a smooth climb; that image then fades into one of digital display that clicks to begin counting down from two hours just as the plane attains cruising altitude. The camera pulls back to reveal that the timer rests at the center of a seething mass of snakes, and then further back through a wall of boxes to show us that the snakes, at least for the next two hours, are concealed within a pallet loaded with boxes of leis that we've previously seen being loaded into the plane's cargo bay. In *United 93*, the hijackers' leader delays their plan, whose execution is then dependent on his equally unreadable decision to proceed. In *Snakes on a Plane*, the visual transition from the instruments measuring a routine flight to the methodical countdown to the explosion that will release the snakes equates the two operations, as if the violence that is to follow is a result of the same technological and economic circumstances that have produced the airline industry. If our ingenuity and ambition can make human flight a commonplace experience, it must follow, the cut implies, that the same forces will at times produce the kind of violence and disregard for life that we are about to witness. Believing that one belongs to the "natural laws" of this world while the other evades them is a self-serving form of denial.

But there remains one element of *Snakes on a Plane* that can be fully explained neither rationally, like the snakes' behavior; marvelously, like the characters' fidelity to type; nor systemically, like the connection between Eddie Kim's pathological actions and the society in which he lives. That element is the hero himself, FBI agent Neville Flynn, played by Samuel L. Jackson. We first encounter him in Hawaii when he rescues Sean from the hit men Eddie Kim initially sends after the witness. Sean has realized the killers are at his door and is standing, paralyzed, on the balcony of his apartment when the arm of a black man snakes in behind him from off-screen and pulls him, mouth covered, into what may be safety or certain death. The next shot is a close-up of Flynn holding Sean tightly against his chest; forestalling any questions Sean might pose as his mouth is uncovered, Flynn warns, "Do as I say, and you live." That's all the explanation we ever get as to how the FBI knew that Sean had witnessed the murder or that Eddie Kim had

FIGURE 2.3. *Introducing Agent Neville Flynn (*Snakes on a Plane, *New Line Cinema, 2006).*

located him. Throughout the film Flynn is theatrically unimpressed by those around him or by his own heroics, to an extent that seems to exceed what we might expect from any such action hero; his air of disdain for the challenges that confront him eventually produces his climactic line, famously added in reshoots after the completion of the film and inspired by suggestions from the film's prerelease Internet fan base: "Enough is enough! I have had it with these motherfuckin' snakes on this motherfuckin' plane."

Fans generated versions of the line as they jokingly rehearsed, in cartoons, on T-shirts, and in their own homemade videos, the spectacle of Samuel L. Jackson in a film called *Snakes on a Plane*.[33] The line belongs, then, not to the character but to a quintessential Samuel L. Jackson who was already fully formed in his fans' minds before they'd heard of Neville Flynn, and whose performances in other films was imagined as wholly predictive of what they would see in this one. When New Line Cinema was moved by the film's prerelease notoriety to shoot additional scenes that would significantly raise the film's level of gore and titillation, the line was added as a kind of tribute to the fans whose engagement with their imagined film inspired the studio to make the actual film look more like it. The line epitomizes Jackson's performance as Flynn, and the fact that Flynn doesn't come across, as the other characters do, as having arrived straight from central casting. His performance doesn't fit into an internally consistent narrative world because we understand it as generated by Samuel L. Jackson in *our* world, without reference to the particular narrative realm of *Snakes on a Plane*. In a way, this is another of the effects that Vivian Sobchack describes as a kind of eruption of the documentary register into a fictive frame. She uses the example of how widespread awareness of the unfolding details of Woody Allen and Mia Farrow's breakup disrupted the audience's reading of their performances in *Husbands and Wives* (Woody Allen, 1992) when it was originally screened; when a line of dialogue seemed more compelling in relation to the pair's real circumstances than to their characters', the film's "fictional space was . . . ruptured and restructured as a space of the real."[34] Like the CNN footage from our world that penetrated into the fictional frame of *United 93*, Flynn's character calls on the "existential and cultural knowledge" we bring with us to the film from the real world. And as in that moment from *United 93*, the relationship between the fictive and the real is more complicated than it might seem. Perhaps, to use Sobchack's formulation, Flynn's character gains its "axiological charge of affects and values from an existential and cultural knowledge that exceeds—and contextualizes—the homogenizing devices of both cinematic and narrative representation."[35] But that "existential and cultural knowledge," in this case the imaginary film generated in the minds of potential viewers simply by placing the film's title in conjunction with the name "Samuel L. Jackson," only proves the extent to which our cultural existence has *already* been shaped by "the homogenizing devices of both cinematic and narrative representation." The character may exceed and contextualize the world of *this* film, but only by virtue of the fact that the idea of Samuel L. Jackson, our expectations of the B movie, and our own compulsion to see variations of the same film over and over again, have all already been implanted within us by *other* films, and by the conventions of cinematic representation more generally.

If we return to examine *United 93*'s "documentary" use of the CNN footage of Flight 175 through this lens, we might emphasize the mediated quality of this footage over its documentary place in our memories. Greengrass may have used the footage to stand for the "real," but of course it is a "real" framed by the televisual medium, conditioned by the logo of the station superimposed on it. The fact of that framing only temporarily troubles the distinction between the "real" world we inhabit and the cinematic world in which we immerse ourselves. When *United 93* uses the CNN logo superimposed over an image to produce the heightened impact of the "real," it conveys the paradoxical message that what is most "real" is an image already mediated for public consumption. And when *Snakes on a Plane*, on the other hand, embraces its fans' influence over the fiction they're consuming, the "real" power they revel in is entirely derived from the cinematic conventions they've mastered, and it can only be expressed within the bounds of those conventions. The latter film, then, avoids the actual events of 9/11 to expose the former's representation of them in "real time" as a denial of the extent to which, even as they first unfolded before our eyes, their "reality" was already embedded within the generic conventions that structure the medium through which we apprehended them; and further that the time in which they took place ("too soon!") already measured against the expectations to which those conventions give rise. If *United 93* allows us to "transcend" the experience of the 9/11 attacks, it does so only because the media's presentation of the attacks had already laid the tracks for their *re*-presentation in a new genre, allowing for a narrative in which they end "right on time."

NOTES

1. Homi Bhabha, "A Narrative of Divided Civilizations," *Chronicle of Higher Education*, September 28, 2001, B12.

2. Sean Smith and Jac Chebatoris, "A Dark Day Revisited," *Newsweek*, April 10, 2006, http://www.newsweek.com/2006/04/09/a-dark-day-revisited.html.

3. James Kendrick, "Representing the Unrepresentable: 9/11 on Film and Television," in *Why We Fought: America's Wars in Film and History*, ed. Peter C. Rollins and John E. O'Connor (Lexington: University Press of Kentucky, 2008), 511–528.

4. Linda Williams, "Film Bodies: Gender, Genre, and Excess," *Film Quarterly* 44 (Summer 1991): 11.

5. Kendall R. Phillips, *Projected Fears: Horror Films and American Culture* (Westport, CT: Praeger, 2005), 5.

6. J. Hoberman, "The New Disaster Movie," *Village Voice*, May 9, 2006, http://www.villagevoice.com/2006-05-09/film/the-new-disaster-movie/.

7. Roger Ebert, review of *United 93*, RogerEbert.com, April 28, 2006, http://rogerebert.suntimes.com/apps/pbcs.dll/article?AID=/20060427/REVIEWS/60419006.

8. David Denby, "Last Impressions," *New Yorker*, May 1, 2006, http://www.newyorker.com/archive/2006/05/01/060501crci_cinema.

9. Hoberman, "New Disaster Movie."

10. A *Newsweek* article of April 10, 2006, typifies these speculations. The manager of a New York City theater that pulled the trailer after audience protests worries, "I don't think people are ready for this," while the daughter of one of the flight's casualties argues against the idea that the film was "exploiting a national tragedy." Smith and Chebatoris, "A Dark Day Revisited."

11. Williams, "Film Bodies," 4.

12. Ibid., 5.

13. Manohla Dargis, "Defiance under Fire: Paul Greengrass's Harrowing 'United 93,'" *New York Times*, April 28, 2006, http://movies.nytimes.com/2006/04/28/movies/28unit.html; Stephanie Zacharek, review of *United 93*, Salon.com, April 26, 2006, http://www.salon.com/entertainment/movies/review/2006/04/26/united_93/index.html; and Kenneth Turan, "Too Real?," *Los Angeles Times*, April 28, 2006, http://articles.latimes.com/2006/apr/28/entertainment/et-united28.

14. Williams, "Film Bodies," 6, 9.

15. Rush Limbaugh, "Paul Greengrass Interview on Rush Limbaugh," FreeRepublic.com, April 28, 2006, http://209.157.64.201/focus/f-news/1623538/posts.

16. Frank Rich, "Too Soon? It's Too Late for 'United 93,'" *New York Times*, May 7, 2006, http://select.nytimes.com/2006/05/07/opinion/07rich.html.

17. Other critics, like Andrew Sarris, see the film as proposing too little "difference" altogether; because the film "giv[es] equal time to the hijackers" and refuses to lionize a few "bigger and younger males . . . at the expense of the rest of the passengers," he argues, "the four hijackers were more individualized than the 40 innocent victims." But Sarris, perhaps, goes too far when he writes that "indeed, at the film's climax, a disinterested observer might be left to wonder who one was supposed to root for: the rebellious passengers breaking down the cockpit door or the hijacker seeking to fly the plane into the U.S. Capitol building before he is interrupted." The fact that it's hard to imagine rooting for the "wrong" side even with no more information than that provided in Sarris's one-sentence description of the adversaries is ample evidence that there can be no "disinterested observer" to events already judged by the language in which they're cast. Like the film itself, Sarris's rhetoric clearly privileges the victims over the hijackers by portraying the former as engaging in spontaneous, autonomous, and collective action while the latter play out a role from which they can imagine no deviation. "Greengrass' *United 93* Gives Terrorists Curious Airtime," *New York Observer*, May 7, 2006, http://www.observer.com/node/38798.

18. In its portrayal of this process, the film's narrative implicitly endorses the argument made by Elaine Scarry that in contrast to our military defense systems' inability to act against the hijackers in a timely fashion, the response of Flight 93's passengers represents a model of effective action based on "informed consent" generated by a body acting as "a small legislative assembly or town meeting." "Citizenship in Emergency," *Boston Review* 27 (October–November 2002), http://bostonreview.net/BR27.5/scarry.html.

19. In this essay, I will refer to the airline and flight number of each flight the first time I refer to it, and thereafter to the flight number alone, to maintain the distinction between Flight 93 and *United 93*.

20. For an example of the latter, see Sarris, "Greengrass' *United 93* Gives Terrorists Curious Airtime," and of the former, Rich, "Too Soon?"

21. Williams, "Film Bodies," 10.

22. Ibid., 11, 12.

23. Vivian Sobchack, *Carnal Thoughts: Embodiment and Moving Image Culture* (Berkeley: University of California Press, 2004), 261.

24. Ibid., 271.

25. Ibid., 285.

26. Ibid.

27. Tzvetan Todorov, *The Fantastic: A Structural Approach to a Literary Genre*, trans. Richard Howard (Ithaca, NY: Cornell University Press, 1975), 25.

28. Jeff Jensen describes the film's production history in "Kicking Asp," *Entertainment Weekly*, July 28, 2006, http://www.ew.com/ew/article/0,,1219727,00.html. Victoria Mielke's website *9/11: Pop Culture and Remembrance* catalogs some of the changes that were made to other films and film advertising campaigns already underway to remove or alter material that seemed to evoke the attacks. See http://septterror.tripod.com/.

29. The buzz about the film started a year before its release when the screenwriter Josh Friedman posted on his personal blog about being asked to work on the script

for *Snakes on a Plane*, to which Samuel L. Jackson was already attached. As word of the proposed film spread around the Internet, people began to design T-shirts, write theme songs, and imagine episodes from the film without knowing anything more about it than its title and lead. Instead of trying to prevent the proliferation of unlicensed material related to *Snakes on a Plane*, New Line Cinema embraced the underground publicity, sponsored a contest to choose a band whose *Snakes*-related song would appear on the soundtrack, and eventually even decided to add five extra shooting days "so that elements culled from the fans' input could be incorporated into the mix." David Waldon, *Snakes on a Plane: The Guide to the Internet Sssssensation* (New York: Thunder's Mouth Press, 2006), 11.

30. Jeff Jensen, "Making Hisssstory," *Entertainment Weekly*, August 18, 2006, http://www.ew.com/ew/article/0,,1228538,00.html.

31. Todorov, *The Fantastic*, 63.

32. Actually, the "gay" flight attendant represents a kind of doubling down on the film's commitment to a "what you see is what you get" narrative ethic; because of his fey affectations, Ken provokes raised eyebrows whenever he mentions his girlfriend, but when the plane finally lands in LA, there she is, a blonde cheerleader type who leaps into his arms, wraps her legs around his waist, and instantly renders Ken's heterosexuality as stereotyped as his homosexuality seemed.

33. Waldon, *Snakes on a Plane*, 37, 60, 73.

34. Sobchack, *Carnal Thoughts*, 277.

35. Ibid., 271.

CHAPTER THREE

Transforming Horror

David Cronenberg's Cinematic Gestures after 9/11

ADAM LOWENSTEIN

From *Shivers* (1975) through *The Fly* (1986), the cinema of director David Cronenberg repeatedly depicted the human body thrust to such violent extremes of physical transformation that he earned nicknames like the "Baron of Blood" among horror fans.[1] Cronenberg's films remained equally disturbing from *Dead Ringers* (1988) through *Spider* (2002), but they tended to channel the notion of transformation in less visceral ways.[2] The result was a series of more critically acclaimed films closer in tone and reception to art cinema than the horror genre.[3]

In the wake of 9/11, a transformation of a different kind occurs in Cronenberg's work. With his remarkable, intimately linked films *A History of Violence* (2005) and *Eastern Promises* (2007), Cronenberg moves toward integrating the two halves of his career. One must add the caveat, however, that to divide his career into "halves" in the first place is not entirely accurate, since the art cinema proclivities were always there in the "horror films," and the horror tendencies remain present in the "art films." Yet the ability of *A History of Violence* and *Eastern Promises* to meld the sensational shocks of his early efforts with the art cinema trappings that characterize his later work, such as the presence of internationally renowned stars and controversial sexual themes, signals something new for Cronenberg. This essay analyzes these two films in terms of how the haunting echoes of 9/11 and the subsequent U.S. "War on Terror" in Afghanistan and Iraq figure in transforming horror genre vocabulary into provocations concerning globalized geopolitics in Cronenberg's cinema. These transformations in Cronenberg's films take on particular importance in the post-9/11 cinematic landscape, where many explicit representations of the War on Terror fail to reach a substantial audience (e.g., most Iraq War films prior to *The Hurt Locker* [Kathryn Bigelow, 2008], and even that Academy Award winner was more of a critics' darling than a sweeping popular success), and many implicit representations face critical dismissal through unfortunate labels such as "torture porn" (see the critical reception of *Hostel* [Eli Roth, 2005] and its contemporary horror film brethren).[4] Cronenberg's post-9/11 films offer valuable opportunities for political engagement with the War on Terror by interweaving popular accessibility, critical admiration, and the confrontational aesthetics honed over more than three decades spent straddling the horror film and art cinema.

Eastern Promises transpires amid the sound and fury of clashing cultures in today's London. The film begins by introducing three bloodied bodies in succession: Soyka (Aleksander Mikic), a captain in the Russian organized crime syndicate *vory v zakone*, has his throat slit in a barbershop belonging to a Turkish immigrant; Tatiana (Sarah Jeanne Labrosse), a pregnant, fourteen-year-old Russian prostitute, bleeds between her legs and faints while asking for help from an Indian pharmacist; and Tatiana's daughter, born as her mother dies in Trafalgar Hospital, emerges tiny and helpless, awash in her mother's blood. The visual image of blood that binds these three scenes, which indicates a continuity between these three bodies, reasserts itself in the film's dialogue shortly afterward. Anna (Naomi Watts), the nurse supervising the birth of Tatiana's daughter, comes home from the hospital and presents Tatiana's diary to her own uncle Stepan (Jerzy Skolimowski). Although Anna's deceased father was Russian, her mother is English and she cannot read Russian herself; she hopes her Russian uncle will translate the diary for her.

Stepan refuses, however, accusing Anna of robbing the dead. He insists that the diary should be buried with Tatiana's "bodies." Anna corrects Stepan's English, reminding him that he means the singular "body," not the plural "bodies." He shrugs off her comment, a gesture that suggests she misses the point viewers already understand: blood connects each body to a series of bodies. By the same logic, Stepan's apparent infelicity with the English language, his inability to master it as an immigrant, points toward another language the audience must learn during the film—neither Russian nor English, both Russian and English—the language, in other words, spoken by Cronenberg's cinema.

When *Eastern Promises* redefines an apparently singular body by showing us the plural bodies that lend it meaning—and writes that redefinition on the body, in blood—it constitutes the latest iteration of Cronenberg's longstanding cinematic project. This project's roots in horror will be recognizable to anyone observing Cronenberg's career since he reframed the intellectual concerns of his experimental mini-features *Stereo* (1969) and *Crimes of the Future* (1970) to enter the commercial arena with *Shivers*. Whether we think of the phallic/fecal-looking parasites that induce sexual dementia in *Shivers*, or the radical psychotherapy that enables emotions of rage to be "born" as murderous children in *The Brood* (1979), or the matter transmitter that fuses human and housefly at the molecular-genetic level in *The Fly*, Cronenberg's horror confronts us with bodies that revolt. These are revolting bodies in a double sense: they rebel against their conventional identities and functions within the films, but they also prove difficult for us to watch. Given the confrontational nature of Cronenberg's cinematic project, it makes a certain amount of practical as well as poetic sense that his films would appeal to their widest audience in many years during the turbulent times dominated by the Iraq War, in the still-unfolding wake of 9/11. In this moment, Cronenberg turns his attention more specifically than ever before to the conjuncture of violence and globalized geopolitics.

According to the cultural anthropologist Arjun Appadurai, the key to defining what makes globalization "strikingly new" over the past century or so is "a technological explosion, largely in the domain of transportation and information, that makes the interactions of a print-dominated world seem as hard-won and as easily erased as the print revolution made earlier forms of cultural traffic appear."[5] For Appadurai, the centrality of media such as cinema, television, and computers to the new global cultural economy demands that we shift our understanding of globalization from standard center-periphery models, where concepts such as Americanization have explained how the center dominates the periphery, to a more "disjunctive" point of view. In disjunctive globalization, global flows move in multiple, uneven, and idiosyncratic directions simultaneously, not just from the center to the periphery. "The complexity of the current global economy," concludes Appadurai, "has to do with certain fundamental disjunctures between economy, culture, and politics that we have only begun to theorize."[6] The events of 9/11 could be seen as inaugurating a heightened awareness of a particular form of disjunctive globalization, one where global flows operate according to the speed of digital media and the visual logic of spectacular violence. After 9/11, in other words, disjunctive globalization looks more than ever before "just like a movie"—a phrase used again and again to describe the awful carnage of that day. Cronenberg's post-9/11 films go to the political heart of this violent, cinematized sense of globalization. The resulting illumination of how violence circulates in a global era where we are *shown* so much but *see* so little represents a crucial political turn for Cronenberg. Analyzing this turn invites consideration of how Cronenberg's presentation of violence, with its connections to his earlier horror films, shapes the way these new films imagine globalized geopolitics after 9/11.

A History of Violence directly precedes *Eastern Promises* and demands contemplation alongside it. Based loosely on a graphic novel by John Wagner and Vince Locke adapted for the screen by Josh Olson, *A History of Violence* distills Cronenberg's most powerful themes and applies them, rather uncharacteristically, to an explicitly American context (as a Canadian director, Cronenberg tends to favor explicitly Canadian or vaguely defined "North American" settings for his films—even so, the locales of Millbrook, Indiana, and Philadelphia in *A History of Violence* were shot in Ontario).[7] *Eastern Promises* extends the history of violence to London, Russia, Afghanistan, Chechnya, and elsewhere, but it, too, inevitably, addresses the United States' role in contemporary geopolitics. *Eastern Promises* insists that when Americanization both gives birth to and gives way to globalization, intertwined histories of violence *become* the global condition. If 9/11 and the Iraq War inform *A History of Violence*, as I will contend below, then the collapse of the Soviet Union informs *Eastern Promises*. What the two films accomplish as one conjoined work stems from how Cronenberg interweaves these two watershed geopolitical events to foster critical reflection on globalization. In both films, this work of reflection depends on the use of gestures first employed in Cronenberg's earliest horror films.

Gesture, as a mode of speaking with the body rather than with words, has always played a vital role in film art. For the philosopher Giorgio Agamben (extending the work of Gilles Deleuze), gesture constitutes not only the bedrock of cinematic expression but also the means by which cinema becomes political. Cinema rests on an "antinomic polarity" between images, which freeze gestural movements, and gestures, which preserve the dynamism of these movements. According to Agamben, "the former lives in magical isolation," while "the latter always refers beyond itself to a whole of which it is a part." Cinema's fundamental investment in the gesture, rather than the image, indicates how film "belongs essentially to the realm of ethics and politics (and not simply to that of aesthetics)." Why is this so? For Agamben, "What characterizes gesture is that in it nothing is being produced or acted, but rather something is being endured and supported. The gesture, in other words, opens the sphere of *ethos* as the more proper sphere of that which is human." Gestures, then, have political and ethical value in that they break with "the false alternative between ends and means that paralyzes morality." The "mediality" of gestures—their preservation of movement that endures and supports (means) instead of subjugating means to the finality of goals that produce and act (ends)—allows them to convey means and ends as a single, ongoing process. The result is that cinema, with the gesture as its core expression, invites spectators to perceive actions as a fluidity encompassing means and ends—"a pure and endless mediality" where ethical decisions present themselves at every juncture, not just the endpoint captured in the frozen image. Agamben concludes that "cinema leads images back to the homeland of gesture," but that "the duty of the director" (a political duty) resides with how that director's film will provoke "the liberation of the image into gesture."[8] To understand how Cronenberg fulfills this duty, one must trace the post-9/11 gestures of *A History of Violence* and *Eastern Promises* through those of *Shivers* and *The Brood*.

A HISTORY OF VIOLENCE AND A NEW SOCIAL ORDER

A History of Violence punctures the dream that the United States can somehow revive its shaken confidence at home by lashing out abroad after 9/11—instead, the film presents an "ideal" American home whose exterior layers peel away to reveal the violence that always lived there, that in fact made the "ideal" possible. The film begins with two thugs "checking out" of a country motel by murdering the staff—an act they perform as nonchalantly as returning keys. Cronenberg emphasizes the routine nature of their brutality by allowing the violence itself to occur off-screen (showing only the aftermath), while we witness instead the thugs inching their car through the parking lot and complaining about the hot weather. Cronenberg's decision to shoot the film's opening four and a half minutes as a long take only accentuates the sluggish atmosphere of stifling drudgery.

When the violence finally appears on-screen, it is unbearable to watch—one of the thugs draws his gun on a whimpering young girl who is clutching her doll inside the corpse-strewn motel office. Our relief when Cronenberg cuts from the gun blast to a different young girl waking up screaming from a nightmare is as palpable as the dread we felt in the previous scene. Perhaps that motel was only a dream, we tell ourselves, hoping to wish it away. Indeed, when this new young girl, Sarah Stall (Heidi Hayes), receives comfort from her father, Tom (Viggo Mortensen), her mother, Edie (Maria Bello), and her teenage brother, Jack (Ashton Holmes), we begin to believe what they tell her—that there is no such thing as monsters, that shadows flee from the light. By the conclusion of *A History of Violence*, however, we know that monsters exist—and not just in the shape of the very real thugs at the motel. We know that the monsters were already there in that cozy room with Sarah, telling her not to fear such things.

FIGURE 3.1. *Reassuring young Sarah in* A History of Violence *(New Line Cinema, 2005).*

Her family, as it turns out, rests on a foundation of violence connected to Tom's buried past life as Joey Cusack, a vicious mobster in Philadelphia. When this past life reawakens in the present, Tom's family must face a history of violence it never knew—but also, even more devastatingly, a history it has always known at some level, no matter how unspoken or unconscious. When Tom becomes/returns to his identity as Joey Cusack, his whole family reckons with itself in a new way—Jack brutally assaults his bullies at school, and Edie enters Tom's darkness in the most intimate way (she has sex with Joey, not Tom, and uses her influence as a lawyer to protect Joey's criminal past rather than expose it). In the film's shattering final scene, when Tom/Joey returns home to the family dinner table after yet another round of killing he hopes will put his past to rest for good, even Sarah seems altered by this history of violence. While Edie and Jack stay still, Sarah rises to set a plate for her father at the table. Only, when she places the silverware beside the plate, she turns the knife the wrong way—it faces toward her father, not away from him. Can the family survive with this new consciousness, this new recognition of its intimacy with violence, this awareness that it *is* the monster it used to dismiss as a phantom? Cronenberg leaves these questions achingly, awfully open—the film's final shot shows Tom looking desperately toward Edie, waiting for a sign from her about who he is in this once familiar but now completely bewildering setting. The reverse shot of Edie never arrives.

Cronenberg has said that *A History of Violence* is the closest he has come to making a film in that quintessential American genre, the Western.⁹ The film does indeed present a version of the Western narrative where an embattled homesteader defends his family and land from hostile outsiders, and it came at a time in the United States when variations on this theme were being mobilized to support the fiction of the Iraq War as a defense of the home, not an act of aggression. Cronenberg was keenly aware of this post-9/11 political context: "When westerns are mentioned by the President as part of his foreign policy, when Osama bin Laden is wanted 'dead or alive,' you have to seriously think about the 'interbleeding' of genre, myth, and *realpolitik*, which, I guess, is not that *real*."¹⁰ The film ruptures illusions of a peaceful home protected from the chaotic violence outside it. Instead, this home's mirage of peace depends on the violence hidden within it, silent but essential. What does the future hold for a family—for a nation, perhaps—that can no longer dwell in the comforting myths of inside and outside? Can it survive in the face of this knowledge? Cronenberg's refusal of the reverse shot at the conclusion of *A History of Violence* offers no easy way out of these questions.

This absent reverse shot functions very similarly to the gesture that concludes *Shivers*, Cronenberg's first horror film.¹¹ When *Shivers* ends, the residents of a luxury condominium have all been infected by slithering parasites that cause their hosts to exhibit wild, sexually "deviant" behaviors paired with a violent need to transmit the parasites through sexual contact. Rather than portraying the triumph of the parasites as a frenzied, terrifying apocalypse, *Shivers* presents the infected residents calmly exiting the condominium in an orderly procession of automobiles, each one carrying a newly formed couple created by the parasites: a doctor who once spurned his nurse's flirtations; a straight housewife who never dared to pursue her friend's lesbian desire for her; a father now incestuously united with his teenage daughter. These couples are no longer the raving, aggressively sexual zombies we witnessed them acting as earlier in the film, but rather a series of peaceful, attractive couples whose gestures (contented smiles, the nurse's lighting of the doctor's cigarette) convey their pleasure in being together. The radio broadcast played over the end credits suggests that the parasite infection has now spread beyond the condominium, with unconfirmed reports of a "citywide wave of violent sexual assaults" now gripping Montreal.

Cronenberg's decision to end *Shivers* with the gestures of the happy couples rather than these "violent sexual assaults" prefigures the impact of the refused reverse shot in *A History of Violence*. In both films, ambivalent concluding gestures raise questions about how to draw lines between old and new social orders, as well as how relatively "better" or "worse" these orders really are. Is the pre-infection social order of *Shivers* better than the post-infection one? The radio report says yes; the gestures of the couples say no. Can a family face its history of violence at home, the very place where it used to dismiss that violence as a childish nightmare? In *A History of Violence*, the gesture of Tom/ Joey's unanswered look offers no solution. Both films end, then, by liberating the image into gesture in Agamben's sense. Whether through the happy couples of *Shivers* or the yearning gaze of *A History of Violence*, concluding actions in these films flow simultaneously backward to earlier scenes we must now read differently, and forward into futures we must imagine for ourselves based on ethical political decisions.

The idyllic advertisement for the condominium that opens *Shivers* rings as hollow by the film's end as the reassurances the Stalls give to Sarah when she wakes from her "nightmare" at the beginning of *A History of Violence*. In *Shivers*, the "good life" promised by the advertisement clashes with a very different vision of a "good life" enabled by parasitic infection. In the ad, this good life stems from equating capitalist consumption with a comfortable lifestyle based on self-enclosed isolation. In the gesture, the good life stems from violent bodily transformations that demand interpersonal contact of the most intimate kind. The move from an illusory denial of violence, wrapped in an atomizing blanket of capitalist consumption, to a terrifying embrace of violence that nonetheless forges a community impossible to realize earlier, invites viewers to ask certain political questions. At what ethical price does the denial of violence exist in the pre-infection social order? Is the ethical price of violent transformation worth paying when a genuine community rises as a post-infection social order?

Similarly, the family gatherings that begin and end *A History of Violence* present alternate versions of violence denied and violence embraced. The warm circle of family members that soothed Sarah when the film began (violence denied) splinters so seriously by the film's end that Sarah, by setting a place for her father at the table, must comfort *them* (violence embraced). Sarah's gesture suggests that the only way this family can continue to exist is by redefining itself as complicit in the violence it once denied. Tom/Joey's parallel gesture along these lines, his unanswered look toward Edie, leaves open the question of resolution. As in *Shivers*, the opportunity to pretend that the old order was simply better, that it was somehow separate from violence, has dissolved. It is no longer available as an illusion. Viewers must now make a choice that mirrors the one the Stalls struggle with: Can we face up to the new order, with its insistence on recognizing our own involvement with the violence within it? Confronting this question after 9/11, when understanding the new order requires new maps of globalized geopolitics, becomes possible in *A History of Violence* through gestures that reach back to *Shivers'* synthesis of physical and political transformation.

EASTERN PROMISES AND THE GLOBAL VILLAGE

Eastern Promises dismantles a myth at least as constitutive of contemporary geopolitics as the post-9/11 myth of the nonviolent American "home" in *A History of Violence*: that the end of the Soviet Union signals a triumph for "freedom" and "democracy" over totalitarian oppression, an enlightened new day in the "global village" made more perfect by removing the major obstacle to global capitalism. I choose the term "global village" deliberately, as its originator, the media theorist Marshall McLuhan, bears certain important similarities to Cronenberg: both are Canadian thinkers whose simultaneous proximity to and distance from the United States provide a valuable critical perspective on transformations in bodies and technologies across the border.[12] McLuhan's influence on Cronenberg can be detected most clearly in *Videodrome* (1983). In that film, a McLuhan-esque media prophet named "Brian O'Blivion" (who may also owe a debt to the French critical theorist Jean Baudrillard)[13] appears on television to utter lines like the following: "The television screen is the retina of the mind's eye; therefore, the television screen is part of the physical structure of the brain; therefore, whatever appears on the television screen emerges as raw experience for those who watch it. Therefore, television is reality, and reality is less than television." Of course, listening to Brian O'Blivion after 9/11 bears a queasy similarity to hearing Bush administration pronouncements on its confident ability to shape reality according to its whims, even if that reality stubbornly contradicts these desires.[14] It follows that Cronenberg would work hard to strip the "global village" concept of its reassuring connotations concerning technologically produced equality and harmonious multiculturalism (electronically enhanced, globally multiplied versions of the U.S. "melting pot" and Canadian "mosaic"). *Eastern Promises* confronts us with a very different global village, one where histories of violence set the terms for any reckoning with who we are or who we wish to be inside globalized geopolitics.

In the London of *Eastern Promises*, the presence of immigrants from all over the world may indeed inspire a number of business transactions—but the price paid, more often than not, comes in blood, and the suspicions and enmities between different cultures have hardly disappeared. Steve Knight, the screenwriter of *Eastern Promises*, explored this territory before in his screenplay for *Dirty Pretty Things* (Stephen Frears, 2002), a film that went a long way toward bringing the cinematic image of London into a more dynamic, complex, and culturally hybridized present than most mainstream films dare. Knight's sensibility seems more straightforwardly humanist than Cronenberg's, and *Eastern Promises* feels, at times, like an unresolved battle between Knight's affection for his characters and Cronenberg's commitment to playing them against each other in ways that highlight the savage violence embedded in wishful fantasies of the global village.[15]

One of the false notes in the film results from a stalemate between these two approaches, as the Russian gangster Nikolai (Viggo Mortensen), under instructions from his boss, Semyon (Armin Mueller-Stahl), visits Stepan to assassinate him. We do not see the encounter between them, but we learn later that Nikolai, who actually works undercover for the Russian desk at Scotland Yard, did not kill Stepan; instead, he sent him to a five-star hotel in Edinburgh to hide. If we had a sharper sense of Nikolai's struggle with this decision—as in an earlier sex scene with a Ukrainian prostitute where he must test his alliances to law and lawlessness, to deceiving others and deceiving himself—then his course of action might not feel so hollow and mechanical. As *Eastern Promises* stands, though, Nikolai's mercy toward Stepan seems as artificial as the film's penultimate scene, a sunny multicultural idyll that forgives and forgets by restoring family (Stepan returns, Anna adopts Tatiana's daughter and names her Christine [!]) and honoring difference (Christine's adopted mother and grandmother speak to her in both Russian and English). Nikolai's absence is the only hint given that all is not neatly, happily resolved.

When we finally do see Nikolai, his image destroys the preceding scene's reassurances. Sitting alone in the restaurant once run by his boss, Semyon, Nikolai has clearly achieved his goal of replacing Semyon as "king" of London's *vory v zakone*. But he expresses only silent, anguished desolation. The stark visual contrast between this coffin-like restaurant, with its enveloping shadows and darkly saturated colors, and the previous scene's warm natural light and invigorating sunshine, makes the very idea, even the dream, of Nikolai joining Anna and her family cruelly impossible. His exclusion from their world feels so complete, so extreme, that we are reminded how Tatiana's desires for what she calls "a better life" in London could only be "realized" as prostitution, rape, drug addiction, and death. Indeed, Tatiana's voice on the soundtrack, reading the words of her diary in Russian-accented English, provides a sound bridge between Anna at home and Nikolai at the restaurant. If Tatiana's "bodies" have now finally come to rest somewhere between these two spaces, Cronenberg demands that we reckon with the cost of the "better life" for Tatiana's daughter: the physical death of Tatiana and the spiritual

FIGURE 3.2. *A devastated Nikolai at the end of* Eastern Promises *(Focus Features, 2007).*

death of Nikolai. These lost lives challenge globalization's false promises concerning migration as mobility. As Tatiana writes in her diary, "I am condemned to give birth to my new life."

What will this "new life" feel like for Tatiana's daughter? *Eastern Promises* provides no definitive answer, but Cronenberg's *The Brood* offers one possibility.[16] Candy (Cindy Hinds) in *The Brood*, like Christine in *Eastern Promises*, inherits the anguish of a traumatic family history. Caught between her separated parents, Frank (Art Hindle) and Nola (Samantha Eggar), while they wage a bitter custody battle, Candy can do little more than stare in shocked silence while her world crumbles. Nola participates in an experimental psychotherapeutic program called "psychoplasmics," which encourages its patients to externalize their inner rage as outer physical manifestations (welts, sores, tumors, and, in Nola's unique case, a brood of murderous, parthenogenetically produced children). Nola's brood kills every person Nola discusses in therapy, including Candy's grandmother and schoolteacher—two murders Candy witnesses firsthand. At the film's climax, Candy herself nearly dies at the hands of the brood when Nola realizes Frank has only pretended to reconcile with her in order to steal Candy away forever. Frank, as desperate to hold on to Candy as Nola is, strangles Nola to death to neutralize the brood. As they drive away from the scene of this murder, Frank reassures Candy, "We're going home." But Candy, her clothes blood-spattered and her face stained with tears, offers no reply. Instead, Cronenberg zooms in to reveal two small welts on Candy's arm—the physical evidence that she cannot

FIGURE 3.3. *A devastated Candy at the end of* The Brood *(New World Pictures, 1979)*.

simply "go home," that she now carries her family's traumatic history inside and outside her own body. The film's final shot captures Candy's eyes in an extreme close-up: silent, staring, devastated, desolate.

Candy's haunted look prefigures Nikolai's at the end of *Eastern Promises*. Their shared gesture of the silent stare conveys similar emotions in both films: profound aloneness, silent suffering, and anticipation of future pain. But most of all, Candy and Nikolai stare together at the impossibility of "going home." The idea of Candy somehow settling into a "normal" family life with her father seems just as remote as the chances of Nikolai joining Anna's household. In *The Brood*, the impossibility of home revolves around family trauma embodied by the welts on Candy's skin. In *Eastern Promises*, the impossible home transforms into the impossible global village. Nikolai's exclusion from Anna's home derives from Tatiana's "bodies" and the globalized geopolitical violence they testify to, just as surely as Candy's exclusion from her father's vision of home emanates from her own scarred body. In this sense, the linked gestures that traverse the conclusions of the two films extend networks of familial violence central to the horror genre to those of political violence.[17] If the gestures that unite *Shivers* and *A History of Violence* remind us that the political issues concerning competing social orders made more horrifically explicit in the earlier film have not simply evaporated in the family setting of the later one, then *The Brood*'s gestural relation to *Eastern Promises* offers an equally powerful reminder in the opposite direction: that the familial anguish of the earlier film has not disappeared amid the globalized geopolitics of the later one. The post-9/11 nature of geopolitical violence in *Eastern Promises* emerges in yet another set of intertextual gestures, this time crossing between *A History of Violence* and *Eastern Promises* via the presence of both films' lead actor, Viggo Mortensen.

DOUBLED IDENTITIES

Mortensen's importance for Cronenberg's vision in both *Eastern Promises* (as Nikolai) and *A History of Violence* (as Tom/Joey) cannot be overstated. Mortensen masterfully conveys, through his wordless articulation of Nikolai's inner emptiness at the conclusion of *Eastern Promises*, a grim recognition that Nikolai can no longer answer the question "Who am I?" Is he an undercover agent working zealously to undermine *vory v zakone*? Or an underworld boss whose Scotland Yard connections provide a convenient rationalization for his need to be "king"? Does he love Anna? Or can he only truly love the vicious criminal world he chooses to live in, over and over again? The shock of lost identity, of knowing no longer who one is, electrifies the endings of *Eastern Promises* as well as *A History of Violence*. In both cases, final expressions of desperate, ravaged confusion about one's identity prevent the films from offering any comforting solutions to these problems as they arise in a globalized world. That Mortensen embodies these expressions silently in both films encourages us to process them as a single linked gesture—one that joins the post-9/11 violence of the United States during the War on Terror with the violence of multicultural London in the shadow of a dissolved Soviet Union. A gesture, in other words, that reveals globalized geopolitics as shared histories of violence.

Mortensen's presence, coming on the heels of his heroic star turns in Peter Jackson's blockbuster *The Lord of the Rings* series (2001–2003), expands Cronenberg's ability to reach a more mainstream audience than he has in the past. The collaboration with Mortensen, coupled with a step back from the more cultish genres of horror and science fiction and a step toward the more accessible genres of the gangster film, thriller, and Western, allows Cronenberg to deliver shocking violence to viewers less accustomed to his disturbing visions. By the same token, Cronenberg's die-hard fans must chew on more heavily foregrounded geopolitical themes than they might expect, even though some version of the director's signature spectacles of sex and violence still occur alongside them. In short, the gestures toward histories of violence in these two films will likely unsettle a number of different kinds of spectators for a variety of different reasons.

The theme of doubled identities, each so relentlessly voracious that one swallows the other until nothing of either remains, goes back much further in Cronenberg's work than his collaboration with Mortensen. In fact, Cronenberg's most notable previous collaboration with a major star that spanned two films also focused on this theme: Jeremy Irons in *Dead Ringers* and *M. Butterfly* (1993). In *Dead Ringers*, Irons plays identical twin gynecologists whose intimately conjoined lives implode when one falls in love with an actress—the twins' relationship cannot withstand this intrusion, so they spin into an ultimately suicidal decline of psychological disintegration. In *M. Butterfly* (based on the play by David Henry Hwang), Irons portrays a French diplomat whose double life includes the roles of a strait-laced government official as well as the secret lover of a Chinese opera singer—a singer who poses as a woman but who is actually a male Communist agent. Irons's character dedicates himself so feverishly to his fantasy of the singer that he does not realize her identities as male or Communist; when he must face these realities, he commits suicide.

The suicides that conclude *Dead Ringers* and *M. Butterfly* mirror each other as strikingly as the identity losses at the end of *A History of Violence* and *Eastern Promises*. Where Irons's characters radiate cerebral repression, Mortensen's enact physical volatility. No matter how psychologically burned-out Tom/Joey and Nikolai may be by the time Cronenberg finally cuts away from their faces and the credits roll, we cannot forget the astonishing feats of embodied violence they performed earlier. Even when these films end, we sense that Mortensen's characters remain coiled, ready to spring into murderous brutality should their bodily instincts get triggered. Irons's characters cannibalize themselves psychologically and take their lives physically, so that the aura of queerness surrounding them ultimately perishes with their bodies. Mortensen's characters resist this equivalence between torn mind and torn body, so their own moments of queerness (the lingering embrace between Joey and his brother; Nikolai's simmering flirtation with his boss's closeted son) explode in violent physical fireworks. As a result, Cronenberg's latest films channel the director's recurring fascination with bodies and minds at war over identity in particular ways: the promise of violence lives on in the body, even if the mind surrenders to tortured uncertainty about identity.[18] In the globalized contexts of *A History of Violence* and *Eastern Promises*, this violent body and defeated mind form a vision of external aggression cut off from internal reflection—of contemporary geopolitics as a sleepwalk from one destructive act to the next.

Not coincidentally, *A History of Violence* and *Eastern Promises* both include a bravura sequence that crystallizes the film's concepts of an instinctive body outpacing a rational mind. In *A History of Violence*, the sex scene between Tom/Joey and Edie condenses all the hatred, mistrust, desire, and need that exist between the characters into an ecstatically punishing fuck on the staircase of their home. Cronenberg films this encounter with stunning eloquence—the line between revulsion and arousal, rage and love emanates from the bruising twists and turns of their bodies on the stairs, attracted and repelled in equal measure. Edie knows Tom lied to her about his past as Joey, just as Tom knows Edie saved him from the law by lying about her knowledge of Joey. Nevertheless, their bodies *act* in ways that make what and how these characters *know* seem impoverished, one-dimensional. Through gestures, their bodies speak the darkest ambivalences of their relationship.

The analogous scene in *Eastern Promises* depicts Nikolai ambushed at a public bathhouse by two assassins who mistake him for Semyon's son Kirill (Vincent Cassel). Semyon sets up Nikolai: the tattoos Nikolai recently received at Semyon's request designate him as a leader within *vory v zakone* at the same level as Kirill, so Nikolai's nakedness in the bathhouse allows the assassins to identify him as Semyon's son. In a breathtaking set of savage physical maneuvers, the nude and unarmed Nikolai kills the two clothed and armed assassins. Cronenberg's images of Nikolai stripped to his essence, both literally naked and metaphorically pure through his complete immersion in violence, pack an embodied shock similar to the sex scene in *A History of Violence*. Again, the body speaks with a gestural power and subtlety toward which the mind can only stumble.

In *A History of Violence*, a third body haunts the sex between Tom and Edie: Joey, the ghost of a violent past whose presence in this scene reminds us so forcefully that he never truly went away, that he never really became ghostly. The fact that this violent sexual encounter on the stairs echoes an earlier, apparently innocent and playful sex scene instigated by Edie—she dresses up as a cheerleader to simulate an imaginary high-school dating relationship she and Tom never had—underlines how a convincing sense of the past was never established between the couple. First, Edie tries to fill that void with clichéd sexual fantasy, but not until Joey emerges do Tom and Edie fully connect physically; only then can a real history take shape between them.

In *Eastern Promises*, the history that haunts the bathhouse scene is written on Nikolai's body, much as Candy's history is written on hers in *The Brood*. Nikolai's tattoos include not only the "stars" recently added at Semyon's behest, but also a number of coded images that tell his criminal history for those conversant in the subculture of *vory v zakone*: the prisons where he was incarcerated, the length of the sentences he served, the kinds of crime he committed.[19] Nikolai's most prominent tattoo, which covers most of his back, shows three towers crowned with cupolas. Although the significance of this tattoo within *vory v zakone* most likely relates to chronicling prison terms (three towers = three terms), the tattoo's immediate iconic reference is, of course, the Kremlin.

Eastern Promises was written prior to the highly publicized murder of the Russian exile (and former KGB agent) Alexander Litvinenko in London on November 23, 2006.[20] But Litvinenko, a dissident writer who strongly criticized President Vladimir Putin, died of radiation poisoning during the London location shooting of Cronenberg's film. So Nikolai's tattoo evokes the Kremlin at a time when its (officially denied) associations with merciless violence on a global stage echo loudly. Litvinenko's death in London presents a deadly aspect of globalization, especially when paired with his particularly vocal criticism of Russia's own "War on Terror" with Chechnya. Indeed, the assassins who attack Nikolai are referred to as Chechen, and Nikolai's conversation with a partner of Semyon just before the bathhouse assault focuses on how American military forces disrupt illegal shipments to London from Afghanistan.

In this way, the American and Russian "wars on terror" frame the wrenching violence in the bathhouse and inflect the histories written on Nikolai's body. By the end of the bathhouse scene, the faded blue of Nikolai's tattoos runs red with blood from his knife wounds—adding his body to the series of bloodied bodies that opens *Eastern Promises*, enlarging and deepening the networks of globalized violence connecting the film's multiple worlds. What Cronenberg achieves so stunningly within and between *A History of Violence* and *Eastern Promises* involves ways of seeing the marriage of globalized geopolitics and violence. These films bring to light something too often invisible in today's world: the imbrications of the United States with Russia, of London with Indiana, of Iraq with Chechnya, at the level of *shared* violence. Shared, that is, in the most intimate sense of the body and its gestures, not some abstractly conceptual "global village." When we fail to see and feel globalized geopolitics in this way, Cronenberg suggests, we risk the worst kinds of political and ethical blindness: "There are so many ways to make murder abstract—or killing, if you don't want to call it murder, or war. . . . You've got language, which is always a great curtain, such as 'collateral damage' and all these other euphemisms for ripping bodies apart, throwing heads around. But if the bodily consequences of war were the first thing you thought of, war wouldn't happen."[21] Agamben, paraphrasing Samuel Beckett, calls cinema "the dream of a gesture."[22] So, the risk lies in missing the opportunity to awaken from this dream into the politics of the cinematic gesture.

In his final act of violence in the bathhouse scene of *Eastern Promises*, Nikolai stabs one of his attackers directly in the eye. This action shocks us viscerally—we feel this assault on vision with an embodied literalism that characterizes Cronenberg's work from its horror genre beginnings to its art cinema present. This director always stabs us in the eye. But now Cronenberg's embodied cinema, while perhaps no longer as brazenly iconoclastic as his early horror films, has developed a newly concrete political sophistication to match its wide-ranging philosophical ambitions. With his latest two films, the stakes of vision, the struggle over what we see and how we see it, concern with an unprecedented urgency the way we live here and now. To deliver this urgency, Cronenberg harnesses cinematic gestures that conjoin horror and politics across the length of his career. Cronenberg has long been one of world cinema's most daring and original voices—with his post-9/11 diptych comprising *A History of Violence* and *Eastern Promises*, he becomes one of our most important artist-critics of globalized geopolitics.

NOTES

An earlier, shorter version of this essay appeared as "Promises of Violence: David Cronenberg on Globalized Geopolitics," *boundary 2* 36 (Summer 2009): 199–208. My thanks to Paul Bové, Meg Havran, and Marcia Landy for their feedback on that essay, and to Duke University Press for permission to draw on that material here.

1. For further discussion of this phase of Cronenberg's career, see Wayne Drew, ed., *David Cronenberg* (London: BFI, 1984); and Piers Handling, ed., *The Shape of Rage: The Films of David Cronenberg* (Toronto: General Publishing, 1983). On Cronenberg's biography, see Peter Morris, *David Cronenberg: A Delicate Balance* (Toronto: ECW Press, 1994). For Cronenberg's own accounts of his films, see Serge Grünberg, ed., *David Cronenberg: Interviews with Serge Grünberg* (London: Plexus, 2006); and Chris Rodley, ed., *Cronenberg on Cronenberg*, rev. ed. (London: Faber and Faber, 1997).

2. On this phase of Cronenberg's career, see Ernest Mathijs, *The Cinema of David Cronenberg: From Baron of Blood to Cultural Hero* (London: Wallflower Press, 2008); William Beard, *The Artist as Monster: The Cinema of David Cronenberg*, rev. ed. (Toronto: University of Toronto Press, 2006); and Michael Grant, ed., *The Modern Fantastic: The Films of David Cronenberg* (Westport, CT: Praeger, 2000).

3. On Cronenberg's relations to genre film and art film, see Adam Lowenstein, "Interactive Art Cinema: Between 'Old' and 'New' Media with *Un Chien andalou* and *eXistenZ*," in *Global Art Cinema: New Theories and Histories*, ed. Rosalind Galt and Karl Schoonover (New York: Oxford University Press, 2010), 92–105; and Adam Lowenstein, *Shocking Representation: Historical Trauma, National Cinema, and the Modern Horror Film* (New York: Columbia University Press, 2005), 145–175. For a consideration of the "literary" Cronenberg, see Mark Browning, *David Cronenberg: Author or Film-Maker?* (Bristol, UK: Intellect Books, 2007).

4. On post-9/11 American film, see Stephen Prince, *Firestorm: American Film in the Age of Terrorism* (New York: Columbia University Press, 2009); and Wheeler Winston Dixon, ed., *Film and Television after 9/11* (Carbondale: Southern Illinois Univer-

sity Press, 2004). On the political implications of "torture porn," see Adam Lowenstein, "Spectacle Horror and *Hostel*: Why 'Torture Porn' Does Not Exist," *Critical Quarterly* 53.1 (April 2011): 42–60.

5. Arjun Appadurai, *Modernity at Large: Cultural Dimensions of Globalization* (Minneapolis: University of Minnesota Press, 1996), 27, 29.

6. Ibid., 33.

7. For an analysis of *A History of Violence* that is particularly sensitive to the film's Canadian context, see Bart Beaty, *David Cronenberg's* A History of Violence (Toronto: University of Toronto Press, 2008).

8. Giorgio Agamben, *Means without End: Notes on Politics*, trans. Vincenzo Binetti and Cesare Casarino (Minneapolis: University of Minnesota Press, 2000), 54, 55, 56, 57, 58, 59. For an insightful discussion of the gesture in film that has influenced my own, see Marcia Landy, "'The Dream of the Gesture': The Body of/in Todd Haynes's Films," *boundary 2* 30 (Fall 2003): 123–140.

9. David Cronenberg, post-screening discussion of *A History of Violence*, Museum of the Moving Image, Astoria, New York, September 13, 2005.

10. David Cronenberg quoted in Amy Taubin, "Model Citizens," *Film Comment* 41 (September–October 2005): 24. A number of other critics also sensed this aspect of political commentary in the film. See, for example, Manohla Dargis, "Once Disaster Hits, It Seems Never to End," in *American Movie Critics: An Anthology from the Silents until Now*, rev. ed., ed. Phillip Lopate (New York: Library of America, 2006), 711–713; and Graham Fuller, "Good Guy Bad Guy," *Sight & Sound* 15 (October 2005): 12–16.

11. For further discussion of *Shivers*, see Robin Wood's (in)famous attack on the film in his "An Introduction to the American Horror Film," in *Planks of Reason: Essays on the Horror Film*, rev. ed., ed. Barry Keith Grant and Christopher Sharrett (Lanham, MD: Scarecrow Press, 2004), 135–136. For an account of the film that contests Wood's claims, see Lowenstein, *Shocking Representation*, 153–164.

12. See Marshall McLuhan, *Understanding Media: The Extensions of Man* (New York: McGraw-Hill, 1964). For a discussion of McLuhan in the Canadian context, see Arthur Kroker, *Technology and the Canadian Mind: Innis/McLuhan/Grant* (New York: St. Martin's Press, 1985).

13. See, for example, Jean Baudrillard, *Simulacra and Simulation*, trans. Sheila Faria Glaser (Ann Arbor: University of Michigan Press, 1994).

14. See, for example, Ron Suskind, "Faith, Certainty and the Presidency of George W. Bush," *New York Times Magazine*, October 17, 2004, http://www.nytimes.com/2004/10/17/magazine/17BUSH.html.

15. For a perceptive review of *Eastern Promises* that also attends to the friction between the sensibilities of Knight and Cronenberg, see A. O. Scott, "On London's Underside, Where Slavery Survives," *New York Times*, September 14, 2007, http://movies.nytimes.com/2007/09/14/movies/14east.html.

16. For further discussion of *The Brood*, see William Paul, *Laughing Screaming: Modern Hollywood Horror and Comedy* (New York: Columbia University Press, 1994), 368–380; and Barbara Creed, *The Monstrous-Feminine: Film, Feminism, Psychoanalysis* (London: Routledge, 1993), 43–58.

17. On the centrality of the family to the modern horror film, see Vivian Sobchack, "Bringing It All Back Home: Family Economy and Generic Exchange," in *The Dread*

of Difference: Gender and the Horror Film, ed. Barry Keith Grant (Austin: University of Texas Press, 1996), 143–163; and Tony Williams, *Hearths of Darkness: The Family in the American Horror Film* (Madison, NJ: Fairleigh Dickinson University Press, 1996).

18. For further discussion of Cronenberg's films as "body horror," see Philip Brophy, "Horrality: The Textuality of Contemporary Horror Films," in *The Horror Reader*, ed. Ken Gelder (London: Routledge, 2000), 276–284; and Steven Shaviro, *The Cinematic Body* (Minneapolis: University of Minnesota Press, 1993), 127–156.

19. See Alix Lambert, *Russian Prison Tattoos: Codes of Authority, Domination, and Struggle* (Atglen, PA: Schiffer, 2003). For additional context on the importance of tattoos to the film, as well as related production details, see Katrina Onstad, "Exploring Humanity, Violence and All," *New York Times*, September 16, 2007, http://www.nytimes.com/2007/09/16/movies/16onst.html?ref=movies.

20. See Alex Goldfarb with Marina Litvinenko, *Death of a Dissident: The Poisoning of Alexander Litvinenko and the Return of the KGB* (London: Simon & Schuster, 2007).

21. David Cronenberg, quoted in Desson Thomson, "David Cronenberg, Dead Serious," *Washington Post*, September 17, 2007, http://www.washingtonpost.com/wp-dyn/content/article/2007/09/16/AR2007091601550.html.

22. Agamben, *Means without End*, 56.

PART 2

HORROR LOOKS AT ITSELF

CHAPTER FOUR

Caught on Tape?

The Politics of Video in the New Torture Film

CATHERINE ZIMMER

By now, it can hardly have escaped attention that surveillance, primarily visual surveillance, has become a frequent contemporary narrative figuration. Films in the action-suspense and horror genres in particular rather hyperbolically highlight the thematic concerns of a surveillance culture; slightly less obviously, they demonstrate the relations between political formations, subjects, and technologies that characterize much current thought on surveillance in a variety of fields. Most recently emerging in the United States are such films as *Vacancy* (Nimród Antal, 2007), *Vantage Point* (Pete Travis, 2008), *Untraceable* (Gregory Hoblit, 2008), *Look* (Adam Rifkin, 2007), *Deja Vu* (Tony Scott, 2006), *Eagle Eye* (D. J. Caruso, 2008), and, in a slightly different tradition, *Cloverfield* (Matt Reeves, 2008), *Diary of the Dead* (George Romero, 2007), *Quarantine* (John Eric Dowdle, 2008), and *Paranormal Activity* (Oren Peli, 2007).[1] All these films, in one way or another, situate surveillance as the central theme or as the primary structuring element of the narrative, and thus demand a degree of attention to the specific ways in which an increasingly diversified surveillance culture is structuring cinematic narrative, and, perhaps more centrally, how narrative formations serve to consolidate the stakes of surveillance technologies and practices.[2]

My focus in this essay is the manner in which these surveillance narratives are coincident with our most recently dubbed horror subgenre: "torture porn." As common as the surveillance film, and frequently overlapping, are those romps through sadomasochism best represented by the *Hostel* (2005–2007) and *Saw* (2004–2010) film series, with a number of other notable examples prompting widespread critical disgust. But rather than simply noting that the intersection of torture and surveillance is a relatively straightforward symptom of the current political zeitgeist, my concern is to explore the way video technologies are being deployed in these narratives, and how the resulting narrative formations might allow us to think through the relations between surveillance and torture with greater specificity. In doing so, I will show how what might seem to be the almost insistently apolitical torture narratives of the *Saw* series function in a contiguous relationship to the more focused critiques of a European corollary: the cinematic meditations on video surveillance of the director Michael Haneke. Haneke's *Caché* (2005) and *Benny's Video* (1992) serve to refocus the willfully ahistorical morality discourses of some of the American torture films into a compelling exploration of the relations between graphic cinematic violence and the production of racial subjects in western European postcolonial surveillance cultures. The contiguities between the American and European films, based on both violence and surveillance, are not just instructive for an understanding of contemporary narrative formations, but also serve to demonstrate the structural politics of surveillance technologies and practices that are both highly coded and historically specific.

The phenomenon of torture porn is widely considered the lowest common denominator in the global reinvestment in horror in the new millennium. The ultra-graphic violence of these films, in combination with narratives that seem predominantly invested in providing the basis for incredibly drawn-out scenes of torture—rather than the rhythmic suspense of a more "traditional" slasher film or the eerie uncanniness of the contemporary Asian or Spanish ghost films—situates them as somehow both the pinnacle and the gutter of contemporary horror. Many of these are American films, often connecting the threat of torture with foreign travel, as in *Hostel* (Eli Roth, 2005) and *Turistas* (John Stockwell, 2006), which present teenagers or young adults as victims of kidnapping and torture during those first youthful escapades abroad characteristic of upper-middle-class Americans. The emergence of these narratives of American youth, frequently men, going abroad and finding themselves immersed in what often amounts to an economy of torture must, I believe, be read as a tremendously projective fantasy—one in which American youth are figured as the victims rather than the perpetrators of this kind of organized violence. Particularly since the events of September 11, 2001, and the ensuing American military actions that resulted in the establishment of the detention facility at Guantanamo Bay and the well-documented abuses at Abu Ghraib, it seems striking to posit Americans as the innocent objects of torture scenarios. At the minimum, the contemporary appearance of so many films about the economies, bodily experiences, and technologies of torture must be viewed in conjunction with the politics of torture that has concurrently occupied the American and world stage. As Dean Lockwood has pointed out in his own discussion of torture porn, critics and filmmakers alike have already made the "obvious contextual links" between such films and recent discussions and representations of real-world torture.[3] The fact that several of these films situate torture as an international affair is also telling, despite the fact that with the exception of *Turistas*, which invokes Latin American economic resentment as a rationale for the harvesting of American organs, these films disavow any explicitly political structure to the torture.

The *Saw* franchise, which emerged in 2004 and is still going strong (with, remarkably, a sequel released annually since then to enormous box office success), notably seems little marked by political commentary; further, unlike the films mentioned above, it situates torture as both domestic and highly personalized and pathologized. And yet the stakes of this continuing and successful series are instructive in relation to the way torture is figured in the larger sub-generic arena. The *Saw* films, clearly influenced by the tremendous success of David Fincher's *Se7en* (1995), tell the story of the serial killer "Jigsaw," who kidnaps people and places them in scenarios that require them to make torturous choices in order to survive or save others, thus, according to Jigsaw, learning the "real" value of life. The choice at the center of the first film involves either having to saw off one's own foot to get out of a chained cuff and kill another person, or allow one's family to die. But the narrative progressions of all the films are not so simple as just to follow the wrangling with these choices. Rather, the narratives are organized around trying to determine precisely what the scenario is, what the choices are, and who is a victim and who is a perpetrator of these violences. The first *Saw* film (James Wan, 2004) hides the identity of Jigsaw until the surprise ending, and thus the central scenario is surrounded by a series of investigations into previous Jigsaw crimes and false leads for both the investigators and the audience. Ultimately, I think it would be reasonable to suggest that the films posit every character as both guilty and innocent.

This universality of guilt and innocence constitutes the more explicit moral-philosophical question at the center of these films: Is Jigsaw himself somewhat right, and are his "trials" for people who are wasting or abusing their lives really "saving" them? This possibility is foregrounded (in the first sequel) when one of Jigsaw's surviving victims becomes his disciple. Thus the films, in what often seems less like a jigsaw puzzle and more like a game of pickup sticks, still manage to incorporate some themes easily extrapolated to contemporary politics: the morality or efficacy of torture, definitions of life, fundamentalist belief systems, and bodily and psychological experiences of violence.

I want to point out that despite the critical marking of these films as a disturbing symptom of the bloodlust of our times, they are also oddly trying to work through some of the complexity of the experience of violence (and the anger with current formulations of and responses to these violences) in a less pedantic way than the more explicitly political films addressing topics such as torture. At the very least, it is highly notable that while films addressing contemporary politics, such as *Rendition* (Gavin Hood, 2007) and *Lions for Lambs* (Robert Redford, 2007), lost money, the *Saw* series has proved consistently marketable: *Saw IV* (Darren Lynn Bousman), the sequel released in 2007, grossed almost two times more than *Lions for Lambs* and *Rendition* combined.[4] It seems worthwhile, then, to examine how *Saw* speaks to contemporary violences in a way that the more directly political films do not. One of the specific ways that the *Saw* films address some of the formulations of torture is by introducing technological mediation, and particularly surveillant structures, into the life-and-death "games" that Jigsaw stages. The series incorporates surveillance as a recurrent feature of Jigsaw's methodology, and one that intermingles with the games of torture in various ways. Lockwood, reading these films within a Deleuzian framework as "allegories of control," has also remarked on the *Saw* films' "emphasis on surveillance and tracking."[5] My focus is the symptomatic nature of this inclusion of the video surveillance apparatus, and how, despite the many other points of reference in the film, it is this factor that connects these films in the most significant ways to political considerations.

The first two *Saw* films best organize a discussion of how surveillance functions. The first film centers on two men who find themselves mysteriously awakening in a filthy and dilapidated industrial bathroom, with another man dead on the floor in a pool of blood. They have no memory of how they got there, and via a series of clues, primarily audiocassettes that provide puzzling instructions in Jigsaw's altered voice, they try to assess their situation and what they must do to escape. As the film progresses, it emerges for both the trapped characters and the audience that the men are being watched on video surveillance, or what seems more precisely to be closed-circuit television (CCTV). The film cuts from the scene of entrapment to a low-resolution video image of the same scene; the unidentified watcher of these images, shot from behind, is clearly implicated as the one orchestrating the entire scenario by virtue of his operation of the surveillance. The as-yet faceless surveillance operator and his seemingly predatory gaze are clearly deployed here in the mode of the killer-to-be-named-later traditional to horror films ranging from *Peeping Tom* (Michael Powell, 1960) to *Halloween* (John Carpenter, 1978). In and of itself, this straightforward deployment of video surveillance as part and parcel of the predation is unremarkable and would seem to be simply a televisually technologized version of the sadistic voyeur killers with whom horror film has long been familiar.

But the surveillance and the video emerge in many additional places in the film—and the proliferation of these moments also complicates the theoretical models with which we can address them. The first time we actually see video technology within the film is when we are presented with a prior victim of Jigsaw recounting her trauma. She awakens trapped in a head-enclosing torture mask, and a video monitor turns on in front of her. The puppet that often serves as Jigsaw's avatar appears on the monitor and informs the woman of why she is there and what she must do to escape. The video serves the same function as the audiotape for the two men we have already seen, and these tapes of various kinds thus become an integral part of the torture scenario. They are essentially the means of a select release of information to the victims, both escalating their horror and serving as a possible means of escape. Thus, whether the video is utilized to monitor torture scenes or incorporated as part of the torture itself, it is clear that the more obvious *intent* of the video technology for the Jigsaw character is to function as an organizational methodology serving to produce and control responses.

This would seem to add to the sadistic voyeur trope a Foucauldian theorization of surveillance as a disciplinary model: Foucault's analysis of the panopticon, introduced in *Discipline and Punish*, has long served as the crux of analyses of surveillance, particularly as it is considered structurally. And though Foucault's account emphasizes the production of "docile bodies" through a shift *away* from torture, *Saw*'s narrative use of surveillance within a torture film as a tool and form of confinement, control, and power has notable resonance with the Foucauldian account.[6]

But as many theorists of surveillance—particularly David Lyon and Kevin Haggerty—have noted, the panoptic model can no longer serve as a singular account of the politics of surveillance, especially as produced technologically. Haggerty provides the compelling critique that "the panoptic model has become reified, directing scholarly attention to a select subset of attributes of surveillance. In so doing, analysts have excluded or neglected a host of other key qualities and processes of surveillance that fall outside of the panoptic framework."[7] And as Lyon more specifically suggests, the dominance of "dataveillance"—the proliferation of digital information as a primary mode of contemporary social sorting and policing—as well as the overarching spectacularity of a world that does not fit into a unidirectional model of power as to who is watching and being watched, makes it hard to rely on the model of visual technologies as functioning in any straightforward way to organize and support institutional power.[8] I would add that even the films' narrative deployment of CCTV and video surveillance, which seems so insistently visual, finds itself, as will be discussed below, somewhat unclear in its functions and effects.

Lyon cites Giorgio Agamben as a thinker who importantly points out that "the panopticon was a distinct and bounded area; now . . . zones of indistinction are crucial, and in fact, are the locus of power." And it is to Agamben that I believe we might turn to examine the complex ways that cinematic surveillance narratives function, even when such formations might seem far more clearly addressed by the explicitly visual structures of panoptics and voyeurism, or even the Deleuzian formation of "control society" through which Lockwood has discussed surveillance in these films.[9] In particular, these "zones of indistinction" show how narrative and technology interpenetrate in somewhat surprising ways. Agamben did not posit the notion of zones of indistinction in the specific formation of a concept of a surveillance culture, but more generally as a way to describe the way that Western politics has constructed itself around the biopolitical categorical pairing of bare life versus political existence, and the inevitable indistinctions that formula raises. In his description of the figure of *homo sacer* (sacred man), Agamben discusses the sovereign formulation of this figure of "bare life" as that which may be killed, but not sacrificed, which is to say it is neither human, nor divine, nor animal precisely. Agamben suggests that this "originary" zone of indistinction is the crux of a series of interrelated zones of indistinction that have become increasingly spatialized in modern politics (in particular, through the construction of the space of the "camp").[10] Theorists have taken up these ideas to look at the way that surveillance technologies and social formations around surveillance models operate with these zones of indistinction. While it is not possible to explore the full complexity of these formulations here, it seems of particular interest that *Saw*'s torturous narrative logic parallels the bare life versus meaningful existence, subject versus object, exclusion versus inclusion formulations that Agamben points to as producing the zones of indistinction that characterize political power structures. Specifically, I want to show that these zones of indistinction characterize the rest of the film's surveillance models and the narrative result: torture and death.

Crucially, surveillance technologies in *Saw* produce characters as part of the mystery of guilt or innocence, and they introduce Jigsaw's self-righteous morality of the life-worth-living through his video and audio lectures. Over the course of the film, we are presented with several possible suspects of who Jigsaw might be: Danny Glover plays a police officer on Jigsaw's trail whom we later discover operating a surveillance operation that is marked as patho-

FIGURE 4.1. *Zep's surveillance system in* Saw *(Lionsgate, 2004).*

logical rather than legal. Holed up alone in a dilapidated apartment, mumbling to himself, and surrounded by newspaper clippings about the Jigsaw murders, the detective engages in both binocular and video surveillance that is coded as obsessively crackpot-ish, and which is clearly not sanctioned by the police as an institutional force. The character, aptly named Detective Tapp, thus himself becomes a suspect by virtue of his operation of a surveillance model. Also, Zep (Michael Emerson), a hospital orderly who had previously appeared suspicious, is seemingly "found guilty" as the killer when we see him operating a complex video surveillance system monitoring the men trapped in the bathroom. And, through flashback, we discover that Adam (Leigh Whannell), one of the men in the bathroom, has been taking surveillance photos of the other man (Cary Elwes). The question of whether Adam is a participant or a victim of the scenario is here also opened up by his own operation of surveillance. But it turns out that none of these people is actually Jigsaw, and, with the possible exception of Detective Tapp (whose surveillance operation turns out to be a vengeance/vigilante mission), all those who appear to be participating are themselves pawns of Jigsaw, suffering their own fates at his hands.

I want to note that not only is there a *guilt* and a *pathology* associated with the operation of surveillance technology here, but more important, it is the surveillance that blurs the distinction between who is the subject or object of torture, and which establishes the victims of the torture as somehow guilty in their own way. To point out that this reverses the general forensic point of surveillance—which is to establish guilt on the side of the surveilled subjects—is clear. But what is significant here is that the narrative structure of the horror, as well as the torturous choices that the victims must make, becomes wrapped up not with a sadistic, voyeuristic, or even panoptic model, but with blurred boundaries, the production of ambiguity, and the formation of narrative zones of indistinction through the introduction of surveillance technologies and practices. Simply put, there is a turn here away from the classic horror formulation that "someone is being watched and there is danger there," to "someone is being videotaped, and we don't quite know what it means, who is operating the technology, and what the association with that technology implies." Or, if extrapolated to a broader vision of how these films narratively reflect video surveillance practices, we can turn to Dietmar Kammerer's conclusion in his essay on CCTV in Hollywood cinema: "It is not a question of 'conspiracy' or 'complicity' but rather of 'complication' and 'complexity.'"[11]

In a somewhat less pronounced manner, video surveillance technology is used to similar effect in several other films from the torture subgenre. In the explicitly torture-focused *Captivity* (Roland Joffé, 2007), for instance, the video surveillance technology follows a trajectory that demonstrates how even the most "traditional" formulation of surveillance within a sadistic voyeuristic model becomes necessarily complicated by the indistinctions circulating through video. *Captivity* is a return to the psychosexual slasher film, but within the torture genre. The film's first segment presents a young model as she is stalked by someone—the stalking is presented as a video camera point-of-view shot, a clear harking back to Michael Powell's *Peeping Tom*, which has been a defining moment for discussions of the coincidence between moving-image technologies and sexual violence. But just as I have argued in an earlier essay that the use of the small-format camera in Powell's film hardly produces any straightforward subject/object relations, the multiple incorporations of video technology within *Captivity* serve to complicate the stalker-voyeur trope even as they remain central to the torture scenario.[12]

After the abduction of the female target, Jennifer (Elisha Cuthbert), the majority of the film takes place in the torture chamber, which is—naturally—outfitted with myriad forms of surveillance technologies, including video monitors, two-way mirrors, and microphones, as well as video screens for playback (we are presented with flat screens for a more contemporary look than the square monitors of the *Saw* films, which are clearly meant to evoke a kind of violent primitivism even in the use of technology). The narrative unfolds as Jennifer is subjected to a series of terror-inducing experiences and what appears to be physical torture. But, as with *Saw*, the surveillance technology is used to *mis*lead; here as well we realize that the video is primarily used as *representation* to heighten her confusion and fear, rather than as only a methodology of voyeuristic excess or as a monitoring tool. She is, for example, shown a video of a prior victim, strapped down exactly as she is herself, as acid is poured on her face. The same process presented on video unfolds for Jennifer in the present, with a spigot beginning to pour the same ominous liquid as on the video. Jennifer is thus experiencing the video as a kind of anticipatory mirror, showing her what she is about to experience. Yet the liquid we see pouring onto Jennifer turns out not to have been acid—after a fade to black, she awakens with bloody bandages on her face, but as she peels them off, she discovers that she is still physically intact. These "games" grow even more complex as another captive is introduced into the scene: Gary (Daniel Gillies), a young man from whom she is at first physically separated and who is also being surveilled through video from the as-yet unidentified watcher. The romance and sexual encounter that develop are presented through crosscutting as captured and enjoyed via video surveillance by a wine-drinking, still-faceless figure. Rather than this merely being another level of voyeuristic enjoyment for the director of this basement play, it turns out that Jennifer's new romantic interest is in on the whole thing, and the entire development of the traditional heterosexual romance narrative is in fact part and parcel of the torture and surveillance—a manipulation. Video here moves firmly into the role of *representation* that stands outside its understanding within a surveillance logic as a purely documentary form. And though we could say here that the representation still performs a disciplinary role, it seems clear that it can do so only by virtue of its status as a highly ambiguous form.[13]

Another central part in this ambiguity is particular to the use of televisual technologies: the slippages and indistinctions that become foregrounded in the second *Saw* film are about whether the image is a live or prerecorded event. *Saw II* (Darren Lynn Bousman, 2005) organizes its entire torturous narrative around a policeman watching his son on closed-circuit television attempt to survive various tests in a house along with other victims. Late in the film it turns out that this is not *live* CCTV, but a recorded video, and the "test"/torture we have been watching is not the son's, but the policeman's. And here, in these particular uses of video, we can get a better sense of how we might define the zone of indistinction—not just a trick or an ambiguity, but something that really is indistinct. The video is a live event, as it unfolds for the police officer and the film's audience, but it is also a past event. The power the video holds over the narrative and the characters within it is in these very zones of indistinction.

The indistinctions produced by the surveillance models in all these films are almost necessarily punctuated by acts of incredible violence, and it is here that we can begin to see how the very ambiguity of the surveillance model relies on the structural logic of torture as both narrative and ideological resolution. The closing montage of the first *Saw* film is particularly instructive. The sequence serves to organize all the prior narrative incoherence in a crescendo of violence in both content and form: as Jigsaw's identity is finally revealed, a series of increasingly quick cuts strings together prior scenes of investigation and violence until a door is literally slammed on the narrative and the credits appear. All the prior ambiguities are shown to be manipulations organized by Jigsaw, and the "truth" of the various characters' positions is demonstrated here not only by the more traditional narrative revelation of the "real" killer, but also stylistically. The high-speed reintroduction and reorganization of a series of images from the film represent the production of narrative clarity, but it seems more than incidental that this ostensible clarity is offered through a violent smashing together of the film's earlier images. The narrative closure and the cementing of clear subject positions—the sense and sensibility that are produced here—are as much about the systematic reproduction of violence as about narrative resolution. Or, more to the point, resolution requires violence reorganized into, and as, a logic.

It is clear that surveillant representation and the proliferation of images of violence *enhance* torture narratives and, indeed, become a part of the deployment of power in torture scenarios. This extends beyond cinematic narrative into the realm of real contemporary tortures. Jasbir Puar highlights this fact in her analysis of the photographs that were emblematic of the abuses of prisoners at Abu Ghraib: "These images not only represent specific acts and allude to the procedural vectors of ever-expansive audiences but they also reproduce and multiply the power dynamics that made these acts possible in the first place."[14] But in addition to suggesting that the surveillance becomes a part of the torture, my point here is that the ambiguous narrative formation around surveillance *asks* for torture, *hailing* it in order to turn the zones of indistinction into resolved deployments of power. Because Jigsaw, as the representative of both ideological formation and narrative organization in the *Saw* films, serves as an organizing regime (rather than as merely the lone pervert), I argue that the film's violence refers not to the breaking of laws, but also to the law itself and the political powers it deploys. As such, Jigsaw's games become not just expressions of pathological violence, but a politics of surveillance and torture.

But it is not merely the fact that there is "an" ideology associated with Jigsaw that necessitates that we read his acts as political: more to the point, and returning to Agamben's increasingly apt discussion in *Homo Sacer*, it is an ideology organized around definitions and designations of what constitutes *life*

that causes this film series to resonate with analyses of biopolitical constructions. In formulating the "originary zone of indistinction" as *homo sacer*, or
bare life, "a life that could be killed," we can begin to see how the zones of indistinction around surveillance in *Saw* are crucially tied to the film's primary
narrative concern with the production/elimination of a life through structural
games of torture.[15] I do not want to suggest necessarily that there is direct
parallel between how Jigsaw asks his designated "subjects" to reconstruct their
own relationships to life through torture—by making decisions about both
their value systems and their very bodies in attempts to escape from various
machines and scenarios—and Agamben's discussion of how the designation
of "bare life" by a sovereign can be thought of as "something like the originary
'political' relation."[16] But in an era when the ostensibly apolitical torture film
is on the rise, it is also worth taking it to heart when Agamben states, "There
is no clearer way to say that the first foundation of political life is a life that
may be killed, which is politicized through its very capacity to be killed," and
dragging these films, kicking and screaming, back to their political context.[17]

Insofar as the *Saw* films narrate torture as an ideological formulation
around constructions of those that may live versus those that may die, they
necessarily maintain themselves in a highly political sphere. But it is not the
act of selection of victims by Jigsaw that suggests a political relation, with
him as sovereign and his victim as the "bare life." In fact, it is the games of
torture—in combination with the surveillance formations and the narrative
development—that all serve to construct for the films' spectators our sense
of who on-screen is deserving of life. The narratives unfold as we try to dis-
cern what the circumstances are that allowed the victims to be chosen for
the "game," and what choices they will make about their bodies, the bodies
of others, and their own relations to their lives. These decisions are organized
through the games of torture and the surveillance technologies that link the
victims, the perpetrator(s), and the films' audiences. Thus the selection of
victims by Jigsaw is only part of the biopolitical formation: the torture, the
surveillance, and the narrative all function in the films as *biopolitical technologies* serving to produce and sort out "bare life." Pairing Agamben's theoretical
formation with the success of these films during an era that is similarly defining uses of torture in relation to highly politicized subjects, it seems clear
that accepting these films' conceit of addressing any "pure" or "instinctual"
experience of life and death would ignore the deeply symptomatic reflection
of not just the relations between surveillance and violence, but also the kinds
of political subjects that emerge out of the zones of indistinction circulating
within and through those relations.

A somewhat more straightforward but closely related way to address these

configurations is to note that what these filmic narratives reflect is that a surveillance culture, far from being a highly controlled deployment of power,
produces such deeply unstable zones of visual, temporal, and ultimately political indistinctions that for a regime (or narrative) overseeing that culture,
the mechanism of torture becomes necessary to cement power relations in
identifiable forms that support the originating regime of surveillance. Or as
Elaine Scarry writes in her discussion of "The Structure of Torture," "It is
. . . precisely because the reality of [a regime's] power is so highly contest-
able, the regime so unstable, that torture is being used."[18] Both narratively
and politically, the surveillance here serves primarily to precipitate a specific
kind of consolidating violence that will give meaning to that surveillance, as
the closing montage of the first *Saw* film forcefully demonstrates. The fact
that video surveillance in particular seems to produce specifically temporal
ambiguities furthers this point by suggesting that the "liveness" of an event
can only really be produced by the terrible presence of a body in pain, a fight
for survival, or the moment of death. For, as Agamben argues in *Homo Sacer*,
"Until a completely new politics . . . is at hand . . . the 'beautiful day' of life
will be given citizenship only either through blood and death or in the perfect senselessness to which the society of the spectacle condemns it."[19] The
Saw series hyperbolically reflects how "blood and death" and the "society of
the spectacle" are not just related options, but also contiguous formulations:
blood and death give a horrible grounding sense (and sensation) to the senselessness of rampant and incoherent spectacularity.

Such a sweepingly negative statement about surveillance culture perhaps sums up the implications of the *Saw* films and a number of those other
torture-porn films that deploy surveillance as a trope; but it is worthwhile to
note that these surveillance models and their resulting formations of violence
can also complicate and unravel the functioning of an oppressively stabilizing
social and ideological system. A film such as Michael Haneke's *Caché* makes
this clear through its very lack of clarity.

Caché might be considered to have a somewhat dubious relationship to the
American torture franchises I have thus far been discussing. But Haneke's
earlier films, such as *Benny's Video* and *Funny Games* (1997), could easily be
seen as the artsy predecessors of the recent American horror market—a point
driven home by the U.S. release of the American remake of *Funny Games* in
2007, directed by Haneke himself, and demonstrating that the earlier films
are now retroactively inseparable from recent trends in American film. *Benny's
Video* and *Funny Games*, both in their own ways, intermingle video surveillance and representation with traumatic, graphic violence scenarios and point
in some highly revealing ways to the use of video as a methodology of torture

and a means of exaggerating cinematic violences. But it is with *Caché*, in its much more subtle, even meditative, use of video as aggression, that we might locate how the implicit political formulations I have pointed to within the American torture narratives become a more explicitly postcolonial model of technological politics and social relations organized around the intersection of surveillance and torture. The logic (or illogic) of video surveillance as seen in torture porn, as well as the stakes raised around regimes, violence, and so forth, do not just take on a racialized and politicized form in *Caché*—instead, that film reveals the political and racial disavowals at the heart of the films discussed above (as well as Haneke's earlier films), and it explains the ways that subjective, narrative, and generic formations are working through one another in surveillance models.

Caché tells the story of a bourgeois host of a literary television show and his family who are being sent surveillance videos of their home, with no clear origin or agenda. For a variety of reasons, some seemingly internal to his own guilty associations, the TV host, Georges (Daniel Auteuil), suspects he is being targeted by an Algerian-French man, Majid (Maurice Bénichou), whom he knew from his childhood and whom Georges's family was considering adopting until Georges caused him to be sent away through manipulative lies. Georges now tracks down Majid and violently accuses him of the present video aggressions; Majid compellingly asserts his own innocence, as does his adult son (Walid Afkir). The spectator's growing view of Majid as now the victim of Georges is complicated by Georges's later receipt of a videotape that was taken of the encounter between Georges and Majid at Majid's apartment. This confusion extends through the rest of the film and remains not only narratively and affectively unresolved, but grows increasingly more complex. The narrative indeterminacies are, however, almost secondary to the extended visual indeterminacies that set up the film and continue throughout.

Ara Osterweil's excellent 2006 review essay on *Caché* aptly describes the manner in which the film's visual logic (or lack thereof) is introduced and developed in the film. Describing the opening shot—"Filmed with a static camera, uninterrupted by editing, and lingering longer than most viewers are accustomed to, this mysteriously ominous glimpse of French street life immediately sets the mood that is the hallmark of Haneke's work: discomfort, suspicion, anxiety"—Osterweil suggests the complexity of the film's visual affect, which is primarily associated with an inappropriately surveillant look.[20] It turns out that we were watching not just the film's establishing shot but also a video within the film—the film's opening shot is revealed, through a sudden fast-forwarding, to be the videotape that Georges and his wife, Anne (Juliette Binoche), are watching after it has been mysteriously delivered to them. As D. I. Grossvogel describes it, "Only after this single take lasting nearly three minutes are we made aware that we are not *outside* the house but *inside* the Laurents' television room, looking with them at the first tape."[21] Thus the purpose and obviousness of an establishing shot is undermined by duration (long take), temporal manipulation (fast-forwarding), and the confusion of spatial parameters (outside is inside). The film's opening here sets the terms for the way the introduction of video surveillance immediately destabilizes coherent structures through the indistinctions raised by narrative and visual interpenetrations. It is the particular indeterminate effects and affects of video technology as surveillance that refer to the systems of torture in the *Saw* films, connecting the American series' myopic and self-contained scenarios to the explicitly racial and politicized implications of *Caché*.

While Haneke's earlier films *Benny's Video* and *Funny Games* might be said to be far more direct statements on the violence of video, one of the reasons *Caché* is so deeply compelling is that its very ambiguity speaks far more directly to the specificities of the use of video. *Caché* importantly makes all the questions and indistinctions I suggest emerge out of the *Saw* series more explicit by removing the explication: guilt and innocence, temporal ambiguity, violent resolution, all figure in this film as centrally as in the torture-porn examples, but without the ostensible clarity provided by the more traditional narrative structures and resolutions of the American films. The narrative zones of indistinction become central and unresolved, and they are particular to a video gaze and visibility. Because the film has a tremendously complex unfolding of affect and politics based in what is in some ways a profoundly simple plot formation, it provides a space to show how the *Saw* films are indicative of larger political formations—ones that either began as or have become racialized in very particular ways.

One of the primary things to understand about the way video functions in the film is the manner in which it provides both the instability and the punctuation of the film, and how the punctuation is not definitional and organizational, but instead elliptical and circular. It is of particular importance here that the "resolution" that video provides is completely irresolute. The opening scene sets the terms for this; not only do we not know who or why someone is being watched, but it is also unclear what the technology is that is producing the image, and whether that technology is intra- or extra-diegetic. At first, we think we are watching "the film," which of course we always are, but then it turns out we are (narratively, as well as technologically) watching the video within the film.[22] What in *Saw* is a narrative feint—are we watching this live or is it recorded, and what does it mean that a character is placed in seeming control of surveillance?—is similarly deployed in *Caché* through this opening

FIGURE 4.2. *The opening shot of* Caché *(Sony Pictures, 2005).*

FIGURE 4.3. *The opening shot of* Caché *in fast-forward (Sony Pictures, 2005).*

long take. Here, it produces an indistinction between whether we are watching this film or a video within the film, and whether the POV is subjective, technologized, or omniscient. This will be repeated in the film's closing shot, which not only refuses to resolve the question of who or what is watching, but also whether the look is a threat. Though *Saw*'s unstable narrative could be considered incoherent (or frankly just stupid) whereas *Caché*'s narrative is thought of more as significantly ambiguous, I think it is not simply coincidence that both forms of instability are centered around video's unclear status as representation or contemporaneous surveillance. In *Saw*, the temporal ambiguity opens up the space for—even demands—torture as a wishfully ahistorical call to violent bodily presence. But as we will see below, in *Caché* the attention to ambiguous temporality introduced by the video within the film calls attention to the historical productions of both pathologized and political violence.

The punctuating moment in the opening sequence—when the tape begins to fast-forward and we realize we are watching video—provides an answer of sorts to the questions raised by the extended length of the opening shot.[23] But, of course, it also simply raises more questions and begins the circuit that continues with more videos and their implicit and explicit references to graphic violence. The following video punctuations follow the same structure of organizing the narrative into incoherence. While more tapes are received, along with childish drawings that indicate to Georges that the tapes have been sent by Majid (insofar as they refer to the lies Georges told about him when he was a boy), the next moment of definite narrative punctuation is when Majid kills himself in front of Georges during Georges's second aggressive visit to the now increasingly beleaguered-looking Majid. But, as Osterweil succinctly puts it, "when a videotape of this clandestine meeting is sent to Anne and Georges's television producer, all bets are off."[24] Shown twice—first from Georges's subjective position, and then from the perspective of a hidden video camera—the suicide of Majid is a perfect example of the manner in which video surveillance and graphic violence work together in this film to process zones of indistinction in a somewhat different manner than American torture porn. Again from Osterweil, "On the one hand, the footage, which shows Georges as a belligerent, threatening presence, is a potentially incriminating piece of evidence that calls into question the audience's (and Anne's) initial assumptions about the true identity of the victimizer. On the other hand, the very fact that a tape has been made by a hidden camera within his low-rent flat suggests the impossibility of Majid's innocence."[25] Here, the violence serves not to resolve the slippages of culpability and narrative coherence produced by the video, but also to produce more, and to do so in particular conjunction with the surveillance and re-presentation of this moment: Majid's suicide would seem to place an almost primordial guilt firmly on Georges, in both his past and present aggressions against the Algerian. Majid's sudden cutting of his own throat is so affectively shocking to both Georges and the film's spectator that the very pace and tenor of the film are ruptured at this point into a moment of horrible presence. But since this incident makes clear that Majid's apartment was equipped with a hidden surveillance camera, which would seem to prove him guilty in the sequence of video aggressions against Georges that led to this moment, the introduction of video has once again established both everyone and no one as guilty and innocent. While in *Saw* and other torture films the violence becomes a moment of clarity, here that moment of clarity is merely reintroduced into the video gaze to highlight the circuit of violence and surveillance that is fundamentally unstable and constantly recoded. In other words, as soon as the cinematic plot would seem to provide some explanation or even resolution, a videotape reemerges to circle the narrative back into a state of total questionability around subject positions and the enactment of violence.

The film's open-ended conclusion provides a further view of this circumstance. Another long-take gaze, an extreme long shot (mirroring and circling us back to the beginning of the film), presents us with Georges's teenage son (Lester Makedonsky) on the steps of his school. There Majid's son approaches him, and the two have a discussion that we do not hear from the distanced position of visual surveillance. The initial question of the possible relationship between these boys is quickly followed up by the corollary question: If Majid's son is in front of the camera, and Majid is dead, with whom is this look from the video camera to be connected? Catherine Wheatley addresses these questions by pointing out that "one problem that poses itself is that the vast majority of the taped scenes are shot from seemingly 'impossible' angles: filmed from outside walls where bookcases stand, or from a position too high for a handycam operator unless they were standing very conspicuously on the roof of a car."[26] Thus what is repeatedly suggested to be a diegetic video camera within the film both isn't and can't be explained by diegetic means. At the end of the film, the incoherence and ambiguity of all that had preceded finally announces itself as a kind of *impossibility*: the production of a video gaze (and its corollary visual field) that appears to be surveillant, with a materiality highly coded as a diegeticized, technologized "real," becomes also highly metaphorical and about the impossibility of all these video gazes. It is a recognizable visual code (voyeuristic, disciplinary, violent) that here decodes itself into abstraction.

In this way, the film ultimately offers up the surveillant gaze as both the primary structuring and de-structuring force, suggesting—in a somewhat different way than *Saw*—that surveillance is often an actual material formation, but one that deconstructs its own premises. Video surveillance establishes nothing but its own codes, until another logic (in many cases, a violent one) turns those codes into systems. Clive Norris and Gary Armstrong have discussed this on the sociological and criminological level in their detailed study of closed-circuit television in the United Kingdom. With the UK deploying more video surveillance cameras than any other nation in the world, Norris and Armstrong note that on the most basic level, "while we are all increasingly under the camera's gaze what this means in practice is that its implications for social control are dependent not so much on the cameras, but on their integration with other technologies, and the organisational environment in which they operate."[27] The narrative abstraction away from the material realities of surveillance video in *Caché*, in other words, is less a metaphor around a totalizing gaze than it is an insight into the very real fact that surveillance systems on their own are barely systemic or deterministic. Or, as Norris and Armstrong put it in relation to how CCTV might operate according to Foucault's account of the panopticon, "the extent to which CCTV produces an 'automatic functioning of power' is questionable."[28] And yet to say that video surveillance becomes dispersed, abstracted, and metaphorized is not to say that surveillance is in itself "neutral" until it is applied—rather, it is a nonsystem that accesses visual, social, and historical codes of power and violence. The nonsystem will often be resolved into a system through the deployment of violence, as in the *Saw* films, or merely point back to its coding, as with *Caché*, in a manner that opens up a series of points of access to the violence and zones of indistinction in a surveilled situation: in this case, the postcolonial European bourgeois family.

The violence against and within that familial space achieved a kind of crescendo in Haneke's 1997 *Funny Games*, the film that most explicitly connects the director's work to the American torture films by virtue of Haneke directing his own faithful remake of the film for the American market in 2007. In these films, two teenage boys—coded by their matching tennis outfits and polite demeanor as privileged white youth—at first insinuate themselves into and eventually forcibly infiltrate an upper-middle-class white family's country home, mount a campaign of psychological and physical violence, and finally murder the entire family (once again, a family comprising two parents with a single male child), one by one, in Haneke's characteristically shocking matter-of-fact style. The films contain no narrativized surveillance and are quite insistent on being limited to the bourgeois domestic space, but here also Haneke refuses to engage in the "straightforward" narrative of torture without reference to mediation and spectatorship. First, occasional direct addresses to the film's audience from the perpetrators of the violence imply a complicity of the spectator in the unfolding scenario. And it is with the television blasting sounds and images (almost as if it were a primary character in the scene) that the film reaches its horrifying pinnacle: the child of the family is executed with a shotgun. What the spectator is offered visually in this scene, however, is not the boy being shot, but the blood-splattered television screen in the aftermath—a none-too-subtle connection between the images on the television screen and the violence of the film we are watching. But even more notably than all this, when one of the aggressors is surprisingly shot and killed, the film ruptures its already somewhat reflexive diegetic space entirely when the other perpetrator, traumatized at the death of his partner in crime, grabs a remote control and rewinds the film we are watching as if it were a videotape. Reclaiming mastery over the narrative, the boy takes the narrative back in time and "rescues" his partner for the continuation of their "funny games." This moment is, of course, a similar gesture to that of the opening shot of *Caché*, when the otherwise cinematically realistic shot is interrupted by a fast-forwarding, reframing (literally) what we're seeing as a video rather than a cinematic narrative. The gesture also similarly signifies the temporal instability of the video image discussed earlier: not only is video used to undermine a clear temporal location, but it is here also used to refuse both visual and narrative realism.

Funny Games, in both its pre- and mid-torture-porn incarnations, is clearly more invested in a direct critique of media violence than it is in the political complexity of circuits of surveillance (which is not to say that these are unrelated issues; the intersection between representation and surveillance is clearly central to this discussion). But of greater interest to me is the casting of the scene of torturous violence as that of the highly mediated bourgeois home, and the perpetrators of the violence not as outsiders to that environment, but as themselves white, educated, "proper" young men. The way in which even a home-invasion narrative is posited as one in which the invaders seem more like insiders than outsiders highlights how internal this violence is to that domestic space.

The violence and disintegration within the European bourgeois family unit that is at the heart of *Funny Games*, as well as virtually all of Haneke's other films, in *Caché* assumes a more explicit focus about what some of that violence contains. The family unit is extended to reveal the repressed element—the "adopted" (colonized) North African who has been simultaneously implicated in and ejected from the white "family." The infantilization, pathologized jealousy, guilt, perversity, and aggression that constitute the personal family narrative of this film here also represent the circuit of racialized violence and projection of contemporary Europe in a postcolonial and now "post-9/11" era. Or, as Osterweil aptly sums up, "Haneke suggests that First-World talk of 'post'-colonialism involves denial and attempted self-exculpation—an effort to defend against any acknowledgement of continuing internal and international oppression and injustice."[29] The way these issues focalize around the video gaze and a lack of clarity about the origin, production, control, meaning, and use of these videotapes suggests not only the manner in which mediation functions both to produce and obscure the particularity of these social relations, but also specifically the way that technologies of surveillance—so weighted with signification around power relations and the visibility of truth—become a point of access, if a violent one, to the circuit of projection and injustice around race in "post"-colonial Europe.

Haneke's earlier film *Benny's Video* introduces racialization as a disavowed production of surveillant violence in somewhat the reverse direction, which proves illuminating for a structural reading of *Caché*. This film, taking place in Austria, quietly tells the story of a white, bourgeois teenager named Benny (Arno Frisch) whose obsession with violent video imagery causes him to organize his life around video rentals, a repeated watching of a video of his family's participation in the slaughter of a pig with an air gun, and the setting up of video cameras to monitor both the world outside his apartment window and within his darkened room. Inviting a young girl home from a video store with no recognizable intent, Benny shoots her with the air gun in what seems like an only vaguely aggressive manner. The scene is caught on the video camera, and eventually he shows it to his parents, who, with a kind of stunned complicity, try to figure out how to manage it. As his father cleans up the mess, Benny's mother takes him on a subdued tourist expedition to Egypt, a "vacation" that serves to reframe the mediated events at home significantly. Although the televisual and videotape imagery is clearly the centerpiece of the film—and suggests, like *Funny Games*, a rather straightforward indictment of the contemporary culture so inundated with television violence that, as if by sleepwalking, Benny simply reproduces—it is the family's covering up of the crime that marks the colonial production of race in those circumstances, one which does so in the interest of the bourgeois family unit.

The aftermath of the violence is most telling in this regard. The son returns from his Egyptian vacation with a tan, a shaved head, and a knit kufi. Benny's visual transformation shows how the sociopathic violence at the heart of the bourgeois European family has become cast as racial other during the cover-up, with a gesture as direct as a vacation. Most simply, we could say that Benny's act of violence leads to his production—*visually*—as racialized other. While the television news shown earlier in the film focuses on the ethnic violence in the collapsing Yugoslavia, here Benny is cast off and reemerges as a more particular remnant of western European ethnic violence. The danger within is sent abroad and returns, as if it had always come from there. While this is already a powerful critique of the projection and disavowal of white European violence, the fact that Benny comes back from this trip and turns himself and his parents in to the police recasts the issue as a return of the repressed in the form of culpability. Benny's visual coding as the colonized other brings the responsibility home to roost not because he *truly* represents the "other" that highlights the structural violence of his culture, but because he represents the very process of visual coding and recoding that has clearly marked the violent production of racialized subjects in colonial and postcolonial Europe: a production, as has so often been noted, tied both historically and experientially to mediated visibility. The account given by Frantz Fanon best communicates the violence in the circuits of visualization at the heart of the colonial enterprise, particularly in relation to mediation: "I cannot go to a film without seeing myself. I wait for me. In the interval, just before the film starts, I wait for me. The people in the theater are watching me, examining me, waiting for me."[30] The fact that for Fanon the experience of cinematic spectatorship is also an experience of the intensive surveillance of him as a racialized object highlights how even narrative cinema, a media form less associated with surveillance, becomes enmeshed in that project specifically through the production of race in the colonial context.

Returning to *Caché*, we can see visual coding, recoding, and, crucially, decoding operating far more explicitly as a function of the surveillant gaze, as stated above, but with the racial and postcolonial issues more centralized. The repeated and ultimately unresolved introductions of the videotapes and video POV shots as simultaneously accusatory, exculpatory, evidentiary, irrelevant, and simply impossible, force the issue: the idea of social identities and relations as produced by a visual-cultural field, particularly one defined by surveillance, makes sense only if we understand those productions as also irretrievably destabilized by that same visuality. Put simply, every time a video image appears in the film, it undermines any prior stability of form or content. Insofar as race is also often visually produced as a marker out of that same surveillant field, it, too, becomes a coded position that is here also decoded even as it is centralized in the zones of indistinction of modern politics and media.

In the end, that now-clichéd phrase "caught on tape" becomes deeply ironic—ultimately, video as surveillance "catches" nothing, but rather opens up spaces for a series of violences. The types and uses of these violences are what remain to be determined. In *Saw*, narrative figuration suggests not only that video surveillance is part of the methodology of torture, but also that torture is hailed as a resolution to ambiguities within the field of surveillance. For its part, *Caché* implies that the surveillance model is so deeply unstable that when followed to its (il)logical conclusion, it deconstructs its own functions in a manner that may well be violent, but possibly in a way that, unlike the *Saw* films, undoes rather than reintroduces the conceit of a stable and deterministic visual field.

Thus my choice to read the ostensibly new genre of torture porn through reference to Haneke's work is a suggestion that the generic codes of cinema are not separate from the coding of subjectivity that is happening around video surveillance—this coding is itself a constant decoding, a manifestation of recognizable boundaries that points only to interrelated structures that have no clear boundaries. Torture porn *must* be read as trans- and international, trans- and inter-generic, trans- and inter-technological, simply because the narrative formations of surveillance and torture insist on the production of boundaries only to blur them, and the introduction of indistinctions only to produce (un)stable resolutions. Despite the hyperbolic insistence on the recognizability of graphic, bloody torture as monitored and produced by video surveillance in American contemporary horror, that very subject matter opens up to the complexity of the international political and technological stages— which are, in fact, the more literal (non)-locations of torture and surveillance in current times.

NOTES

My thanks to Catherine Mills and Ani Weinstein, whose input on various aspects of this argument were extremely helpful, and particular thanks to Zahid Chaudhary, who not only helped me think through these issues, but who also (almost willingly) sat through a number of these films with me.

1. *Quarantine* is the American remake of the Spanish film *[Rec]* (Jaume Balagueró and Paco Plaza, 2007).

2. Even several years before this most recent spate of surveillance films, John Turner noted that "surveillance as a narratival and structural device in popular cinema is indeed ubiquitous." "Collapsing the Interior/Exterior Distinction: Surveillance, Spectacle, and Suspense in Popular Cinema," *Wide Angle* 20 (October 1998): 94. And as Thomas Levin has so compellingly argued, "A socio-political understanding of surveillance at the dawn of the new millennium must also include an analysis of the striking proliferation of the *rhetorics* of surveillance—at both the thematic and the formal level—in virtually all contemporary media ranging from cinema and television to cyberspace." "Rhetoric of the Temporal Index: Surveillant Narration and the Cinema of 'Real Time,'" in *CTRL [SPACE]: Rhetorics of Surveillance from Bentham to Big Brother*, ed. Thomas Y. Levin, Ursula Frohne, and Peter Weibel (Cambridge, MA: MIT Press, 2002), 581.

3. Dean Lockwood, "All Stripped Down: The Spectacle of 'Torture Porn,'" *Popular Communication* 7 (January 2009): 42. For another discussion of the relation of these films to the political context of real-world torture, see Gabrielle Murray, "*Hostel II*: Representations of the Body in Pain and the Cinema Experience in Torture-Porn," *Jump Cut* 50 (Spring 2008): http://www.ejumpcut.org/archive/jc50.2008/TortureHostel2/index.html.

4. http://boxofficemojo.com/. The domestic gross for *Saw IV* was $63.3 million.

5. Lockwood, "All Stripped Down," 45.

6. As Foucault states, within the modern system of discipline and punishment, "the body as the major target of penal repression disappeared." But the interaction of torture and surveillance within these films proves illuminating for a discussion about how, despite the move away from public spectacles of bodily abuse, surveillance practices are intersecting with torture in new formations. *Discipline and Punish: The Birth of the Prison*, trans. Alan Sheridan (New York: Vintage, 1977), 8.

7. Kevin D. Haggerty, "Tear Down the Walls: On Demolishing the Panopticon," in *Theorizing Surveillance: The Panopticon and Beyond*, ed. David Lyon (Cullompton, UK: Willan Publishing, 2006), 23.

8. David Lyon, "The Search for Surveillance Theories," in Lyon, *Theorizing Surveillance*, 3–20.

9. Ibid., 11, and Lockwood, "All Stripped Down," 45.

10. Giorgio Agamben, *Homo Sacer: Sovereign Power and Bare Life*, trans. Daniel Heller-Roazen (Stanford, CA: Stanford University Press, 1998).

11. Dietmar Kammerer, "Video Surveillance in Hollywood Movies," *Surveillance and Society* 2, nos. 2/3 (2004): 473.

12. See my earlier essay "The Camera's Eye: *Peeping Tom* and Technological Perversion," in *Horror Film: Creating and Marketing Fear*, ed. Steffen Hantke (Jackson: University Press of Mississippi, 2004), 35–51.

13. *Vacancy* builds its narrative in the reverse trajectory but for the same end: the realization from two motel guests that the videos in their room are not just disturbing horror films left for their entertainment, but documents of prior violent murders in their own room, serving to escalate their fear as they become the objects of the production of a new "snuff" video.

14. Jasbir K. Puar, "On Torture: Abu Ghraib," *Radical History Review* 93 (Fall 2005): 31.

15. Agamben, *Homo Sacer*, 86.

16. Ibid., 85.

17. Ibid, 89. Lockwood, in his Deleuzian account of torture porn mentioned above, has similarly noted (through reference to the work of Benjamin Noys) that it is difficult to consider these films outside the formulation of "bare life" that Agamben posits. But despite his invocation of Noys and Agamben, as well as his noting of the *Saw* films' surveillance aspects, Lockwood goes on to argue primarily for an understanding of torture porn as a cinema of affect that in its extremity represents a transformative and liberatory masochism. "All Stripped Down," 44–45.

18. Elaine Scarry, *The Body in Pain: The Making and Unmaking of the World* (New York: Oxford University Press, 1985), 27.

19. Agamben, *Homo Sacer*, 11.

20. Ara Osterweil, review of *Caché*, *Film Quarterly* 59 (Summer 2006): 35.

21. D. I. Grossvogel, "Haneke: The Coercing of Vision," *Film Quarterly* 60 (Summer 2007): 38.

22. As Catherine Wheatley points out, this technological confusion is significantly produced by the use of high-resolution digital video. While earlier video images within film are often marked off as low-res, and thus stamped with the mark of a gritty reality, Haneke's turn to digital video here also introduces indistinction between the subjectivized, diegeticized video surveillance gaze, and the narrative and visual verisimilitude of the cinematic image. It is not of neutral interest that this apparently

"aesthetic" (or simply commonsense) choice is made not only when narrative films are increasingly composed of digital production and postproduction, but also when surveillance is increasingly composed of a relation between visual and informational technologies. "Secrets, Lies, and Videotape," *Sight & Sound* 16 (February 2006): 32–36.

23. Interestingly, the high-resolution video is now a VHS tape, which is a bit incongruous.

24. Osterweil, review of *Caché*, 36.

25. Ibid.

26. Wheatley, "Secrets, Lies, and Videotape," 35.

27. Clive Norris and Gary Armstrong, *The Maximum Surveillance Society: The Rise of CCTV* (Oxford: Berg, 1999), 59.

28. Ibid, 91.

29. Osterweil, review of *Caché*, 38.

30. Frantz Fanon, *Black Skin, White Masks*, trans. Charles Lam Markmann (New York: Grove Press, 1967), 140.

CHAPTER FIVE

Cutting into Concepts of "Reflectionist" Cinema?

The Saw *Franchise and Puzzles of Post-9/11 Horror*

MATT HILLS

The *Saw* franchise (2004–2010), on its seventh installment at the time of writing, has been one of the success stories of noughties horror. Writing of trends in contemporary horror cinema, the scholar and critic Kim Newman suggests that there have been a relatively small number of "films and film-makers responding with dark, brutal gut-punches that define the times. . . . The contemporary US horror canon, which we can loosely term the *Grind-house* school . . . , includes Eli Roth's *Hostel* films . . . and James Wan's *Saw* (and sequels by other hands), perhaps the only modern American horrors which will be remade a generation after the sequels run out."[1] Positioning the *Saw* titles as possessed of at least some cultural value, Newman nevertheless argues that modern horror is not generally as politicized as its predecessors. Whereas canonical genre movies such as *Night of the Living Dead* (George Romero, 1968) or *The Texas Chain Saw Massacre* (Tobe Hooper, 1974) encouraged audiences "to make connections between what they'd just seen and what was happening in the world . . . these films were really 'about' Vietnam or social class in America," Newman argues that, by contrast, the noughties "is not an era that cares for films which are 'about' anything. . . . The 'message' of horror in the 1970s tended to be that there was something seriously wrong with society; the 'message' of 2000s horror is that Other People Are Shit. . . . Too much current horror cinema adopts apparently contradictory positions of solipsism and misanthropy that need to be outgrown."[2]

In this chapter, I want to develop Newman's concerns by focusing in more detail on the *Saw* movies, analyzing to what extent they can be interpreted as being "about" contemporary political and cultural contexts. The question, then, is one of how we can relate horror texts to cultural contexts—here, particularly, the contexts of post-9/11 U.S. (media) culture. I want to begin by addressing the range of ways in which we can theorize horror as relating to its society—through what are sometimes dubbed "reflectionist readings"—before moving on to consider the textual and sub-generic specificities of the *Saw* franchise as an example of what the journalist David Edelstein has termed "torture porn."[3]

Ultimately, I will argue that the *Saw* movies suppress and marginalize readings through which their scenes of torture might be related to real-world political contexts. But at the level of their narrative problematics—returning obsessively to the meanings and contradictions of supposedly "righteous torture"—the *Saw* films can be read as recodings of U.S. political debates. Neither allegories nor metaphors for U.S. foreign policies leading to and following 9/11, the *Saw* movies are nonetheless not wholly divorced from post-9/11 contexts, especially debates over whether the United States' treatment of "prisoners of war" can be construed or defined as torture, along with media coverage of Abu Ghraib. As torture porn, these movies circle thematically around contemporary political controversies, without quite being "about" them. As such, I will argue that we need to analyze *Saw*'s spectacular "traps"—and its absence of magical or supernatural forces[4]—as a type of exaggerated, heightened modality, exploiting the horror genre to "tackle highly volatile issues . . . at a remove from reality."[5] What is called for here is a more liminal, nuanced approach to text/context "reflectionism," which can move beyond alternatively dismissing specific horror texts as mere fantasy, or concretely revalorizing them as "serious" political commentary. And it is this wider issue of historicized text and context that I want to consider first, setting the stage for my subsequent analysis of the *Saw* franchise.

CUTTING INTO "REFLECTIONISM"; OR, HOW CAN THE PIECES OF THE TEXT/CONTEXT PUZZLE FIT TOGETHER?

The notion that horror can be read in relation to its societal and cultural contexts is well established as an interpretative strategy among media sociologists and cultural historians of the genre. For example, Andrew Tudor asserts that there "is no doubt that the modern horror movie, like all popular culture, tells us something about the society in which we live."[6] But the nature of any text/context articulation is rarely as clear-cut as this argument might seem to imply. Tudor himself identifies three different "levels" of articulation: "First there are those accounts operating at a relatively low level of abstraction which lay claim to a direct thematic link between specific features of the genre and aspects of agents' . . . social experience. Second, there are those which focus upon genre developments . . . seeking to demonstrate their congruence with more macroscopic currents of social change. And lastly there are arguments about the relation between whole horror discourses and the typical structures of social interaction which they presuppose and to which they contribute."[7] Tudor places Mark Jancovich's *Rational Fears* at the first level, aspects of Noël Carroll's *The Philosophy of Horror* at the second, and his own *Monsters and Mad Scientists* at the third level.[8] Analyzing the *Saw* franchise as torture porn, and considering "thematic links" to post-9/11 political debates over torture, seems to place this essay at Tudor's "relatively low level of abstraction." Even at this level, though, there can be instabilities of meaning and interpretation. For, as Jancovich notes in his work on 1950s B movies, an established reading where Cold War invasion narratives equal cultural fear of communism can be complicated: "These claims about the 1950s invasion narratives have virtually achieved the status of an orthodoxy, but there are considerable grounds for challenging, or at least qualifying, them. . . . The alien's association with the Soviet Union did not necessarily imply an affirmation of American society. Indeed, the concerns with the Soviet Union were often merely a displacement or a code which different sections of American society used in order to criticise those aspects of American life which they feared or opposed."[9] Instead of simply othering communism as a way of life, Jancovich argues that a range of 1950s B movies displaced or coded critique of American industrialism, such as Fordist mass production: "Rather than legitimating Fordism and its application of scientific-technical rationality to the management of American life, these texts often criticised this system by directly associating the alien with it."[10] In this "level one" *re*reading, the alien comes to stand in for, and code, aspects of *both cultural self and other*. In other words, there is a multiple coding, or over-coding, which resists easy interpretation as a straightforward "message"; the monstrous alien invader can stand for two seemingly opposed terms simultaneously.

Relating texts and contexts of the *Saw* movies, we should therefore take note of this interpretative problem and perhaps refrain from attempting to arrive at, or force into place, any univocal "message." Instead, *Saw*'s codings of torture may also be connotatively multiple, relating to both contemporary cultural selves and others. I will return to this matter in the next section.

Any attempt to fit together textual and contextual themes needs to negotiate not just the semiotic multiplicity of textual codes, but also the possible openness of contextual meanings. As Brigid Cherry points out of the first *Saw* (James Wan, 2004), "The enigma at the start of the film is that, as Lawrence ponders, 'they must want something from us, the question is what?' There is a sense of meaninglessness (a metaphor for the emptiness of post-modern life, perhaps) set up from the very start."[11] The alleged nihilism of the

Saw movies means that exactly which cultural contexts are being referenced is somehow unclear. Instead, a "postmodern" lack of meaning calls up a range of interchangeable cultural anxieties about the collapse of cultural narratives of the future: "The postmodern condition is such that, as Crane says, 'it is impossible to end a horror film with any plausible orientation to the future.' We are 'inhabiting a world in which the future has vanished before everyday signs of the last things'—we could consider gun crime, knife crime, AIDS, bird flu, the war on terror, and climate change, amongst others, as some of these signs, 'watching a horror film is a reality check.' Indeed, there is no redemption even for Adam and Lawrence at the end of *Saw*."[12] By virtue of textual openness or nihilism, a variety of contextual, cultural anxieties can be cued.

Jason Colavito similarly argues that vastly different cultural contexts can be read into torture-porn movies:

> In *The Monster Show*, David J. Skal suggests that horror movies' "life and death issues very often have their roots in war and its aftermath." . . . [To his schema we can add that] Torture Films (2002—present) [seemingly correspond to the] War on Terror (2001—present) [and the] Iraq War (2003—present) . . . [yet] there is no easy correlation between horror films and periods of war, which with the inclusion of the nebulous Cold War and War on Terror meant that the United States would have been at war of some sort for nearly all of the years covered by horror films. . . . No matter when a horror movie was made, it would be near enough to *some* war for Skal's purposes.[13]

Indeed, Colavito rules out this supposedly "spurious correlation" by displacing it with one "between horror film florescence and economic volatility . . . [including] Torture Films (2002–present) [correlating with] Dot-Com Bust and Recession (2000–2003)."[14] This argument, along with those of Jancovich and Cherry, points out that there can be no singular cultural context against and through which to read horror texts. The B movies of the 1950s can be about communism or fears of U.S. industry; the *Saw* franchise can be about a "postmodern" collapse in projected cultural futures, or the "War on Terror," or economic recession and associated fears within U.S. society. For example, *Saw VI* (Kevin Greutert, 2009) aligns itself denotatively with anxieties over the provision of American health care, offering up a seemingly more direct cultural-political resonance than other entries in the franchise.

What thus becomes important in any attempt to piece together the semiotic jigsaw of text and cultural context is twinned (con)textual instability. In effect, this amounts to a scenario where the two puzzle pieces one is trying to slot together—text and context—can both change shape depending on one's viewpoint. As such, any claim to have finally or definitively fitted these pieces together should be met with profound skepticism. Reflectionism, I would suggest, itself frequently needs to be cut into more nuanced, complex components, or approached reflexively as a deliberate halting of semiosis. Rather than retreating altogether from historicized and societal readings, one might take account of Robin Wood's cautionary note on horror's ideologies: "Any work . . . will reveal—somewhere—areas or levels of incoherence . . . [because] so many things feed into it which are beyond the artist's conscious control—not only his personal unconscious . . . but the cultural assumptions of his society. Those cultural assumptions themselves have a long history (from the immediate social-political realities back through . . . history . . .) and will themselves contain, with difficulty, accumulated strains, tensions, and contradictions."[15] This offers an alternative to either reading horror films for a clear "message" or dismissing some noughties horror for a supposed lack of political engagement. Rather, we can explore the incoherence and ambivalence of the *Saw* franchise in relation to post-9/11 U.S. culture, addressing it as a coded sequence of "guilt-trauma" films, in Joan Hawkins's term.[16] And as Robert Solomon has suggested, the relationship of horror to the "real" may characteristically be one of symbolic distanciation, with a semiotic gap, and hence indeterminacy, between text and context being essential to the genre's operation:

> Art-horror cannot be *too* real. The scheduled release of "action" movies was seriously disrupted after September 11th. . . . Hollywood editors were busily editing out shots of the Twin Towers and even postponing new releases because they were "just too real" and evocative of the real-life horror. Thus, while one consideration for art-horror may be that its object must be close to a real object, another is that for there to be any pleasure at all, art-horror must remain at a safe distance. Getting these two demands in balance is the (rarely met) challenge of horror filmmakers.[17]

Indeed, when Adam Lowenstein's reading of horror as Benjaminian "allegory" addresses the coding of an "immediate" cultural moment after 9/11, it is perhaps indicative that he turns away from horror and looks, instead, at war movies.[18] It is as if the lack of distance between text and context temporarily disallows the horror genre's effectivity in this case.

The question left in place, however, is why some horror movies are canonically recuperated and read as "social commentary" while others are attacked as "sadistic pornography."[19] Indeed, as I will go on to argue in the next section, the *Saw* movies have not generally been taken seriously in academic and journalistic commentary, being predominantly viewed instead as highly commercial (and thus uninteresting) exploitation cinema, and as franchise horror that is formulaic, "graphic," and of limited sociological interest.

While remaining cognizant of the issues of multiple (con)textual meaning and incoherence highlighted thus far, I will suggest that the *Saw* franchise can be read differently by examining the narrative and character-psychological rationales for the Jigsaw killer's actions. Focusing on how torture is (fantastically) narratively rationalized allows us to reread the *Saw* franchise as a symbolic coding of post-9/11 debates over the meaning of "torture." Both semiotic distanciations from the "real" and the self/other doublings of horror[20] may well work against clear political messages of "social commentary," but I will argue here that they also work against any clear depoliticization of the franchise as mere "sadistic pornography." In short, narrative examinations of "torture" and its cultural meanings in "torture porn" can be brought into focus, rather than reception being drawn to attacking or defending alleged "porn."

"TORTURE PORN"; OR, THE NARRATIVE PUZZLE AND INCOHERENCE OF "RIGHTEOUS TORTURE"

To be sure, the *Saw* franchise does not deal directly or denotatively with that element of noughties U.S. society that might be termed post-9/11 culture. Though the character of Eric Matthews (Donnie Wahlberg) spends *Saw IV* (Darren Lynn Bousman, 2007) literally on thin ice while dressed in an orange jumpsuit, this iconography—potentially visually cueing imagery of Guantanamo prisoners—goes unremarked on. Writing on the use of a related image of "orange overalls" in a torture scene in the science fiction television series *Doctor Who*, Anne Cranny-Francis and John Tulloch suggest that the "series was not operating in a critical media vacuum for its . . . audiences."[21] Nor, we might say, does the *Saw* franchise operate in such a vacuum, though it seemingly works to minimize parallels and resonances with such real-world politics. *Saw II* (Darren Lynn Bousman, 2005) features fleeting mentions of a "movie on TV" featuring a reporter in a "war zone" who "spent nine years in captivity," as well as brief references to "Tokyo subway attacks," but these citations of real-world referents of war and terrorism are merely incidental moments that are not textually emphasized. Likewise, the "war zone" remains unspecified, invoking the idea of being a prisoner of war in the vaguest of associative terms rather than via any concrete reference to cultural context.

Saw II also features threats of torture to extract information, quite unlike the Jigsaw killer's usual modus operandi, but these come from Detec-

FIGURE 5.1. *Reflections of Guantanamo in* Saw IV *(Lionsgate, 2007).*

tive Matthews as he tries to discover what Jigsaw, John Kramer (Tobin Bell), has done with his son. The tortures set up by Jigsaw, by significant contrast, are typically neither ongoing nor about extracting information. Instead, Jigsaw's traps are always timed—that is, precisely finite, a race against time—and concern his victims' will to live rather than the gathering of any form of intelligence. As such, the "torture" of this torture porn is defined by its very symbolic distance and difference from that carried out in the name of the War on Terror at the likes of Abu Ghraib and Guantanamo. The philosopher Adriana Cavarero defines this real-world torture as "horrorism," by which she means the redefinition of violence in excess of murder's finality, aimed instead at causing ongoing, potentially endless pain: "Torture belongs to the type of circumstance in which the coincidence between the vulnerable and the helpless is the result of a series of acts, intentional and planned, aimed at bringing it about. Several peculiar aspects of horrorism are thereby fully disclosed. The center of the scene is occupied by a suffering body, a body reduced to a totally available object or, rather, a thing objectified by the reality of pain. . . . There is no alternative or reciprocity. There is no way out, only the infinite and prolonged repetition of unilateral suffering."[22] What the George W. Bush administration defined as "interrogational torture," marking out a supposed difference separating "harsh but legal interrogation techniques from the degeneration of these techniques into torture,"[23] is held very strongly at a distance from the representations of the *Saw* franchise. Instead, these forms of finite, non-interrogational torture are also heightened and exaggerated—

distanced from a modality of referential realism—by virtue of Jigsaw's staging of traps. Though Jigsaw's apprentices Amanda (Shawnee Smith) and Lieutenant Hoffman (Costas Mandylor) sometimes alter the rules of these artificial stagings, their artificiality nevertheless persists. These many traps have been extratextually embraced by fans as a key part of the franchise's horror spectacle, and the films' distributor, Lionsgate, has promoted them as such through DVD extras.

The traps of the film series are significantly akin to what Cynthia Freeland terms horror's "numbers" in an analysis of the *Hellraiser* movies. By "numbers," Freeland is likening moments of horror spectacle to the song-and-dance numbers in a musical. These represent points where the narrative is somewhat displaced in favor of displaying grand set-pieces: "Films employ brilliant special effects, but the numbers in them are not just there as spectacles of mindless gore. They convey information about the monster, its nature and its desires, and who it will attack and why. As we watch the numbers, we can try to learn the laws about these monsters, so as to classify them and address the evil that they represent. Also, the numbers provide . . . specialized aesthetic pleasures for fans."[24] Jigsaw's traps similarly reveal his nature as a "monster" to the audience—that is, whom he will attack and why. At the same time, the character and his multiple surrogates are linked to the setting up of spectacle: "The monster is . . . like the filmmakers, a magician who makes the visual spectacles possible. The monster is associated with the creativity behind the numbers that constitute the aesthetic pleasures of graphic horror."[25] These convoluted "numbers" involve the likes of a razor-wire maze in *Saw*; a Venus flytrap "head trap" in *Saw II*; the pig vat in *Saw III* (Darren Lynn Bousman, 2006); *Saw IV*'s series of four tests undergone by Rigg; *Saw V*'s (David Hackl, 2008) tests experienced by the "Fatal Five" group; and *Saw VI*'s carousel trap involving six "Umbrella Health" workers.

Freeland goes so far as to explain the appeal of Pinhead (Doug Bradley) in the *Hellraiser* movies in these terms: "Fans like Pinhead because of the very particular role he plays in the graphic spectacles of *Hellraiser*, a role that can be played only by good monsters in horror: He both reveals and punishes human monsters or evildoers."[26] And I would suggest that Jigsaw can be read as a non-supernatural Pinhead, to the extent that he, too, aims to expose and punish human "monsters" who have not lived their lives well. Reinforcing the fact that horror fans tend to read these traps as aesthetic spectacle, there is even a horror fan website that lists its favorite ten traps, according first place to the "needle tub" from *Saw II*.[27]

But scholarly interpretations of the *Saw* franchise have read its traps somewhat differently than the fans' emphasis on aesthetic spectacle or the producers' readings given in DVD extras, such as Oren Koules's statement that "there is a morality that Jigsaw feels."[28] For instance, Jason Colavito rejects any interpretation that accepts Jigsaw's rationale for his tortures:

> It turns out that the Jigsaw killer is dying of cancer, and it really made him *appreciate* the value of life. He wants to share this sweetness and light by torturing innocent people to make them . . . really *feel* how great it is to live. . . . Though the killer claims to have a reason for his tortures, this is superficial coloring. He kills because he can kill. He is dying, so he does not care what happens to him. But even this is just a superficial reason grafted onto a film series that the Motion Picture Association of America worried was too dark for an R-rating (restricting viewers under seventeen).[29]

These meanings are disqualified by Colavito, ruled out as absurd and as mere alibis for the films' violence. Such "superficial coloring" is hence ignored, leading to a strongly dismissive reading of the franchise. Though taking a less evaluative approach, Brigid Cherry also argues that the rationale presented for Jigsaw's killings is undermined both by Amanda's alteration of the "rules," and by the fact that most victims do not escape their traps: "Despite the fact that Jigsaw intends his traps to be 'tests' or 'games' that will teach the victim a valuable lesson, this never seems to work. The one victim for whom it does seem to work is Amanda, but then in later films she . . . rejects his underlying principle by ensuring the victims can never escape death even if they escape the trap. The only thing the victims are expected to do is enter into the game that is being played without fully knowing the rules or the motivation of the game-master."[30] Colavito rules out Jigsaw's reasons in order to read the films as sadistic pornography, a style of dismissive interpretation to which Cherry also comes close: "Subsequent *Saw* films have significantly increased the levels of pain and torture inflicted on victims. . . . Devices for the torture and dismemberment of the body are increasingly the sole raison d'etre of the films."[31]

Against these types of scholarly reading, I want to argue that Jigsaw's character psychology cannot simply be ruled out, as Colavito suggests, or read as textually subverted, in line with Cherry's interpretation. Instead, Jigsaw's worldview can be read as a key part of his monstrosity. Deborah Knight and George McKnight have laid the groundwork for such a reading: "We might say that what characterizes [non-supernatural killers such as] Bates, Lecter, and Bateman is not their fantastic biologies, but their *fantastic psychologies*. Indeed, in films such as *Psycho*, *The Silence of the Lambs*, and *American Psycho*, psychology becomes thematized in the figure of the horror villain."[32] This is equally true for Jigsaw and his apprentices, who are constantly tested by, as well as testing, the mind-sets of others in exaggerated, spectacularly unpleasant ways.

If we don't immediately rule out Jigsaw's "fantastic psychology," then the franchise becomes legible in a very different way. Instead, we might take seriously Jigsaw's assertion that he has "never murdered anyone" in his life, as he responds when accused by Matthews of "killing and torturing people for your own sick, fucking pleasure" in *Saw II*. In other words, there is a central narrative puzzle here: Should the audience grant any validity to Jigsaw's view? Is there such a thing, as a result, as "righteous torture," in which the morally unworthy, the human "monsters," are punished? It is this question, I would suggest, that forms the crucial problematic of the franchise, one that is rendered invisible if Jigsaw's perspective is a priori negated in scholarly readings.

Curiously enough, Edelstein raises related questions in his journalistic definition of torture porn. Though his classification groups together very disparate films (not all of them clearly horror movies), he actually articulates these titles within a post-9/11 context: "Fear supplants empathy and makes us all potential torturers, doesn't it? Post-9/11, we've engaged in a national debate about the morality of torture, fueled by horrifying pictures of manifestly decent men and women (some of them, anyway) enacting brutal scenarios of domination at Abu Ghraib. And a large segment of the population evidently has no problem with this. Our righteousness is buoyed by propaganda like the TV series *24*, which devoted an entire season to justifying torture in the name of an imminent threat: a nuclear missile en route to a major city."[33] But even as he raises this coded relationship with post-9/11 culture, Edelstein makes the same sort of (pre)judgment as Colavito: "Back in the realm of non-righteous torture, the question hangs, Where do you look while these defilements drag on?"[34] The line between "righteous" and "non-righteous" torture is assumed, thereby enabling torture porn to be devalued and critiqued as sadism, as well as other media being firmly positioned as "propaganda" for the Bush administration's policies. What goes missing is, again, the very *narrative puzzle* of "righteous torture"—whether such a thing can *ever* culturally exist, and how we might evaluate and respond to claims made for its existence. For, at the very moment that the Jigsaw killer claims his traps are justifiable, he becomes symbolically and connotatively articulated with the Bush government's post-9/11 policies.

There is thus both a distance from the post-9/11 "real" via the finite, non-interrogative, and artificial modality of Jigsaw's traps, and a closeness to the "real" via the narrative problematic of torture claimed as morally justifiable.

As Solomon argues of effective art-horror, *Saw*'s narratives are precariously poised between these two meaning-making possibilities.[35] But the objects of Jigsaw's game are not othered as terrorists, enemy combatants, or Islamic fundamentalists. Quite to the contrary, these victims represent versions of U.S. audiences' cultural selves: they are implicitly or explicitly identifiable as American citizens. As a producer on *Saw II*, Mark Bury, argues, "He's killing these people who don't appreciate how good they have it in life, as most people in America don't realize."[36] Cherry similarly notes that in the first *Saw* movie, "Adam is set up in the film as a passive observer in life (a variation on the postmodern zombie, perhaps). . . . *Saw* . . . depicts a society that is stagnant and corrupt."[37] Just as Jancovich has argued that 1950s B movies may have coded cultural anxieties over aspects of U.S. culture, so, too, I would suggest, does the *Saw* franchise.[38] It symbolizes fears over the alleged decadence and amorality of contemporary America, suggesting that threats to the culture operate from within rather than without. Making the self rather than the other an object of problematically righteous torture is also readable, though, as a further textual strategy for achieving symbolic distance from the "real"; it is an ideological inversion that seeks to leave military and legal definitions of "interrogative torture" securely outside the textual parameters of genre entertainment. But recall that Jancovich's work cautions us to consider how self and other can stand in for each other: the other can code anxieties about the self as part of the horror genre's doublings and incoherence. In the case of *Saw*, we might argue that self and other are symbolically collapsed together in the figure of the torture victim, despite textual and denotative strategies seeking to enforce a strict separation of the two.

This doubling can be seen even more clearly in the figure of John Kramer. Jigsaw is a torturer who assumes his own righteousness and legitimacy, and who repeatedly refuses to consider himself a murderer—just as the United States doesn't legally commit murder when it is at war. But there is something unusual about the *Saw* franchise: Jigsaw is not its sole, iconic killer. In order plausibly to continue the franchise following his demise in *Saw III*, the device of looping back in diegetic time is used, but Jigsaw also has a number of apprentices and emulators (e.g., Amanda and Hoffman) who continue Jigsaw's work. Unlike many other iconic horror monsters, then, Jigsaw's "evil" is propagated as a belief system. His "deviant" beliefs, within which the United States is corrupt, decadent, immoral, and in need of punishment, are inculcated in others who have undergone his testing. In short, Jigsaw's role as a horror villain is not merely embodied: he has converts to his way of thinking who carry on his campaigns against the unworthy. Though this is a relatively secularized moral campaign—again providing symbolic distance from the "real"—Jigsaw and his converts are readable as coded versions of Islamist "extremism," representing a belief system attacking the United States for its decadent immorality and threatening to spread via "radicalization."

Both the monster *and* the victims in the *Saw* franchise are therefore marked by over-coding or doubling; both symbolically collapse self and other at the connotative level, creating a series of films that, far from being wholly apolitical, are structured through thoroughgoing political incoherence, being open to a multiplicity of different politicized anxieties as the franchise unfolds. Jigsaw can stand in both for the Bush administration's defense of "righteous torture" and for terroristic radicalization; his victims appear to invert the position of the other against whom the American state directs "interrogative torture," but their victimization also articulates them symbolically with this very other. Rather than restaging a critical dynamic via the "smoke screen" of its genre codings,[39] *Saw* restages an entire field of political debate without appearing, denotatively, to be in any way "political." And this, I would suggest, is the measure and mark of its success at tapping into cultural and political anxieties. The franchise's great popularity may otherwise appear to be something of an enigma—it is not a star vehicle; not a series of big-budget blockbusters; not a film-history-making genre innovation. Explanations of the franchise's success may, problematically, rely on explicitly or implicitly pathologizing audiences as sadistic gorehounds addicted to ever more gruesome and graphic horror. But if we address the profound incoherence of the text, then its particular ability to resonate with a range of contemporary, post-9/11 fears is brought into focus.

The skill of these films lies in how they cut into "reflectionist" views of horror. Immense over-coding enables the *Saw* movies to operate as a lightning rod for conservative fears of radicalization and anti-American belief systems; for liberal fears of "righteous torture"; and, of course, for apolitical fears of bodily violation, as Jonathan Lake Crane has described: "The perfectly broken body . . . is the most interesting and most vital special effect in any contemporary horror film."[40] And all of this is achieved while body horror is aestheticized within the artificial modality of traps, and Republican/Democratic political anxieties are coded at a symbolic distance from the real, thereby enabling the *Saw* phenomenon to function as a form of bloody, anxiety-containing entertainment.

The gaming, ludic nature of the franchise has also been remarked on, as in Mikel Koven's commentary on *Saw* for *101 Horror Movies You Must See before You Die*:

The first of the *Saw* films evokes, through its title, not just the Jig*saw* killer and the hacksaw Elwes uses to cut off his own foot . . . but also the act of "seeing" itself. What do the characters "see"? What do we in the audience "see"? Throughout the film is a strong game element, playing with sight and what is hidden from sight. The final revelation . . . can be dismissed as a narrative trick, but given . . . the rules of the game . . . it is the most logical of all the trumps. . . . What we don't see has been right in front of our eyes the whole time.[41]

This narrative-as-game, resulting in a final twist or "reveal," marks each entry in the series to a degree: *Saw II* tricks its audience by playing games with "live" and "recorded" mediation; *Saw III* makes Jigsaw's death part of a hidden test; *Saw IV* reveals another Jigsaw convert, as well as playing tricks with assumed narrative sequencing; *Saw V* inverts the usual form of the traps by making the space outside a contraption lethal, rather than the space within its confines. Even *Saw VI*, though perhaps lacking the bravura narrative feints of its predecessors, turns the tables on Hoffman to provide another last-gasp narrative development. Typically, each of these twists reinforces the sense that the viewers themselves have been subjected to a type of aesthetic trickery, making the films' ludic nature recurrently diegetic and extra-diegetic—that is, playing with audiences' expectations as well as setting in motion games of life and death for characters. Indeed, contra the torture-porn characterization, which implies that the "numbers" of graphic bodily spectacle are the attraction, the *Saw* franchise is powerfully focused on narrative machinery. Its moments of heightened, artificial spectacle are also exaggerated moments of narrative crisis, enforced life-or-death choices made against the clock.

Another part of *Saw*'s success, I would argue, lies in this extreme condensation of narrative and spectacle via traps. Unlike Cynthia Freeland's theorization of Pinhead's appeal, Jigsaw and his converts are not only sources of horror's visual spectacle; they are also, at the same time, agents of narrative construction. Jigsaw resembles a potent puppeteer, controlling and manipulating other characters, anticipating their decisions and setting a variety of plans in motion—something captured via the repeated use of order-giving cassettes and the literal use of a puppet avatar. Through Jigsaw and his acolytes, the *Saw* franchise creates a narrative world of highly legible symbolic order and meaning. Rather than denotatively representing cultural disorder, debate, and ambiguity, *Saw* installs a series of nonnegotiable diegetic certainties. As such, it offers a micro-staging of moral order and agentive action where characters are compelled to prove their worth and decide their fates.

FIGURE 5.2. *Machinery of horror (*Saw, *Lionsgate, 2004).*

"Torture narrative" or "torture story" would be a more appropriate term, in this sense, than torture porn, given that *Saw*'s traps offer an immediate, visceral shortcut to the basics of storytelling: suspense generated by action against the countdown, and meaning created by the binary of life/death or redemption/punishment. But this micro-narrative staging of moral order occurs at the artificial level of each trap, implying diegetically that zones of cultural disorder, chaos, and corruption surround these manic, ostentatious attempts to fix meaning and moral order. Jigsaw and his followers inflict moral judgment on their victims, rather than moral worth being naturalized through specific characters, as is more typically the case in popular culture's Manichean structures. Though the *Saw* franchise may often be read as a machinery of visual body horror, it is simultaneously a narrative machine, offering storytelling shocks as much as graphic gore. Its "monstrous" figures of near-magical potency and power are not just the masters of spectacle; they are also the masters of narrative meaning.[42] Jigsaw, even in death, always has another trick to play on audiences and characters alike. And this emphasis on narrative trickery is stressed through the repeated use of Charlie Clouser's "Hello Zepp" music cue. This piece of music, in a variety of realizations, plays over key dramatic twists in every entry in the franchise. It is as much a part of the series' format as Jigsaw and his traps, sonically reinforcing the *Saw* brand not as graphic horror per se, but rather as a series of audacious, heightened narrative games and reveals.

Adriana Cavarero argues that under the contemporary cultural conditions of "horrorism," "the Abu Ghraib tormentors and their victims appear as . . . personified citations of horror. . . . Torture in this case, materially perpetrated on bodies but no longer concealed, indeed acted out for that worldwide audience that the Internet guarantees, becomes spectacle."[43] But this "citation of horror" is not just spectacular but also narrational: a micro-narrative of humiliation, as the torture victim is forcibly and violently allocated a place in a specific cultural script. Meaning is artificially made in and through the body of the victim, just as Jigsaw and his acolytes convert the bodies of their victims into a staged moral order.

Assuming that there may be one explanation of *Saw*'s success—that audiences are voyeuristic gorehounds—misses the fact that the social and cultural contexts within which movies mean will always be multiple. As such, contemporary horror's appeal may be "cognitive and constructivist in emphasis. Elements of the fiction resonate, as it were, with features of the social experience of its consumers."[44] In this essay, I've argued that the *Saw* franchise's focus on narrative puzzles and problematics of "righteous torture" allow it to resonate with post-9/11 U.S. culture, while its incoherence and self/other doubling allow for highly diverse political and apolitical perspectives to be incorporated. Rather than viewing this franchise as either carrying a "message" about post-9/11 America or as being dangerously apolitical and "not . . . 'about' anything,"[45] its greatest trick is to be denotatively apolitical and, at one and the same time, connotatively hooked into a multiplicity of post-9/11 cultural-political anxieties surrounding the United States' imputed decadence, the spread of threatening or "monstrous" belief systems, and the "justifiable" use of torture.

Caught between a symbolic distance from the "real" and a closeness to "real" objects of fear, the *Saw* films don't merely "reflect" post-9/11 concerns. Instead, they code these concerns through ideological incoherence: they represent Jigsaw as a dangerous legitimator of righteous torture *and* as the source of a value system attacking America's decadent immorality; they represent his victims as American citizens *and* place them within the "horrorism" of the "enemy combatant" other. The *Saw* franchise doesn't have "a message"; it isn't singularly pedagogical or political. Yet it is not nihilistically meaningless, mere gore-filled torture porn. Here, I've argued that we need to see text/context articulations differently, cutting into "reflectionism" debates in a way that allows for the very instability of horror's meanings, spectacles, and narratives, while refusing to cleave contemporary horror a priori into the "meaningful" versus the "meaningless," or "social commentary" versus "sadistic pornography." In the end, all the pieces of the text/context jigsaw don't fit together quite so neatly.

NOTES

1. Kim Newman, "Horror Will Eat Itself," *Sight & Sound* 19 (May 2009): 37.

2. Ibid., 38.

3. David Edelstein, "Now Playing at Your Local Multiplex: Torture Porn," *New York*, January 28, 2006, http://nymag.com/movies/features/15622/.

4. Newman, "Horror Will Eat Itself," 38.

5. Isabel Pinedo, "Playing with Fire without Getting Burned: Blowback Reimagined," in Battlestar Galactica *and Philosophy*, ed. Josef Steiff and Tristan D. Tamplin (Chicago: Open Court, 2008), 175.

6. Andrew Tudor, "From Paranoia to Postmodernism? The Horror Movie in Late Modern Society," in *Genre and Contemporary Hollywood*, ed. Steve Neale (London: BFI, 2002), 116.

7. Andrew Tudor, "Why Horror? The Peculiar Pleasures of a Popular Genre," in *Horror, the Film Reader*, ed. Mark Jancovich (New York: Routledge, 2002), 50.

8. Ibid., 51; Mark Jancovich, *Rational Fears: American Horror in the 1950s* (Manchester, UK: Manchester University Press, 1996); Noël Carroll, *The Philosophy of Horror; or, Paradoxes of the Heart* (New York: Routledge, 1990); and Andrew Tudor, *Monsters and Mad Scientists: A Cultural History of the Horror Movie* (Oxford: Blackwell, 1989).

9. Jancovich, *Rational Fears*, 17.

10. Ibid., 26.

11. Brigid Cherry, *Horror* (London: Routledge, 2009), 201.

12. Ibid., 203.

13. Jason Colavito, *Knowing Fear: Science, Knowledge, and the Development of the Horror Genre* (Jefferson, NC: McFarland, 2008), 415–416.

14. Ibid., 416-417.

15. Robin Wood, *Hollywood from Vietnam to Reagan . . . and Beyond*, rev. and exp. ed. (New York: Columbia University Press, 1986), 42.

16. Joan Hawkins, "Culture Wars: Some New Trends in Art Horror," in *Horror Zone: The Cultural Experience of Contemporary Horror Cinema*, ed. Ian Conrich (London: I. B. Tauris, 2010), 134–135.

17. Robert C. Solomon, "Real Horror," in *Dark Thoughts: Philosophic Reflections on Cinematic Horror*, ed. Steven Jay Schneider and Daniel Shaw (Lanham, MD: Scarecrow Press, 2003), 250–251. See also Daniel Shaw, "A Reply to 'Real Horror,'" in Schneider and Shaw, *Dark Thoughts*, 260–263.

18. Adam Lowenstein, *Shocking Representation: Historical Trauma, National Cinema, and the Modern Horror Film* (New York: Columbia University Press, 2005), 12–13, 177, 180.

19. Ibid., 154-155.

20. Solomon, "Real Horror," and Jancovich, *Rational Fears*.

21. Anne Cranny-Francis and John Tulloch, "Vaster Than Empire(s), and More Slow: The Politics and Economics of Embodiment in *Doctor Who*," in *Third Person: Authoring and Exploring Vast Narratives*, ed. Pat Harrigan and Noah Wardrip-Fruin (Cambridge, MA: MIT Press, 2009), 346.

22. Adriana Cavarero, *Horrorism: Naming Contemporary Violence*, trans. William McCuaig (New York: Columbia University Press, 2009), 32, 31, 114.

23. Ibid., 114.

24. Cynthia A. Freeland, *The Naked and the Undead: Evil and the Appeal of Horror* (Boulder, CO: Westview Press, 2000), 266.

25. Ibid., 267.

26. Ibid., 268.

27. "Top 10 Saw Traps," *Horror Fan Zine*, January 6, 2009, http://horrorfanzine .com/top-10-saw-traps/.

28. "Jigsaw's Game," *Saw II* (2005; Santa Monica, CA: Lionsgate, 2007), DVD.

29. Colavito, *Knowing Fear*, 391–392.

30. Cherry, *Horror*, 201.

31. Ibid., 203–204.

32. Deborah Knight and George McKnight, "*American Psycho*: Horror, Satire, Aesthetics, and Identification," in Schneider and Shaw, *Dark Thoughts*, 217 (italics mine).

33. Edelstein, "Now Playing at Your Local Multiplex."

34. Ibid. See also Rick Worland, *The Horror Film: An Introduction* (Malden, MA: Blackwell, 2007), 266.

35. Solomon, "Real Horror." See also Matt Hills, *The Pleasures of Horror* (New York: Continuum, 2005), 135.

36. "Jigsaw's Game."

37. Cherry, *Horror*, 202.

38. Jancovich, *Rational Fears*.

39. See Pinedo, "Playing with Fire."

40. Jonathan Lake Crane, *Terror and Everyday Life: Singular Moments in the History of the Horror Film* (Thousand Oaks, CA: Sage, 1994), 141.

41. Mikel Koven, review of *Saw*, in *101 Horror Movies You Must See before You Die*, ed. Steven Jay Schneider (London: Quintessence, 2009), 402.

42. See Shaw, "A Reply to 'Real Horror.'"

43. Cavarero, *Horrorism*, 111.

44. Tudor, "Why Horror?," 52–53.

45. Newman, "Horror Will Eat Itself," 38.

CHAPTER SIX

The Host versus *Cloverfield*

HOMAY KING

This essay explores collective images of global disaster in two films—Bong Joon-ho's *The Host* (*Gwoemul*, 2006), the highest internationally grossing Korean film of all time, and Matt Reeves's *Cloverfield* (2008). In these films, certain historical traumas and disasters, both man-made and ostensibly "natural" in cause, become intertwined with one another and ramify across national boundaries—politically, economically, and in a global popular imagination. As Joshua Clover has observed, the practice in the post-9/11 era of connecting filmic images to the historical events that have shaped them feels too easy: "The sphere of culture is always 'based on a true story' . . . [however] this version of film criticism seems of late like child's play. The geopolitics decoder ring always works, and with a minimum of twiddles: 1-2-3 Baghdad! (Alternately, the count can go 9-11 New York!)."[1] One would think that it would be self-evident that a narrative film can engage with history, and with a sociopolitical world outside its own diegesis, through means other than a one-for-one encoded correspondence to a major headline that is temporally and spatially proximate to its production. But as Clover's observation implies, a reminder of this fact may be useful, and it seems important to pose anew the question of film's relationship to the historical. *The Host* and *Cloverfield*, I suggest, engage with the post-9/11 era of history in a more complex way than is evident at first glance. Both films condense images and affects from multiple historical traumas into aggregate, globally resonant visual forms.

COLLECTIVE IMAGES

Certain highly iconic images appear in *The Host* and *Cloverfield*, ones that bring to mind unforgettable, traumatic, and widely circulated pictures from the first decade of the twenty-first century. Crowds of people rush through city streets in terror, in flight from an unknown threat looming from behind. Mourners grieve beside a wall covered in photographs of the missing and deceased. Pedestrians head to work clad in business attire, their faces obscured by surgical masks. Workers in hazmat suits sift through an area filled with waterlogged debris. Such images evoke and reference catastrophic media pictures from a group of temporally adjacent disasters: the attacks of September 11, Hurricane Katrina, the SARS epidemic, and the 2004 Indian Ocean earthquake and tsunami. They are images that belong resolutely to the early twenty-first century, yet they are characterized by the lack of a singular or true historical analogue. What is most noteworthy about them is that they have been overdetermined, that they resist being solved as if by decoder ring.

Some critics have argued that *Cloverfield* represents a traumatic repetition of the attacks of 9/11.[2] But the film also seems to reference FEMA's drastic, public failure during Hurricane Katrina. Like New Orleans, Manhattan is abandoned at the end of the film by the federal government and left to fend for itself against the monster in its most desperate hour. Similarly, one could claim that *The Host*'s title and contagion theme make it about the SARS epidemic (the fact that this disease is directly referenced in dialogue within the film supports such a reading).[3] Others have suggested that the film offers, in the words of one reviewer, an "allegory of the psychic wounds engendered by Korea's division into North and South . . . presented through themes of ruptured families."[4] Such a reading makes sense in the context of New Korean Cinema's engagement with the "two Koreas" theme and the series of binary oppositions that separate them.[5] Rather than choose between a global reading and a local one, though, we might instead explore how this very concatenation of meanings exhibits a noteworthy characteristic of recent commercial cinema, one that is perhaps especially prominent and pertinent in recent examples of the horror film.

The tendency to concatenate meanings is also a characteristic of traumatic modes of representation. Such modes, as Freud suggests in his earliest writings on traumatic neurosis, involve not only displacement ($X = Y$, monster virus = SARS) but also condensation ($X + Y + Z$ = condensed image). In his case study of Frau Emmy von N., Freud refers to a "compulsion to associate" and goes on to describe how this compulsion manifests both in the discourse of his hysterical patients and in his own dreams, which reveal a "compulsion to link together any ideas that might be present in the same state of consciousness."[6] This observation forms the basis for Freud's theory of condensation, a fundamental operation of the dream-work. In *The Interpretation of Dreams*, Freud refers to a process of working out "connections between the two sets of impressions of the previous day" and combining them "into a single situation"; the dream-work, Freud continues, "is under some kind of necessity to combine all the sources which have acted as stimuli . . . into a single unity."[7] Later in that text, in his analysis of the dream of Irma's injection, Freud refers to a category that he calls the "collective image": a composite figure rendered as if "by projecting two images on to a single plate, so that certain features common to both are emphasized."[8]

The films I propose to analyze are like these collective images in more than one sense. The traumatic scenes they evoke are multiple and resist being paired with any single point of historical reference, or with any single mass-media image from that history. In this way, they speak to what Cathy Caruth describes as "the possibility of a history that is no longer straightforwardly referential (that is, no longer based on simple models of experience and reference) . . . aimed not at eliminating history but at resituating it in our understanding."[9] The manifold and serially superimposed referents for these cinematic images have circulated globally, repetitiously, and virally, in multiple news media formats, including print, television, and the Internet. Despite undeniable elements of regional specificity, I would like to suggest that such images speak to a notion of historical trauma and mass disaster as shared, global phenomena whose shocks reverberate beyond the immediate victims of catastrophe, and beyond the municipal boundaries of any given city, region, or national cinema. These films thus reflect not only the psychodynamics of collective trauma, but also cinema's condition as a global medium with transnational ramifications.[10]

In this essay, I identify and unpack images and motifs like these that appear in *The Host* and *Cloverfield* and group them into three categories: military failure, mourning, and viral contagion.[11] Some of these images, like that of running crowds, seem explicitly to quote or invoke disaster footage from the mass media; others comment on this footage in more oblique ways. My method of analysis also takes a cue from a reading in Adam Lowenstein's *Shocking Representation*. In his analysis of Wes Craven's *The Last House on the Left* (1972), Lowenstein describes the affinities between an advertisement for the film and John Filo's widely circulated, Pulitzer Prize–winning photograph of the tragic 1970 incident at Kent State when National Guardsmen opened fire on student demonstrators.[12] Like this advertisement, the images I analyze in this essay refer not to historical events themselves but to widely circulated photographs and media forms associated with these events. Both the ad and the images I discuss may provoke what Lowenstein calls an "allegorical moment . . . a shocking collision of film, spectator, and history where registers of bodily space and historical time are disrupted, confronted, and intertwined."[13] While my method draws from *Studies on Hysteria*, I aim to interpret both *The Host* and *Cloverfield* not according to a method of symptomatic reading that treats films as though they were patients rife with unconsciously motivated symptoms, but rather as texts that—to different degrees—are consciously searching for allegorical images that can give concrete, visible, and localized form to situations that are abstract, camera-shy, and de-centered.

Reviewers have noted similarities between *The Host* and *Cloverfield* (some adding that the former fares better in a face-off).[14] Both films are creature features, and their monsters resemble each other visually. These monsters are themselves collective images of a sort: enormous, amphibian, somewhat dragon-like, insectoid mutants that assemble aspects of Godzilla, the creatures from the *Alien* franchise, the monstrous maternal, and the prehistoric into aggregate digital form. They superimpose the dinosaur onto the urban metropolis, suggesting the kind of "not straightforwardly referential" temporality of which Cathy Caruth speaks. Each is more Jaws-like than King Kong in its lack of empathy-inducing faciality. Both monsters terrorize large cities (New York and Seoul), and both claim lead female characters in a sacrificial way. Both threaten not only with physical strength but also as carriers of disease, and in both films, our protagonists take search-and-rescue operations into their own hands due to the failure of state-sponsored relief efforts (even as, in both films, the state proves itself remarkably adept at marshaling a military response to the threat).

While similar in genre and narrative structure, the two films differ starkly in their aesthetics. *Cloverfield* takes the form of a mock home video shot by the character Hud (T. J. Miller), who is documenting a good-bye party for his friend Rob (Michael Stahl-David) when the monster attacks. His footage is framed by expositional text that labels it a classified military document; the tape has been discovered after the attacks in a rubble-strewn area "formerly known as Central Park." *Cloverfield*'s style involves visceral, handheld liveness. The film is illusionistic, rife with the gritty realism of amateur disaster-reporting footage. There is no extra-diegetic music. The acting style invokes the casual, "unscripted" feel of reality television, and the camera remains in a relentlessly embodied first-person point of view, like that deployed in *The Blair Witch Project* (Daniel Myrick and Eduardo Sánchez, 1999).[15]

The Host, by contrast, is unabashedly stylized. It deploys a variety of genre conventions in a mash-up. As Julian Stringer notes, this "generic indeterminacy is a factor built in to the very assembly and promotion of many of the titles now widely classified under the rubric New Korean Cinema."[16] Christina

Klein suggests that "appropriating from Hollywood and other national cinemas has long been a feature of 'authentic' commercial Korean cinema."[17] Jeeyoung Shin adds that "contemporary Korean cinema . . . shows that the contact between different cultures results in hybridisation, not homogenisation."[18] This hybrid aesthetic is on full display in *The Host*. In addition to horror, the film draws extensively on the tropes of the domestic melodrama and makes frequent use of mood music. A score reminiscent of Nino Rota accompanies comedic moments; other pieces evoke the artifice and weeping strings of a Korean soap opera. The cinematography and editing are polished, and the performances are non-naturalistic. Bong punctuates key moments in the family's story with slow-motion cinematography and unusually high or low camera angles, elements that draw attention to the fictionality of the film world. Both films maximize the visceral experience of moviegoing that is often associated with the horror genre. But while *Cloverfield* relies on an anxious hyper-presence and immediacy, *The Host* deploys a unique combination of distanced anti-illusionism and sensory, affective fullness that is characteristic of many examples of New Korean Cinema.

THE BUSH DOCTRINE

Both *Cloverfield* and *The Host* depict the U.S. military as brutal, uncaring, secretive, and destructive, even (and perhaps most) when its purported aim is to offset destruction. *Cloverfield* represents the U.S. military machine as harsh and unfeeling but ultimately effective, necessary, and right. The area formerly known as Central Park is gone, and we are meant to understand that the island of Manhattan has been sacrificed in a final effort to destroy the monster. Despite these harsh consequences, the world at large has apparently been saved: the fact that an audience is alive to view the film attests to the correctness of the military's decision and the success of their campaign. With this conceit, *Cloverfield* implicitly takes the side of the military in the binary opposition between army and scientists that Bruce Kawin associates with the genres of horror and science fiction. In the mid-century horror film version of this face-off, Kawin notes, "the army is right and the scientist is an obsessive visionary who gets in the way of what obviously needs to be done."[19] Those who wish to study the monster are woefully naïve, oblivious to the impending fight to the death from which only monster or humans, not both, will emerge alive. According to this don't-think-just-act logic, all too familiar in the early twenty-first century United States, swift, aggressive military action offers the only chance for survival, and those who stop to observe, ponder, collect information, or weigh their options end up dead.

Hud, our videographer and guide in *Cloverfield*, is a case in point. His desire to record the monster on film is what ultimately causes his demise. His name seems to reference the fecklessness of the eponymous 1963 Paul Newman character. It is also a homophone for the technology known as a head-up display (HUD), a visual interface comprising gauges, crosshairs, or other instruments and "screen litter" superimposed on a window or viewfinder, and thus onto the landscape viewed through it. The display provides information to a user at eye level, removing the need to look down at a dashboard. The HUD technology was originally developed for use by fighter pilots, but it is familiar to civilians from its use in digital cameras and video games, particularly those employing a first-person perspective. *Cloverfield*'s gaze at times seems to mimic the embodied, highly mobile, narrowly focalized point-of-view camera associated with first-person shooter games.[20] Contrary to the conventions of classical cinema, this mode of filming signifies extreme vulnerability, emphasizing the limitations of human vision and soliciting paranoia regarding off-screen space. It thus implicitly works to justify the film's combat-survivalist rhetoric and to make the military's superior technologies of vision seem necessary and welcome.

The Host, on the other hand, portrays both the military and scientists—represented in the film primarily by U.S. occupying forces and members of the World Health Organization, respectively—as cruel, hobbled by bureaucracy, either stupid or lying, and neither necessary nor effective. The virus that the monster purportedly carries—and which has resulted in the quarantine that restricts the movements of the film's hero, Park Gang-du (Song Kang-ho), and impedes his efforts to rescue his daughter Hyun-seo (Ko Ah-sung)—turns out never to have existed. Gang-du is an ordinary citizen—a "loser character," as Bong refers to him in his DVD commentary—who is called to extraordinary rescue efforts that are actively hindered by authorities. His failure to save his father and daughter from the monster can be read in the context of a cinematic pattern described by Chris Berry: a "long series of 'masculinity in crisis' films of the South Korean cinema . . . that have questioned the legacy of forced modernisation projects and macho nationalism associated with the military dictatorship that ruled until democratisation."[21] The monster is finally slain neither by the army, nor by the misinformation-spewing American researchers from the World Health Organization, but rather by the family members in a team effort. Gang-du's brother Hae-il (Park Nam-il) is an unemployed academic who imagines himself to be a revolutionary, and who has learned little in school except for how to make a Molotov cocktail. His sister Nam-joo (Bae Doo-na) is the third-ranked competitive archer in the country (archery being a sport in which Korea has excelled, but which, like table tennis or curling, is not understood by outsiders to be particularly virile). Overcoming trigger-shyness, she manages to launch a perfect flaming arrow into the monster's mouth after her brother has primed it with gasoline.

In both *The Host* and *Cloverfield*, female characters lose their lives to the monster. The female victim in *The Host* is Hyun-seo, the young daughter of Gang-du. She is first kidnapped by the monster and brought to its lair in the sewer system near the Han River; there, she meets another survivor, a young orphan named Se-ju. Hyun-seo effectively dies protecting this young boy, who is later adopted into the Park family. The film's final images flash-forward to Gang-du caring for him in the snack shop during winter. Gang-du's hair is shorter and no longer dyed a silly shade of orange, and he now carries a gun, all signs that his encounter with the monster has led to increased maturity and cynicism. In an inversion of the "final girl" horror scenario identified by Carol Clover, the family that remains at the conclusion of *The Host* is one without women.[22] It seems to represent a future Korea, having sustained heavy losses from its military occupation, political split, and foreign economic control, and finally, for better or worse, more vigilant in its defense against monstrous intruders.

Sacrificial in nature and ultimately allowing for the emergence of a new kind of family structure, Hyun-seo's death is also tragic and accompanied by a sense of poignant waste. In the scene where she is finally released from the monster's grasp, her father rushes toward her in an anguished, even manipulative slow-motion shot. In *Cloverfield*, by contrast, sacrifice is figured as necessary and heroic; the loss it entails is presented as something best not dwelled on. Marlena (Lizzy Caplan), a partygoer whom Hud has been unsuccessfully courting, flees with the group into the New York City subway tunnels and becomes infected while fighting off a parasite released by the monster. Hud expresses surprise and gratitude that she has remained behind to help him; she responds, mildly indignant, "You think I'm the kind of person who wouldn't do that?" Her humanitarian efforts turn out to be costly. Later, the group finds a triage station set up by the military. When they inform the uniformed officers that Marlena has been bitten by one of the parasites, she is quickly escorted to a curtained area. In silhouette, we see an ambiguous explosion, Marlena's last presence in the film. Her death is tragic and invites speculation about military complicity, but we are meant to understand the sacrifice as heroic and necessary.[23] Without her, we would not have Hud, and without Hud, we would not have the eyewitness record of the monster.

LOSS

While *The Host* conveys this far more explicitly than *Cloverfield*, both films offer something that we rarely see in horror: open expressions of grief at unfolding tragedy. The generic constraints of the horror film usually preclude characters stopping to mourn the loss of their companions for more than a short beat. But *The Host* features a prolonged funeral scene following the initial kidnapping and assumed death of Hyun-seo. A memorial is set up in a gymnasium to commemorate the victims of the monster's initial attack and to provide a gathering place for survivors. One wall, in an image that recalls memorial displays following 9/11, is covered in photographs of the deceased.[24] Hyun-seo's family members gather around her portrait and begin a wailing lamentation. "Have any of you heard it?," asks her grandfather Hie-bong. "When a parent's heart breaks, the sound can travel for miles." As the family members weep, collapse to the floor, and begin to writhe around in agony, mourning turns to slapstick. The camera assumes a jarring bird's-eye angle on their prone bodies as people turn to snap photos of the grieving family.

The scene is one of the most heavily stylized in the film. A riot of affects erupts violently into the horror milieu, as if it represented a return of the latter genre's repressed. The reference to the iconic collective image from the September 11 attacks seems almost to function as a historical conduit onto the world: an opening that creates a space within the horror genre for the expression of grief. The scene's descent into comedic farce appears to comment on the prior unimaginability of this mode of expression within horror. The memorial scene is soon interrupted by the entrance of a team of hazmat workers in bright yellow suits. They have come to arrest Gang-du, claiming that he had been infected with a virus during his encounter with the monster. Their entrance, however, seems like an intervention into the mourning scene, as if tears were a contagion that must be stopped.

Cloverfield is also quick to put the brakes on its own internal eruptions of elegiac affect. These appear not explicitly within the diegesis, as in *The Host*, but rather in the form of small bits of previous footage that we glimpse briefly whenever Hud shuts down and restarts the camera (we are informed through dialogue that he has accidentally been taping over this footage). The older material is from a day approximately one month earlier that Rob and his love, Beth (Odette Yustman), spent at Coney Island, a place that seems to signify nostalgia for an idyllic and simpler past. If we didn't already understand as much, the abrupt glimpses on the tape convey the message that this past is now irretrievably lost, and they do so with an economy of effort and screen time.

FIGURE 6.1. *Public mourning: the family in* The Host *(Magnolia Pictures, 2006).*

APR 27 6:17PM

FIGURE 6.2. *Elegiac affect: Odette Yustman and Michael Stahl-David in* Cloverfield *(Paramount, 2008).*

A similar brief eruption of sadness occurs at the end of the film, when Rob and Beth have resigned themselves to their fate and speak their last words to the camera, as if writing their own video epitaphs. Beth is reluctant to speak and Rob has to coax her, as if she is aware that doing so constitutes a recognition and authorization of her impending demise. This final testimony is followed by another glimpse of Coney Island, where the "last words" theme is repeated. From their elevated cabin on the Wonder Wheel, Rob turns the camera to Beth and says, "We've got about three seconds left. What do you want to say, last words to the camera?" Beth smiles and responds, "I had a good day," just as the tape runs out. This epitaph forms the last image of both the videotape and the film.

VIRAL HORROR

Fans of *Cloverfield* have noted that in the final images shot from the Ferris wheel at Coney Island, a mysterious object is just barely visible in the background, splashing into the ocean just off the shoreline.[25] This image provides a clue that connects with and is partially explained by the film's highly successful viral marketing campaign.[26] The marketing plan involved a series of cryptic Internet sites, some of them for fake products and companies. Claude Brodesser-Akner describes the campaign thus: "Slowly, websites bubbled up, all strangely industrial, enigmatic and, maddeningly, unacknowledged by the producers—a Japanese deep-sea drilling company called Tagruato, an addictive iced beverage called 'Slusho!'"[27] The Tagruato website included fake updates about a Japanese government satellite known as the "ChimpanzIII," pieces of which had reportedly broken off and fallen into the ocean.[28] This and other clues imply that the monster is somehow of Japanese origin, or at least associated with Japanese corporate practice, government research, and technological progress. This story of origins references that of the monster in Ishirō Honda's *Godzilla* (*Gojira*, 1954), but with the nations reversed. In *Godzilla*, the monster is the product of radioactive poisoning from the U.S. atomic bombings of Hiroshima and Nagasaki. As Chon Noriega notes, *Godzilla* also seems to reference postwar U.S.- and Soviet-conducted nuclear testing, including the detonation of H-bombs off the coast of Japan during the occupation years and their immediate aftermath.[29] Here, we have a nice example of how *Cloverfield*'s monster functions as a collective image in Freud's sense: an image that references both 9/11 and World War II and condenses these traumas onto each other, layering multiple historical traumas that ramify across and, in this case, projectively reverse national boundaries.

The Host's monster is likewise an overdetermined by-product of a callous military, with equally layered origins. The film's opening sequence shows an American official in a white coat ordering his staff to dump bottles of chemicals into the Han River, against concerns voiced by his Korean colleague. Bong based the film's framing narrative on the 2000 scandal surrounding Albert McFarland, a mortician on a U.S. military base in Seoul who improperly disposed of embalming chemicals and thereby polluted the Han River.[30]

The outrage over the handling of the incident—U.S. officials refused to hand McFarland over to the South Korean legal system and instead conducted their own investigation, which resulted in a light, ultimately commuted sentence—are reflected in the film's theme of U.S. distrust as well as its ironic depiction of habeas corpus violations. Hsu cites an additional origin story for the monster: a businessman who commits suicide by jumping from a bridge into the Han River at the start of the film. If military occupation spawns the monster, then economic neoliberalism aids its growth and development. As Hsu notes, "Through its intertwined genealogies of monstrosity, contagion, and biological hazard, *The Host* presents a critique of U.S. and international interventionism that stretches from the Korean War and the post-1997 structural adjustments imposed by the IMF to the biological and environmental harm caused by toxic dumping and chemical warfare."[31] The knots of causality are firmly intertwined and resist untangling, as if the monster were a dense, cryptic symptom of a virus called globalization.

Like Marlena, Gang-du is rushed into quarantine by the military. As we will soon learn, though, the virus purportedly carried by the monster—unlike the virus of globalization—is a hoax, a mere distraction, and the quarantine wholly unnecessary. The family members demand Gang-du's release and finally manage to smuggle him out of the compound in a van. The scenario is almost noirish in its wrong man–style plot. In its invocation of unlawful detention, the film seems to comment on the practice of extraordinary rendition and the extraterritorial "black hole" sites of Guantanamo Bay and Abu Ghraib. "Infection" is a metaphor for social unruliness. "Quarantine" is a euphemism for political detainment.

One scene close to *The Host*'s conclusion makes these metaphors explicit. A group of protesters has gathered on the banks of the Han, carrying signs and wearing T-shirts that read, "Free Park Kang Doo," "Stop Testing Now," and "No Virus!" In English, an amplified voice gives a warning about Agent Yellow, a chemical weapon, obviously evocative of Agent Orange and other rainbow herbicides deployed by the U.S. military in Korea and Vietnam, and also clearly an allusion to the Yellow Peril and racially coded Western fears of Asian hoards. In this scene, authorities are about to spray Agent Yellow in the area, supposedly in order to kill the monster and its fictional virus. The chemical, however, turns out to be more effective as a tear gas against the protesting crowds. In a scene reminiscent of Nagisa Ōshima's *Night and Fog in Japan* (1960), the protestors raise banners and signs amid a cloud of smoke.

The scene's most obvious referent is the SARS virus epidemic, specifically the distrust of government authority that resulted when Chinese officials attempted to downplay its extent. The Yellow Peril–style paranoia surrounding

FIGURE 6.3. *Demonstrators sprayed with Agent Yellow in* The Host *(Magnolia Pictures, 2006).*

that virus (and the attribution of contagiousness to East Asian countries in general when, as of July 2003, there were only 3 reported cases in Korea versus 251 in Canada)[32] is also evoked in the film's images of pedestrians walking the streets in surgical masks. But the film seems to comment not only on SARS, but more generally on the way that viral outbreaks and other "natural" disasters intersect with the politics of globalization and the spread of global information networks. That news of *The Host*'s virus spreads so quickly and horrifically links it to circulation of news surrounding the anthrax scares in the United States following 9/11. Like grief, the film seems to say, terror is contagious, and this ease of transmission is both effect and cause of its own proliferation.

The virus carried by the *Cloverfield* monster is not technically a virus but rather a parasite. However, like *The Host*, *Cloverfield* provides an allegory of another kind of viral transmission, in this case viral video. Noël Carroll has noted that *King Kong* (Merian C. Cooper and Ernest B. Schoedsack, 1933) is a reflexive text in two ways: first, on Skull Island, characters create a film within a film, a travel documentary inside the larger diegesis; second, when the monster is transported back to New York and made the star attraction of a live spectacle, *Kong* becomes a film about "putting on a show."[33] Similarly, *Cloverfield* leverages various contemporary forms of media spectacle, primarily amateur digital video. The Internet and television campaigns for the film constitute an extra-diegetic example of *Cloverfield*'s reflexive relationship to digital media forms. This ad campaign also seems to mimic the effects of

FIGURE 6.4. *Viral marketing:* Cloverfield *(Paramount, 2008).*

traumatic images. Like a traumatic implantation, the ads are unintelligible, "maddening," and capitalize on an element of surprise or shock (websites "bubbling up" as if from nowhere), producing an anxious excitation. Their very ambiguity makes them ideal sites for the projection of trauma's characteristic concatenation of meanings, as well as for conspiratorial fantasies about their origin and purpose.

The film's theatrical trailer provides yet another example of *Cloverfield*'s engagement with characteristically digital forms of media networks and their modes of spectatorship. The trailer featured the decapitated head of the Statue of Liberty crashing through downtown streets, an image inspired by the poster for *Escape from New York* (John Carpenter, 1981). This trailer, along with the film's startling footage of the headless statue standing in New York Harbor, connects to the phenomenon of terrorist beheading videos that appeared on jihadist websites following the murders of Daniel Pearl, Nicholas Berg, and others.[34] While bearing no formal resemblance to these videos, the *Cloverfield* trailer seems to invoke their message, the triumph of terror over American-style freedom, as well as their affect of acute horror. The rapid circulation and repetition of these images could be described as akin to a "screen memory" effect—a secondary traumatic reaction that refers back to and amplifies the original historical event, but that, like a viral video, also proliferates and assumes a life of its own.

The allegory of digital media offered by *Cloverfield* reflects on two aspects of new media networks. On the one hand, digital media is associated with the "YouTube generation," characterized by the democratization of publicity and the assumption of broader access to the means of digital production, as well as by the notion that identity is increasingly dependent on one's capacity to appear in networked spaces (I blog/Facebook/Twitter, therefore I am). In a digital era, existence is tied to one's Internet presence; one can easily imagine the party footage from the first twenty minutes or so of Hud's videotape uploaded into this type of publicity structure. On the other hand, the fate of the *Cloverfield* videotape, its repossession by military intelligence and filing as a classified document, brings to mind the Patriot Act, FISA, and federal wiretapping provisions that make all such acts of self-presentation, communication, and expression, on the Internet or elsewhere, potentially the property of the state—or, equally troubling, of corporate hosts, and thus subject to their bloated end-user licensing agreements and contractual provisions. As mentioned above, *Cloverfield* is slippery on the question of whether military seizures of control and information are effective and worthwhile; *The Host* is far more direct both in its critique of the state and extra-governmental organizations, and in its message about the potential consequences of not limiting their powers.

Although the actual causes of and events leading to their deaths are complicated, the sacrificial characters in *The Host* and *Cloverfield* both die of infections, Marlena from a biological virus, and Hyun-seo from a viral media hoax. In both cases, the circulation of these diseases is thoroughly mediated by the state. And around their deadly effects are woven images of an inept and callous military machine, of quarantine as detention, and of terror as virus and grief as contagion. As Harry M. Benshoff has observed, the 1980s horror monster served as a metaphor for the AIDS crisis.[35] The creatures in *Cloverfield* and *The Host* stand for a different kind of virus, one that, true to its digital cinematic mode of production, is neither strictly organic nor strictly electronic, neither purely natural nor purely artificial. It is a monster created by a host of globally networked institutions, corporate and military, economic and political, digital and biochemical, a monster perhaps more at home in this century than in the previous one. These monsters give fleshly form to the abstract, invisible, de-centered totality of these institutions, and to their failure to assume responsibility for the destruction they sow.

In conclusion, it is important to note that in the contemporary era, any large, commercially viable film, like these monsters, has usually been the product of a group of globally networked institutions. The notion that any such film could be the product of a single national entity and reflect a uniform, homogenous set of national concerns is clearly untenable, increasingly so in the post-9/11 era. *The Host*, which involved direct collaboration with New Zealand's Weta Workshop and San Francisco's the Orphanage film production and effects houses, demonstrates this point in more immediate ways than *Cloverfield*, but the fact of globalization is more pertinent when understood in the context of the interdependent multinational financing entities that underwrite most large commercial film projects. This interdependency, which was dramatically revealed in the economic collapse of late 2008, suggests the need to re-pose the question not only of cinema's relationship to the nation, but also of its relationship to history, and in particular to historical trauma. The two films that I have discussed in this essay speak to that question in very different ways. But both suggest that the Godzillas of the twenty-first century are not spawned by a single enemy; rather, they emerge through a tangled web of networked institutions, whose crossed lines of causality and responsibility sometimes only become visible, if at all, in the aftermath of the disasters they create.

NOTES

I thank Aviva Briefel, Matthias Konzett, and all the participants in the Global Cinema workshop at the 2010 Northeast Modern Language Association convention for their feedback. For inspiration and prior mentorship, I thank Carol Clover.

1. Joshua Clover, "All That Is Solid Melts into War," *Film Quarterly* 61 (Fall 2007): 6.

2. For example, Daniel North writes, "*Cloverfield*'s monster might be seen to give head, limbs and torso to a morass of nightmares about terrorist attack. . . . We could even see *Cloverfield*'s monster as a truly post-9/11 beast." "Evidence of Things Not Quite Seen: *Cloverfield*'s Obstructed Spectacle," *Film & History* 40 (Spring 2010): 90. Stephanie Zacharek writes, "*Cloverfield* takes the trauma of 9/11 and turns it into just another random spectacle at which to point and shoot." Review of *Cloverfield*, Salon. com, January 18, 2008, http://salon.com/entertainment/movies/review/2008/01/18/cloverfield/.

3. Hsuan L. Hsu suggests that *The Host* can be interpreted as an example of what Priscilla Wald calls "the outbreak narrative." Hsu, "The Dangers of Biosecurity: *The Host* and the Geopolitics of Outbreak," *Jump Cut* 51 (Spring 2009): http://www.ejumpcut.org/archive/jc51.2009/Host/index.html.

4. Jamie Russell, review of *The Host*, *Sight & Sound* 16 (November 2006): 60.

5. Michael Robinson, "Contemporary Cultural Production in South Korea: Vanishing Meta-Narratives of Nation," in *New Korean Cinema*, ed. Chi-Yun Shin and Julian Stringer (Edinburgh: Edinburgh University Press, 2005), 16.

6. Josef Breuer and Sigmund Freud, *Studies on Hysteria*, trans. James Strachey (New York: Basic Books, 1957), 69n1.

7. Sigmund Freud, *The Interpretation of Dreams*, trans. James Strachey (New York: Avon Books, 1965), 212.

8. Ibid., 327, 328.

9. Cathy Caruth, *Unclaimed Experience: Trauma, Narrative, and History* (Baltimore: Johns Hopkins University Press, 1996), 11.

10. Some scholars have already described how *The Host* actively reflects and critiques contemporary forces of globalization and their impact on international film markets. Hye Jean Chung nicely summarizes the problem: "It is difficult to sidestep the facile trap of essentialist notions of national identity, while simultaneously avoiding the pitfall of over-emphasizing the importance of transnational flows"; she also describes how certain contemporary South Korean films "reinsert national ideas into concepts of transnationality, an effort that often conflicts with their rigorous endeavors to categorize and promote themselves as global products." "*The Host* and *D-War*: Complex Intersections of National Imaginings and Transnational Aspirations," *Spectator* 29 (Fall 2009): 48–49. Christina Klein describes Bong's ambivalent attitude toward Hollywood cinema; citing his participation in the protests against the 2007 U.S.-Korea Free Trade Agreement that reduced the number of screens dedicated to Korean films, she argues that "Bong's textual appropriation *from* Hollywood is inseparable from his material defeat *of* Hollywood at the Korean box office." "Why American Studies Needs to Think about Korean Cinema, or, Transnational Genres in the Films of Bong Joon-ho," *American Quarterly* 60 (December 2008): 895. For an exploration and critique of the term "national cinema" in general, see Andrew Higson, "The Concept of National Cinema," *Screen* 30 (Autumn 1989): 36–47.

11. Richard Harland Smith also notes that the theme of viral contagion is common to these two films. See "The Battle Inside: Infection and the Modern Horror Film," *Cineaste* 35 (Winter 2009): 42–45.

12. Adam Lowenstein, *Shocking Representation: Historical Trauma, National Cinema, and the Modern Horror Film* (New York: Columbia University Press, 2005), 114.

13. Ibid., 3.

14. For example, Peter Travers writes in his review of *Cloverfield*, "I've heard the excuse that people running for their lives rarely stop to be pithy. . . . But I'm not ready to concede that it's impossible to make a monster movie with a meaning that cuts deep and characters we can see ourselves in. In 2006, South Korean director Bong Joon-ho did just that with *The Host*, a film of transfixing power." "Scare Tactics," *Rolling Stone*, February 7, 2008, 88.

15. Daniel North calls *Cloverfield* a "found-footage horror film" in the tradition of *The Blair Witch Project* and notes that in this subgenre, "the camera operator invariably dies." "Evidence of Things Not Quite Seen," 88.

16. Julian Stringer, "Putting Korean Cinema in Its Place: Genre Classifications and the Contexts of Reception," in Shin and Stringer, *New Korean Cinema*, 99. Stringer also notes that New Korean Cinema is often "de-genred," or marketed differently, for overseas audiences (100). On a related note, Kyu Hyun Kim observes that the marketing campaigns for two other South Korean films, *Tell Me Something* (Chang Yoon-hyun, 1999) and *Sympathy for Mr. Vengeance* (Park Chan-wook, 2002), "scrupulously avoided the 'horror' label. . . . *Tell Me Something* was confusingly marketed as a 'hardcore thriller' . . . *Sympathy for Mr. Vengeance* [was] struck with an equally strange tagline, 'authentic hardboiled movie.'" "Horror as Critique in *Tell Me Something* and *Sympathy for Mr. Vengeance*," in Shin and Stringer, *New Korean Cinema*, 106.

17. Klein, "Why American Studies," 873.

18. Jeeyoung Shin, "Globalisation and New Korean Cinema," in Shin and Stringer, *New Korean Cinema*, 57.

19. Bruce Kawin, "The Mummy's Pool," in *Planks of Reason: Essays on the Horror Film*, rev. ed., ed. Barry Keith Grant and Christopher Sharrett (Lanham, MD: Scarecrow Press, 2004), 6.

20. Will Brooker offers a refinement on this point, noting that *The Blair Witch Project* and *Cloverfield* "seem to come closest to feature-length FPS [first-person shooter], [but] differ in that their point of view is explicitly a camera, which shakes, blurs, can be set down and passed from one character to another—quite distinct from the smooth, steady view of gaming." "Camera-Eye, CG-Eye: Videogames and the 'Cinematic,'" *Cinema Journal* 48 (Spring 2009): 128. On how first-person point-of-view conventions in cinema relate to those in video gaming in general, see Alexander R. Galloway, *Gaming: Essays on Algorithmic Culture* (Minneapolis: University of Minnesota Press, 2006).

21. Chris Berry, "All at Sea? National History and Historiology in *Soul's Protest* and *Phantom, the Submarine*," in Shin and Stringer, *New Korean Cinema*, 153. In "Dangers of Biosecurity," Hsu reads the moments of masculine failure in *The Host* in terms of their relation to the Korean economy: "Battling the creature misogynistically compensates for anxieties about masculinity embodied by characters like the incompetent Gang-du, his unemployed alcoholic brother, and their father—a patriarch who dies after literally drawing a blank. . . . These crises of masculinity, in turn, register anxieties about economic failure (unemployment, families lacking support, the emigration of women and their employment in the informal economy)."

22. See Carol Clover, *Men, Women, and Chain Saws: Gender in the Modern Horror Film* (Princeton, NJ: Princeton University Press, 1992), 35–42.

23. In this way, *Cloverfield*'s message and gender politics differ from those of a film like *Alien* (Ridley Scott, 1979), in which Ripley's discovery that corporate officials have been complicit in her crewmates' sacrificial deaths is met with revulsion and rebellion.

24. A similar memorial wall appears in the reimagined television series *Battlestar Galactica* (Ronald D. Moore and David Eick, 2003–2009), following a genocidal attack on the planet Caprica, the home of many onboard the spaceship.

25. "DVD Easter Eggs—Splashdown," *Cloverfield Clues*, April 8, 2008, http://cloverfieldclues.blogspot.com/2008/04/dvd-easter-eggs-splashdown.html.

26. Daniel North comments at length on the marketing campaign and suggests that the experience of sorting through its data resembles "apophenia, a perceptual process whereby, in the absence of a clear set of connected evidence, people infer or imagine patterns and links between disparate phenomena." He also compares this process to fan activities surrounding other productions by the *Cloverfield* producer J. J. Abrams, such as the television series *Lost* (2004–2010). "Evidence of Things Not Quite Seen," 82.

27. Claude Brodesser-Akner, "Cloverfield," *Advertising Age*, March 17, 2008, 58.

28. "Tagruato Headlines—Altercation," *Cloverfield Clues*, January 3, 2008, http://cloverfieldclues.blogspot.com/2008/01/tagruato-headlines-altercation.html.

29. Chon Noriega, "Godzilla and the Japanese Nightmare: When 'Them!' Is U.S.," *Cinema Journal* 27 (Autumn 1987): 65.

30. Bruce Wallace, "Who's the Monster?" *Los Angeles Times*, November 1, 2006,

http://articles.latimes.com/2006/nov/01/entertainment/et-host1. Klein notes that it is the obedient Korean assistant, not his American boss, who actually pours the chemical down the drain, and she suggests that it is finally the "political posture of subservience . . . [that] creates the monster." "Why American Studies," 887.

31. Hsu, "Dangers of Biosecurity."

32. World Health Organization, "Summary of Probable SARS Cases with Onset of Illness from 1 November 2002 to 31 July 2003," December 31, 2003, http://www .who.int/csr/sars/country/table2004_04_21/en/index.html.

33. Noël Carroll, "*King Kong*: Ape and Essence," in Grant and Sharrett, *Planks of Reason*, 225.

34. On the phenomenon of execution videos on the Internet, see Michael Ignatieff, "The Terrorist as Auteur," *New York Times*, November 14, 2004, http://nytimes .com/2004/11/14/movies/14TERROR.html.

35. Harry M. Benshoff, "The Monster and the Homosexual," in *Horror, the Film Reader*, ed. Mark Jancovich (New York: Routledge, 2002), 91-102.

CHAPTER SEVEN

"Shop 'Til You Drop!"

Consumerism and Horror

AVIVA BRIEFEL

A few weeks after September 11, 2001, George W. Bush prescribed shopping as a patriotic form of resistance: "We cannot let the terrorists achieve the objective of frightening our nation to the point where we don't—where we don't conduct business, where people don't shop."[1] Advertisements deployed an unmistakably nationalist rhetoric to disseminate an ideology of salvation through consumerism; echoing Todd Beamer's iconic "Let's roll," General Motors assured viewers that it would "Keep America Rolling," while during the 2002 Super Bowl broadcast Budweiser ads featured images of the Clydesdale horses bowing before the Manhattan skyline. According to Christopher Campbell, "The mythical world of post 9-11 advertising encouraged consumerism as the appropriate counterpart to stepped-up military action."[2] In line with this ideology, Americans were urged to protect themselves against another attack by stocking up on such "essential" items as duct tape, canned food, and bottled water. This new regime of home-brewed terror situated fear itself as a "style of consumption."[3]

The commodification of patriotism creates a challenge for post-9/11 horror films that—as explored by several essays in this volume—seek to critique the American response to the attacks. How might these films reconcile their (more or less) radical agendas with the fact that they themselves have become increasingly desirable commodities after 9/11? Does their status as profitable consumer items divest them of the ability to challenge mainstream political reactions to real or imagined terrorist threats? While all horror films that take up the orthodoxy of the Bush regime have had to confront these questions in some way, I identify a group of films that self-consciously try to come to terms with their own dual status as sites of social critique *and* potentially lucrative commodities: Danny Boyle's *28 Days Later* (2002), Zack Snyder's *Dawn of*

the Dead (2004), George Romero's *Land of the Dead* (2005), and Frank Darabont's *The Mist* (2007). I argue that these horror narratives negotiate their
paradoxical status by looking to the past: they reference a film that has become synonymous with its critique of consumer culture, Romero's *Dawn of
the Dead* (1979). Counterintuitively, these post-9/11 films isolate a moment
of Romero's film that demonstrates an ambivalent stance toward consumerism: a blissful montage that briefly seems to showcase the liberating aspects
of consumer behavior. The first two films I discuss, *28 Days Later* and the remake of *Dawn of the Dead*, explicitly rewrite this sequence to endorse a radical form of consumption that can extend to their own status as cinematic
commodities. On the other side of the spectrum, *Land of the Dead* and *The
Mist* invoke Romero's montage to express skepticism about the revolutionary effects of consumerism after 9/11. In so doing, they try to mask their own
status as modern commodities by opting for anachronistic self-presentations.
The varying strategies through which these horror films come to terms with
themselves as radical consumer items extend beyond the level of plot to shape
the aesthetics of the genre itself.

MALL ZOMBIES

The original *Dawn of the Dead* features four human characters (Fran, a television reporter; Stephen, her helicopter-pilot boyfriend; Peter, an African
American member of a SWAT team; and Roger, a white member of the same
SWAT team) who try to survive a nationwide zombie attack by hiding out
in a shopping mall in suburban Pittsburgh. The film has attained canonical
status as an anti-consumerist manifesto, a prime example of the horror genre's
capacity for social engagement; in Romero's words, it takes a "satirical bite at
American consumerism."[4] Critics and lay viewers alike have long identified
the zombies as blatant symbols of this critique, as the monsters are hell-bent
(however mindlessly) on returning to the consumer environment they had
frequented when they were alive. One of the most quoted lines of the film
explains this compulsion as "some kind of instinct. Memory. What they used
to do. [The mall] was an important place in their lives." According to Robin
Wood, the zombies' "most obvious characteristic is their need—apparently
their sole need—to consume. They represent, that is, the logical end-result,
the reductio ad absurdum and ad nauseum, of Capitalism; the fact that they
consume flesh is but a literal enactment of the notion that under Capitalism
we all live off other people."[5] Dressed in suburban garb, the creatures at once

threateningly and pathetically press against the mall's glass doors and wander to the sounds of its PA system, as if in search of one last bargain. Their urge to shop is stronger than death.

And yet the film seems to feature conflicting images of consumerism as enlivening rather than deadening, a source of communal joy rather than isolating numbness. Inasmuch as it presents the dark side of the mall, the narrative also offers a glimpse at a seductive fantasy of being trapped within its walls and having luxury items of all kinds at one's disposal. Our main characters rely on the mall for far more than bare necessities: they seize items that they could not afford in their regular lives; raid the gourmet food department, sampling caviar, rare cheeses, and expensive liquors; dress in exclusive jewelry and clothing; play with sports equipment and video games; and furnish their shelter with bourgeois objects, including a fondue pot and a state-of-the-art (for the late 1970s) stereo. These visions of consumer pleasure reach their climax in a "Bliss Montage" that sets the characters' free-shopping escapades to lively extra-diegetic music. I borrow the term "Bliss Montage" from Jeanine Basinger, who uses it to describe the ebullient images featuring the heroine's fleeting moments of happiness in the classical Hollywood woman's film. These images show her having all sorts of irresponsible fun, often with the leading man, in ways that conflate romance with consumerism: purchasing new clothing, traveling, dining out, and so forth. According to Basinger, the "visual presentation" of the Bliss Montage (which she also terms the "Happy Interlude") "finds the cinematic equivalent of its own meaning: the rapid and brief passage of time in which a woman can be happy."[6] Given that, according to Tony Williams, Romero's film extends the pleasures of shopping—which are conventionally gendered female—to the three central male characters of the film, the comparison to the woman's film seems apt.[7] Also striking is the ephemerality of the Bliss Montage of the woman's film and of *Dawn of the Dead*: romantic or consumer pleasures are fleeting (as Basinger notes, the Happy Interlude is "a representational piece of editing that allows [the heroine] maybe two minutes' running time of joy")[8] and usually precede periods of darkness. In Romero's film, the shopping montage marks a sharp turn toward the decline (in some cases, fatal) of the characters.

These images of blissful consumerism are some of the most contested in Romero's film. For many viewers, they are undeniably seductive: Tom Savini, the film's special-effects director, described being "holed up in a shopping mall" as a "fantasy come true," while Edgar Wright, director of the homage/parody *Shaun of the Dead* (2004), posits that *Dawn* presents the "sense of the apocalypse becoming some adult playground, that for all the bleakness and uncertainty, there are chances to play out long held fantasies, the knowl-

FIGURE 7.1. *Roger in Romero's Bliss Montage (*Dawn of the Dead, *UFDC, 1979).*

edge that essentially you can do anything."[9] More frequently, critics tend to acknowledge the appealing aspects of the scene only to subsume them rapidly within Romero's anti-consumerist message. Kyle William Bishop, for instance, refers to the montage as a "fantasy of gluttony" that holds up the promise of pleasure and "play" but ultimately offers an existence that is as stultifying as that of the monsters': "They [the human characters] are largely going through the motions of a lost life, just like the zombies."[10] For his part, A. Loudermilk contrasts his childhood fantasies of "Mall Fantasia . . . of four people having a mall all to themselves, and I remember prioritizing all I would do and possess," with the realization that "Mall Fantasia proves to be a sort of consumer dementia."[11]

What critics are less likely to accept is the very ambiguity of the scene, the fact that it can be read as a fantasy of consumer behavior even though it is surrounded by a narrative that critiques consumerism. Stephen Harper is one of the only scholars who acknowledges the productive ambivalence of parts of *Dawn of the Dead*: "The film's scenes of carnival license [which he compares to the "medieval legend of the Land of Cockayne"] are among its principal attractions, and they appear to have a particular resonance for the film's audience. . . . The audience reaction to this film suggests that people can have an ambiguous relationship with consumer culture." Harper argues that the film seems to offer opposing perspectives on the "consumerism debate," on the one hand delivering a strong Marxist critique of consumerism, and on the other venturing the "postmodern" idea that "consumerism empowers capitalist subjects by granting them a limited, but politically important space in which to live out utopian fantasies of autonomy."[12] The latter interpretation is plausible in light of the contrast between the multi-racial, multi-gendered community of "free shoppers" in the mall, and earlier scenes of urban strife and racial violence shown in the conflict between a SWAT team, led by a sadistically racist police officer, and the African American and Puerto Rican inhabitants of an inner-city project. The Bliss Montage may offer an antidote to this earlier scene by representing shopping as a site of social harmony, where characters set aside their differences in the act of acquiring free stuff. The fact that they pretend to *pay* for the items they seize, as they (gratuitously) check out the price tags on clothing and weigh coffee beans and candy, implies that their consumer ritual might extend to everyday situations as well as to apocalyptic extremes.

My language is tentative here—I write that the montage "may" represent a form of liberatory consumption—because I want to dwell on the significance of its ambiguity, the fact that it continues to cause such interpretive struggles. In this sense, it also follows Basinger's description of the Bliss Montage as one of the multivalent moments of the woman's film. She advises against reading the typically normalizing conclusion of the genre—in which the heroine must typically give up her digressions and return to her husband or children—as erasing earlier images of her liberation: "It's obvious that seeds of unrest, even rebellion, were planted in some female minds by the evidence they saw on-screen despite the conventional endings that turn a story into a conventional tale. When morality has to dramatize its own opposite to make its point, the opposite takes on a life of its own. The film becomes accidentally ambivalent, contradictory."[13] While I do not mean to link the moral domestication of the heroine with Romero's anti-consumerist message, I do want to suggest that both types of film show a resistance to resolving the ambiguous moments they establish. What if *Dawn of the Dead* were not to be settled one way or the other, venturing that in its general oppressiveness, consumerism may offer moments—however isolated—of pleasure and liberation?

In turn, these brief, ambiguous moments of pleasure seem to justify the film's critical potential despite its own status as a commodity that would eventually be screened in shopping malls across the country.[14] Loudermilk acknowledges the possible contradiction between *Dawn of the Dead*'s anti-consumerist message and its commercial success, pointing out that the film may have helped to boost the sales of the real mall in which it was set. Loudermilk tries to mitigate this point by arguing that "what Romero criticizes in *Dawn of the Dead* is the false security of consumer society, not necessarily consumer culture itself, or notions of financial reward. *Dawn*'s huge success as a commodity disproved its era's assumption that an independent and unrated film is fated to remain underground and illegitimate. Credit is due, then, to the innovative and stubborn Romero whose apocalyptic vision of consumer society *was successful* in subverting consumer norms."[15] While plausible, this view also represents an impulse that we find so frequently in Romero scholarship: an attempt to attribute a consistently and unwaveringly radical politics to the director. This type of reading overlooks the contradictions and ambiguities that occur in any text, radical or otherwise, those moments in which the "message" may not be univocal at all.

One crucial aspect of Romero's Bliss Montage is that the liberatory consumption it temporarily seems to present offers a meta-narrative perspective on the means of production of the film itself. Anticipating his characters' use of the mall to acquire goods that they could not otherwise afford, Romero obtained permission to shoot *Dawn* in a location that would ordinarily exceed his means as an independent filmmaker. The owners of the Monroeville Mall were friends of the director who did not charge him for his nightly shootings. They gave him keys to the mall's stores and facilities and allowed him free rein over its many consumer and leisure spaces. In the words of the producer Richard Rubinstein, "There is no way for us to pay, in dollar value, what the use of the mall is worth."[16] Romero himself described his free access to the mall in effusive terms: "I could have shot forever in that place! . . . It was just *constant* invention. We'd get there and we'd wind up in front of a store, and there'd be a display, or whatever, that we'd want to use. It was so much fun—I could have just kept shooting that movie!"[17] The director's enthusiasm echoes his characters' when faced with free stuff. In both cases, acts that are generally situated within a capitalist economy—shopping and filmmaking—seem temporarily (however illusively) detached from these structures. For Romero, free shopping can be an adversarial form of *both* consumption *and* cinematic production.

The conflicts and ambiguities of Romero's Bliss Montage have proved appealing to post-9/11 films seeking to evaluate their own status as adversarial commodities. Its scenes, which leave themselves open to interpretation and rewriting, seem particularly subversive at a time in which shopping represents a patriotic duty rather than a form of self-expression or leisure. As Jennifer Scanlon argues about the post-9/11 context, "Unlike the days of wars of old, when people sacrificed by having less, by stretching the dollar, contemporary Americans could sacrifice by filling the stores, increasing credit card debt, and displaying material goods as symbols of morality and civic duty."[18] This imperative to spend, whatever the cost, illustrates Jean Baudrillard's notion that "the best evidence that pleasure is not the basis or the objective of consumption is that nowadays pleasure is constrained and institutionalized, not as a right or enjoyment, but as the citizen's *duty*."[19] Both *28 Days Later* and Snyder's remake of *Dawn of the Dead* resurrect Romero's Bliss Montage to identify a liberatory model of consumerism that rebels against the idea of patriotic or moral duty, and that extends to their own identities as cinematic commodities. These rewritings offer the self-contained and temporary act of free shopping as an important site of political resistance and subversive self-invention.

TWENTY-TWO YEARS LATER

It is fitting that post-9/11 horror films use the repetition offered by intertextual flashbacks as a mode of political critique. In her introduction to the anthology *The Selling of 9/11*, Dana Heller writes that the commemoration of the event through consumer objects and activities reflects a "collective compulsion to repeat, to engage in a particular acting out of the trauma through specific practices of consumption that administered to the national hunger for meaning—for images and stories of the attacks."[20] The films *28 Days Later* and the new *Dawn of the Dead* enact this repetition compulsion in a double sense: by allegorizing the events following 9/11 and by rewriting the Bliss Montage from Romero's film. In turn, this twofold repetition allows for a dual exploration: of the role of consumerism in a post-9/11 context and of whether the horror film as cinematic commodity can enact such a critique.

Danny Boyle's *28 Days Later* offers a bleak portrait of a society that has succumbed to an attack of the deadly "rage" virus. The narrative draws simultaneously from Romero's film in its presentation of the infected as ominous, zombielike beings, and from the events of 9/11 to depict a nation in decline. While in this case, the nation in question is England rather than the United States, Boyle assembles a pastiche of images that recall the attacks on Manhattan: London replaces New York as a city whose famous monuments loom over scenes of devastation, its streets are filled with posters pleading for news of the missing, its inhabitants are decimated by a strange disease reminiscent of the anthrax scare, and so on. The violent and irresponsible military response to these events in the film harbors a biting critique of American and British reactions to 9/11. Control of the nation has fallen into the hands of a military apparatus whose cruelty and violence surpass the terrors of the infected. Despite the relatively upbeat ending of the original theatrical release of the film, the audience is left with somber images of a world in decline.

Amid this desolation, there is an exuberant—and brief—Bliss Montage,

FIGURE 7.2. *Selena and Hannah in Boyle's Bliss Montage (*28 Days Later, *20th Century Fox, 2002).*

a clear allusion to *Dawn of the Dead*. On their way out of London in a di-lapidated taxicab, our four main characters (Jim, a bicycle carrier; Selena, a young black woman; Frank, a taxi driver; and his daughter, Hannah) come across an abandoned Budgens supermarket. At first, Boyle bathes the scene in ominous light as the characters tentatively enter the space with the fear that it might hide the infected. He soon allays this apprehension by cutting to the store's colorful display of brand products, accompanied by the euphoric opening notes of Grandaddy's song "A.M. 180." Selena, until now marked by her remoteness, gleefully pronounces, "Let's shop!," and initiates the consumer montage. As in Romero's original sequence, the characters grab items that they could not previously afford or that had been denied to them in the apocalyptic climate. What is more, they also engage in an elaborate consumer performance rather than a blind seizure of items; as Frank explains regarding his selection of an expensive whiskey, "You can't just take any crap." Similarly, Selena modifies her announcement—"If I don't see another bar of choco-late again it will be too soon" (candy bars are among the only food items to which she has had access recently)—with an exclamation that sounds like an advertising slogan: "Not counting Terry's Chocolate Oranges, of course!"[21] The montage ends with another pointed reference to Romero's scene when Frank leaves his credit card on the counter before he and his companions exit the store with their shopping carts. This humorously futile gesture evokes the beginning of the Bliss Montage in *Dawn of the Dead*, in which Peter, grabbing money from the mall's bank, announces, "Hey, you never know," before he and Stephen exit by dutifully filing through the circuitous ropes of the empty queue. Even though currency has lost its value (one of the early scenes of Boyle's film shows British pounds fluttering through London streets), the characters preciously retain their consumer gestures.

Like Romero's montage, Boyle's is a temporary reprieve followed by disaster: Jim is attacked by a zombie when he enters another store, Frank dies soon afterward, and the female characters nearly fall prey to a depraved group of army men. It may thus be tempting to read the Budgens scene as a fool's paradise for those (spectators and characters) who have placed their faith in one shopping basket. Boyle joins Romero in presenting scenes of consumerism gone bad in his depiction of the gothic military bunker in which the true villains of the film reside; filled with pilfered cans of food and electronic equipment, the space emerges as a horrific double to Budgens. But such a univocal reading overlooks the fact that Boyle seizes on the very *ambiguity* of Romero's montage, its clash with the tenor of the rest of the narrative. It offers a temporary space of fantasy in which subversive consumer performance serves as a refuge against the monstrous and military dangers that have overtaken the nation. Selena's "Let's shop!" at once echoes and defies the mainstream injunction to consume as a defensive response to 9/11. The communal joy inherent in this enterprise, which, as in Romero's film, challenges social divisions by bringing together a diverse group of characters, represents an important alternative to the violent and exclusionary military world we find later on. The army's stockpiling of consumer goods is confluent with its blatantly sexist and racist ideology, illustrated by the soldiers' attempts to rape Selena and Hannah in order to harness their reproductive capacities, and by their enslavement and torture of a black member of the infected.[22] Boyle presents the Budgens scene as a fantasy of what an alternative form of consumerism might look like when removed from its oppressive capitalist context.

The unconventional consumerism of Boyle's Bliss Montage also serves to justify his film's role as an adversarial commodity. Like Romero's, the scene represents a self-reflexive moment that (partially) exposes its own means of production. While *Dawn of the Dead* showcases the "free" cinematic shopping that allowed for the production of an otherwise unaffordable film, *28 Days Later* flaunts the capitalist structures that made it possible. In contrast to Romero's sequence, which does not show actual brand names, the scene in Budgens is full of recognizable trademarks, such as Rice Krispies, Kellogg's Corn Flakes, Pop-Tarts, and Toblerone. The scene is a treasure trove for the characters and for the cinematic narrative through its concentrated product endorsement. We can read the sequence as one of cinematic exhibitionism in which Boyle exposes the commodities that have made his film possible, and thus the status of his own film as a commodity. This structure allows for an interesting meta-narrative interplay: the consumer items that the characters seize with revolutionary abandon pay for their ability to do so. Of course, while it exposes the film's material history, the montage also conceals this history by rewriting it into a scene of free shopping rather than capitalist exchange.

The idea of subversive repetition is even more central to Zack Snyder's *Dawn of the Dead*. In addition to its title and basic narrative structure, the film acknowledges its status as remake through the multiplicity of in-the-know references to the original: one of the stores in the mall is named "Gaylen Ross," after the actress who played Fran; there are cameos by Romero's special-effects director Tom Savini and by Ken Foree, who starred as Peter; and many lines are virtually identical ("Why do they come here? Memory, maybe, instinct."). In this version, the survivors' decision to hide out in the mall appears as an imperative to return to the first film. When asked what he and his companions are going to do next, given the zombie attack, one character states matter-of-factly, "We're going to the mall," as if this were the only logical place to go. Meghan Sutherland argues that repetition is central to the zombie genre, writing that "every zombie film is a kind of remake." In her view, these repetitions ultimately uphold the power structures that these films appear to challenge: "It is the immanence of political power in raw flesh that we see revealed, precisely on the set of its own structural crisis. Zombies do not pay for merchandise and neither do those escaping them; they do not vote and no executive or military apparatus remains to punish or rescue them. But these apparati and their politics survive nevertheless in every living and dead body."[23] What Sutherland does not address, however, is how this compulsion to repeat comes into conflict with the fear of mimesis inherent in a genre in which becoming a zombie is a fate worse than death. As Steven Shaviro writes of the original *Dawn*, "The living characters are concerned less about the prospect of being killed than they are about being swept away by mimesis—of returning to existence, after death, transformed into zombies themselves."[24] Like its characters, the cinematic remake must avoid a zombifying imitation.

And so, Snyder modifies his version of the narrative to adapt to a post-9/11 context. He alludes to this new circumstance in various references to national disasters, inefficient leadership (we can only smirk at one character's misguided comment that "America always sorts its shit out"), and coercive religious fanaticism (Foree cameos as a televangelist who scapegoats the decline in mainstream values for the zombie takeover). One of the most blatant critiques of American authority is embodied in CJ, a racist, sexist, and homo-phobic mall cop who, in order to prevent "anyone sneaking around stealing shit," locks up the main characters in a furniture store. CJ's very presence in the mall establishes a crucial difference from Romero's authority-free shop-ping center. Power and surveillance are everywhere. These post-9/11 modifica-tions culminate in a subtle yet crucial revision of the original narrative. While in Romero's version the characters do not live in the retail areas of the mall, but rather furnish its upstairs offices with the goods they have seized, Snyder's protagonists make themselves at home in consumer spaces. They sleep in an upscale furniture store, turn the branch of a coffee-shop chain into a com-munal dining area, and (in the case of an expectant couple) set up a nursery in a baby store. This difference uncovers the directors' divergent responses to the mall—for Romero it is a space of acquisition, while for Snyder it is one of habitation. This latter function, I want to argue, reflects a post-9/11 fantasy of appropriating and altering consumer culture from within.

Snyder's version of the Bliss Montage showcases a strategy of change through infiltration. Performed to the tune of Disturbed's relatively upbeat song "Down with the Sickness," the sequence consists of buoyant images of the characters using the mall in subversive ways. We see, for example, one heterosexual couple filming itself in provocative sexual positions with the mall's camera equipment, and an elderly male church organist trying on women's stockings and shoes. Strutting in front of a mirror, he rewrites Fran's masquerade from the original (she evaluates outfits and later applies makeup in front of store mirrors) into a subversive cross-dressing performance. The makeover encourages him to come out to the other characters. A few scenes later, he narrates the story of how he discovered his sexuality as a teenager when observing a man named Todd, "with the most beautiful blue eyes," building a deck in his backyard. The homophobic CJ, who has now been im-prisoned by the other characters, is forced to listen to this confession and mutters, "Oh God, I'm in hell." CJ himself seems to have been transformed during the montage, however, as the otherwise macho game of poker he plays with his buddies is undermined by the feminine presence of a *Cosmopolitan* magazine (which the men will later consult for dating advice) on their game table. The sequence ends with a direct challenge to the panoptic structures of post-9/11 society. A young woman, who had been shown graffiting the walls of the mall, spray paints a security camera to blackness. However tem-porarily—as here, too, things decline after the montage—Snyder depicts the susceptibility of consumer spaces to parasitic transformation.

The new *Dawn of the Dead* fantasizes about creating an adversarial mode of consumption removed from mainstream injunctions to support the economy by acquiring goods. Its Bliss Montage illustrates John Fiske's description of mall shopping as having the power to cause a "crisis of consumerism: it is where the art and tricks of the weak can inflict most damage on, and exert most power over, the strategic interests of the powerful."[25] While Romero merely flirts with this idea in his Bliss Montage, Snyder extends it to other parts of his film. The mise-en-scène of the mall offers a visual equivalent for a strategy of radical infiltration; it displays fake yet familiar brand names and logos that construct an aesthetics of consumer subversion. Apart from a few authentic trademarks, the mall consists of stores that only resemble their real-world counterparts: Metropolis looks a lot like Pottery Barn, Carousel like Gymboree, Hallowed Grounds like Starbucks, Bookmark like Borders, and so forth. These fictitious consumer spaces de-privatize the commodity and transform it into a generic site of consumer critique. In their transformed state, the brands take on the vulnerability of those zombies in the film who resemble famous celebrities. Some of the living characters use these zombies as target practice, challenging one another to identify and shoot a monster who looks like a famous person: Jay Leno, Burt Reynolds, Rosie O'Donnell, and so on. Likewise, Snyder encourages his viewers to isolate a fake brand, identify its real-world counterpart, and target its regular associations. This type of subversive resistance can only take place in the mall—once the characters leave, they fall prey to the zombie invasion that has spread throughout the nation and possibly the world. Snyder's remake thus seems to revoke the temporary nature of the Bliss Montage found in Romero's and Boyle's films, isolating the consumer space of the mall (and, in the case of his film, of cinema) as the ideal site of resistance to post-9/11 hegemonies.

BLISSLESS

But not all post-9/11 horror narratives share the faith in an adversarial consumerism demonstrated by *28 Days Later* and *Dawn of the Dead*. Romero's *Land of the Dead* and Frank Darabont's *The Mist* reject shopping as a countercultural act by building and then thwarting viewers' expectations for a Bliss Montage. They assert that the radical and communal mode of consumerism set forth—however temporarily—by this cinematic device is no longer possible in a political climate in which shopping can only reinforce the status quo. In rejecting the politics of the Bliss Montage, however, these films have to come to terms with their own status as commodities that might become subsumed in post-9/11 consumer ideology. Both narratives seek to surmount this obstacle through anachronistic and even nostalgic self-presentations, deploying elements of plot and mise-en-scène to situate themselves as pre-9/11 artifacts.

Romero was one of the first to reject the implications of his Bliss Montage. In an interview that appeared shortly after the release of his *Dawn of the Dead*, he commented, "What bothers me most about the movie is that I've seen audiences get off on the idea of having possession of the mall. That's a dangerous fantasy, just as I think the most damaging thing about television is that it breeds familiarity with affluence. It causes people to think, 'Oh, it's right there next to me, and it should belong to me.'"[26] Romero anticipates the reclaiming gestures of critics of his film, who are reticent to accept a moment of cinematic ambiguity that seems to veer away from the anticonsumerist impulse of the rest of the film. Romero waited until the post-9/11 climate of 2005 to offer a full-scale retraction of his earlier vision. *Land of the Dead* offers a cinematic apologia for *Dawn*'s Bliss Montage; here, consumerism lacks redemptive value. The film blatantly critiques the Bush administration's exchange of individual freedoms for quixotic ideals of safety and wealth. Following a zombie invasion, Pittsburgh's wealthiest citizens have retreated to the mall/condo complex Fiddler's Green—to which the critic J. Hoberman refers as "a sort of domestic Green Zone"[27]—ruled by Kaufman, a ruthless financier who sacrifices the city's poor to his greed. In subsequent interviews, Romero elucidated that he based Kaufman on Donald Rumsfeld and his henchmen on members of the Bush administration.[28] The dialogue is replete with lines whose references to 9/11 are far from subtle, such as, "We don't negotiate with terrorists," and "I'm gonna do a jihad on his ass."

In the state of emergency depicted by the film, consumerism can no longer be joyful or liberating. Early on, we witness raids on abandoned stores, sequences that seem to purposefully refute the Bliss Montage, as the stores' products and displays are as bleak as the apocalyptic world outside. In sharp contrast to the Budgens scene from *28 Days Later*, a character leaves a drab, abandoned supermarket and comments, "Mostly canned goods—I'd stay away from the fish." A raid on a liquor store undertaken by the mercenaries adds fatality to the gloominess of the earlier scene. The leader's injunction to "shop 'til you drop" takes on a literal meaning when one of his men receives a deadly zombie bite as he tries to seize expensive cigars. Nor is there any bliss available in Fiddler's Green, despite its promise of "luxury living in the grand old style." The complex is a warped version of the mall from *Dawn of the Dead* where capitalism has been established in the most coercive of forms. Although it serves a similar function as a refuge from zombie attacks, it operates under an ethnic and social exclusivity that Romero links to post-9/11 panoptic xenophobia. When a mob of zombies breaks through the glass surface of Fiddler's Green, a mechanized female voice on the loudspeaker says with misplaced reassurance, "A disturbance has been reported on the outskirts of the city. There's no reason to believe that Fiddler's Green could ever be compromised. But we suggest that residents report any sightings of unusual behavior."

Romero dispels the liberating possibilities of this new mall by offering a montage that dramatically rewrites the one from *Dawn*. Instead of a diverse group of characters gleefully seizing items that are beyond their means, we see the rich spending the money that bought them entrance to Fiddler's Green in the first place. With the return of traditional capitalist structures, shopping is no longer free; in fact, it is one of the many ways in which "the living are kept in line by . . . diversions"[29] manufactured by Kaufman. As Adam Lowenstein points out, Romero made a symbolic decision in his casting of Kaufman: "The fact that Dennis Hopper, a countercultural icon of the 1960s for his role in *Easy Rider* (Dennis Hopper, 1969), appears in *Land of the Dead* as Kaufman speaks cynical volumes about how counterculture becomes dominant capitalist culture."[30] Romero also mocks the subversive aspects of consumerism that Snyder celebrated in his film. After the zombies break into the mall, one of them extracts a woman's belly-button ring with his teeth. The camera's gruesome focus on her profusely bleeding navel dramatizes her dual victimization: to the zombies *and* to her desire to radicalize her identity by wearing an empty signifier of cutting-edge fashion.

Romero does value one form of consumer resistance in *Land of the Dead*: a scavenger and secondhand economy, which he uses to convey the subversive possibilities of his film. His heroes in this apocalyptic world are those who make use of the already used, the trash that others have left behind. The slum outside Fiddler's Green, segregated from the luxury complex by armed guards and metal detectors, seems to belong to a different era altogether. It is a Dickensian, anachronistic world in which children watch a Punch and Judy puppet show performed in the recycled carcass of a broken television, used-book and -clothing sellers hock their wares, and street vendors feed the masses. The slum is also the site of grassroots political campaigns; Mulligan, an activist with an Irish brogue, riles up his listeners to rebel against Kaufman. This retrograde and politically charged world functions as a double for Romero's 2005 film, which also deploys recycling as a form of resistance. Beginning with its recognizable title, *Land of the Dead* regenerates elements of the director's earlier films, modified to a post-9/11 context and suspicious of consumerism. By aligning himself with this anticapitalist world on the margins of the mall/condo, Romero obscures the commodity status of his film. This move suggests that the only way to critique the new consumer order is from an outsider perspective, not from the heart of the mall itself (as was the case with both versions of *Dawn of the Dead*).[31]

Although it has been described as "America's definitive post-9/11 movie,"[32] Darabont's *The Mist* also looks to the past to masquerade its own status as a modern commodity. It couches its obvious critique of the Bush administration within a form and content that herald classic Americana. Darabont had originally wanted to release his film in black-and-white, a fitting aesthetic for a sci-fi horror flick featuring bug-like, B-movie creatures that have emerged from a menacing mist. The majority of the film takes place in an old-fashioned, small-town Maine supermarket instead of a sleek mall. The Food House is stocked with mundane groceries organized in quaint categories like "Wine 'n' Spirits," "Milk 'n' Eggs," and "Bread 'n' Cakes." When disaster strikes following the onset of the mist, the store seems to collapse further into the past: the breakdown of its cash registers and coolers leads one cashier to announce, "Welcome to the Dark Ages, and bring your checkbook." David, the film's protagonist, is a movie-poster artist who favors traditional, hand-produced methods over the efficiency of modern technology. Early on, after a storm destroys one of his meticulously painted posters, he complains to his wife that the movie studio "could whip up a Photoshop poster in an afternoon." *The Mist* aligns itself with this traditional artist on his way to being edged out by an increasingly technologized movie industry.

Darabont uses this mist of nostalgia to execute his attack on post-9/11 America. In addition to directing his criticism at the failed leadership, secret dealings, and destructive religiosity of the Bush administration, he focuses on the coercive effects of consumerism. The film specifically rejects the idea that consumer spaces have the potential to become sites of communal support in a post-9/11 context. Scanlon explains that Americans in the United States and abroad turned to big-box stores such as Wal-Mart for "community and consumption," gathering within its vast spaces to exchange news and express patriotism through the purchase of commodities bearing images of the American flag.[33] Although it does start off as a site of refuge, gossip, and sustenance, the Food House in *The Mist* soon proves antithetical to this "town square" ideal. The characters who hide out in the supermarket enact a pop-culture version of a Hobbesian struggle, summarized by one of the supermarket workers in the following way: "As a species, we're fundamentally insane. . . . Put us in a room and we start to think of reasons to start killing one another." The refugees form dangerously divisive factions, accuse one another of stealing food, and plot against and assault one another. When early on some of the characters decide to organize a barbeque with the (free) supermarket food—an event that in another cinematic context might have initiated a Bliss Montage—their efforts are thwarted by a monster attack. Any attempt to form a close-knit consumer community fails. The only type of community that does succeed is the divisive—and ultimately destructive— religious contingent led by the delusional Mrs. Carmody. With its poisonous suspicion and persecution of anyone who does not mirror its ideals, this community reproduces post-9/11 right-wing fanaticisms.

Nor does the apocalyptic shopping fantasy initiated by *Dawn of the Dead* ever materialize in *The Mist*. Rather than inciting the acquisitional desire of the earlier film, the consumer items in the Food House call for an oppressively regimented form of shopping. This is the case even before the monsters attack: we see characters scrutinizing their shopping lists and dutifully standing in long lines, thus obviating the possibility of impulse purchases. When crisis strikes, the shoppers wait to be told the aisle number for particular products, which for the most part are utilitarian in nature (aspirin, blankets, etc.). When some characters help themselves to less pressing items, such as beer, the store manager threatens to report them. In critiquing the oppressive effects of shopping, Darabont looks back to the strong anti-consumerist message found in the 1980 Stephen King novella from which he adapted his film. King writes that "like most modern markets, the Federal [Food House in the film] was constructed like a Skinner box—modern marketing techniques turn all customers into white rats."[34] In the post-9/11 film, this regimentation extends to the consumer activities that Americans were asked to perform to guard themselves against future attacks. One character expresses skepticism at the "duct tape and food bags" that his companions pile against the store windows with the naive hope that they will stave off the monsters.

On the other hand, when they are removed from these consumer constraints, the items on display become monstrous. The film poses uncomfortable parallels between the commodities and the grotesque appearance of the creatures: the camera juxtaposes a chicken wing to one of the flying beasts, the monsters are attracted to the supermarket's plateglass windows, and they swoop through its aisles and displays. Darabont draws from King to establish the monstrosity of things. The novel repeatedly asks its readers to make connections between the supermarket items and the abject creatures: "There was a graveyard of chicken bones on her plate. She was drinking either blood or V-8 juice"; one of the monsters "crashed into the spaghetti sauces, splattering Ragú and Prince and Prima Salsa everywhere like gouts of blood"; another "looked a little like one of those strange creations of vinyl and plastic you can buy for $1.89 to spring on your friends."[35] These gruesome analogies may have been particularly appealing to Darabont's critique of a belief in the redemptive effects of consumerism after 9/11. He signals that the commodities

FIGURE 7.3. *Monstrous consumerism in* The Mist *(MGM, 2007).*

through which we are supposed to save ourselves against a nebulous "enemy" harbor a troubling resemblance to that enemy. Most popular sources condemned the attacks on the World Trade Center as a war on capitalism, all the while overlooking the capitalist basis of these attacks. Frederic Jameson challenges this shortsightedness by describing Osama bin Laden as a figure of capitalism run amuck, the "very prototype of the accumulation of money in the hands of private individuals and the poisoned fruit of a process that, unchecked, allows an unimaginable autonomy of action of all kinds."[36] For Darabont, the peculiar position that commodities occupy between the quotidian and the grotesque prevents them from having a redemptive potential; they are either tools to stultify the masses or monstrous items of retribution.

These dual alternatives for the commodity may begin to explain why films like *Land of the Dead* and *The Mist* situate themselves within pre-twenty-first-century contexts, when packaging political critiques within consumer forms was, allegedly, a less tricky affair. Craig Bernardini's description of the "nostalgia" and yearning for a "return to tradition" that characterizes *Dawn of the Dead* can also be applied to Darabont's film. We are left looking "for a time when making movies outside the Hollywood system seemed less compromised, and not yet fully co-opted as a Hollywood fantasy itself; before the boundaries between center and periphery, power and powerlessness, were blurred; and before the oppressive conditions of production were obscured by an ideology of creative consumer liberation."[37] This impulse is shared by those films that use the Bliss Montage to endorse certain forms of consumerism;

while their nostalgic gaze may not go as far back as Romero's Dickensian universe or Darabont's 1950s world, it turns to the 1970s as a less complicated period for consumer culture. There is something idealistic about this faith in the relative innocence of commodities before 9/11, one that subscribes to the spurious—yet common—belief that the world fundamentally changed from one day to the next. The reliance on retrospection tells us something about the horror film's uneasy relationship to the commodity, even when the genre seems to endorse radical forms of consumerism.

Another strategy deployed by post-9/11 cinematic texts is to emphasize that film is a different form of commodity altogether, remote from other items on the market. This is the case with films that adopt a self-consciously degraded, non-Hollywood, handheld aesthetic, such as *Diary of the Dead* (Romero, 2007), *Cloverfield* (Matt Reeves, 2008), and *Quarantine* (John Erick Dowdle, 2008). *Cloverfield* in particular contrasts the oppressiveness of mainstream consumerism—Bloomingdale's has become a militarized zone for the violent elimination of the infected—to the truth-seeking, survivalist filmmaking of its main characters. The "difference" of film as a commodity is vividly illustrated in Francis Lawrence's *I Am Legend* (2007). While Robert Neville, the last remaining man in New York City, seizes all the food, expensive supplies, and famous artworks (including Van Goghs and Warhols) he desires, there is one category of thing he cannot appropriate: film. Every day he dutifully returns the DVD he had borrowed from his local abandoned rental establishment, a gesture that suggests that films cannot be owned, even if they are there for the taking. This impulse to represent film as another kind of commodity altogether betrays an anxiety about its function in a post-9/11 economy. To deny its exceptionality would entail accepting its paradoxical status as a consumer product that may sustain (willingly or not) the very structures it critiques.[38] And that would be a very scary thing indeed.

NOTES

1. Quoted in Jennifer Scanlon, "'Your Flag Decal Won't Get You into Heaven Anymore': U.S. Consumers, Wal-Mart, and the Commodification of Patriotism," in *The Selling of 9/11: How a National Tragedy Became a Commodity*, ed. Dana Heller (New York: Palgrave Macmillan, 2005), 175.

2. Christopher P. Campbell, "Commodifying September 11: Advertising, Myth, and Hegemony," in *Media Representations of September 11*, ed. Steven Chermak, Frankie Y. Bailey, and Michelle Brown (Westport, CT: Praeger, 2003), 56.

3. Joe Lockard, "Social Fear and the *Terrorism Survival Guide*," in Heller, *Selling of 9/11*, 223.

4. Quoted in Barry Keith Grant, "Taking Back the *Night of the Living Dead*:

George Romero, Feminism, and the Horror Film," in *The Dread of Difference*, ed. Barry Keith Grant (Austin: University of Texas Press, 1996), 202.

5. Robin Wood, "Neglected Nightmares," in *Horror Film Reader*, ed. Alain Silver and James Ursini (New York: Limelight, 2000), 126. Wood is only one of many critics who have read *Dawn of the Dead* in this way; for other examples, see Tania Modleski, "The Terror of Pleasure: The Contemporary Horror Film and Postmodern Theory," in *The Horror Reader*, ed. Ken Gelder (London: Routledge, 2000), 285–293; Tony Williams, *The Cinema of George A. Romero: Knight of the Living Dead* (London: Wallflower Press, 2003), 84–98; and Kyle William Bishop, "The Idle Proletariat: *Dawn of the Dead*, Consumer Ideology, and the Loss of Productive Labor," *Journal of Popular Culture* 43 (April 2010): 234–248, to list only a few.

6. Jeanine Basinger, *A Woman's View: How Hollywood Spoke to Women, 1930–1960* (New York: Knopf, 1993), 8.

7. Williams, *Cinema of George A. Romero*, 91.

8. Basinger, *Woman's View*, 8.

9. "Dead Will Walk," *Dawn of the Dead* (1979; Troy, MI: Anchor Bay, 2004), DVD; and Edgar Wright, "The Church of George," *Virginia Quarterly Review* 81 (Winter 2005): 42.

10. Bishop, "Idle Proletariat," 242.

11. A. Loudermilk, "Eating 'Dawn' in the Dark: Zombie Desire and Commodified Identity in George A. Romero's 'Dawn of the Dead,'" *Journal of Consumer Culture* 3 (March 2003): 93. See also the work of Gregory Waller, who argues that the "celebration of conspicuous consumption" transforms the characters into beings who are no better than zombies, as shopping turns into a "tedious, deadening routine." *The Living and the Undead: From Stoker's* Dracula *to Romero's* Dawn of the Dead (Urbana: University of Illinois Press, 1986), 312, 313.

12. Stephen Harper, "Zombies, Malls, and the Consumerism Debate: George Romero's *Dawn of the Dead*," *Americana* 1 (Fall 2002): http://www.americanpopular culture.com/journal/articles/fall_2002/harper.htm.

13. Basinger, *Woman's View*, 11.

14. Modleski, "Terror of Pleasure," 290.

15. Loudermilk, "Eating 'Dawn' in the Dark," 95, 97.

16. *Document of the Dead* (Roy Frumkes, 1985).

17. Quoted in Paul R. Gagne, *The Zombies That Ate Pittsburgh: The Films of George A. Romero* (New York: Dodd, Mead, 1987), 94.

18. Scanlon, "'Your Flag Decal Won't Get You into Heaven Anymore,'" 179.

19. Jean Baudrillard, "Consumer Society," in *Consumer Society in American History: A Reader*, ed. Lawrence B. Glickman (Ithaca, NY: Cornell University Press, 1999), 49.

20. Dana Heller, "Introduction: Consuming 9/11," in Heller, *Selling of 9/11*, 6.

21. These expressions of consumer preference echo Jim's request for a Tango soda, instead of the other brands Selena offers to him, during a break from one of their zombie escapes.

22. In this sense, the army's dangerous consumption demonstrated in the bunker reflects the takeover of the mall by a motorcycle gang at the end of *Dawn of the Dead*. The gang's members demonstrate a mode of acquisition that perverts the joyous scenes of shopping from the beginning of the film. Waller describes their acts as a "parodic

repetition" of the earlier scene, with the important difference that their looting is as destructive as their perverse killing of the zombies; they are "saturnalian revelers celebrating the end of civilization or at least the lifting of all extrapersonal sanctions on behavior," or "mock-adolescent survivors" who are "obviously sadistic, stupid, and inept." *The Living and the Undead*, 317, 318.

23. Meghan Sutherland, "Rigor/Mortis: The Industrial Life of Style in American Zombie Cinema," *Framework* 48 (Spring 2007): 64, 72.

24. Steven Shaviro, *The Cinematic Body* (Minneapolis: University of Minnesota Press, 1993), 97. See also Philip Horne, "I Shopped with a Zombie," *Critical Quarterly* 34 (Winter 1992): 97–110.

25. John Fiske, "Shopping for Pleasure: Malls, Power, and Resistance," in *The Consumer Society Reader*, ed. Juliet B. Schor and Douglas B. Holt (New York: New Press, 2000), 307.

26. Quoted in Steve Swires, "George Romero: Master of the Living Dead," *Starlog* 21 (April 1979): 47.

27. J. Hoberman, "Unquiet Americans," *Sight & Sound* 16 (October 2006): 23.

28. "Undead Again: The Making of *Land of the Dead*," *Land of the Dead* (2005; Universal City, CA: Universal, 2005), DVD.

29. Linnie Blake, *The Wounds of Nations: Horror Cinema, Historical Trauma and National Identity* (Manchester, UK: Manchester University Press, 2008), 97.

30. Adam Lowenstein, "Living Dead: Fearful Attractions of Film," *Representations* 110 (Spring 2010): 115.

31. Interestingly, this detachment from consumerism, coupled with its much more obvious political agenda, may explain why *Land of the Dead* was far less successful in the box office than the related films *28 Days Later* and Snyder's *Dawn of the Dead*. Ibid., 108.

32. John Patterson, "The Human Race Is Insane," *Guardian* (London), June 27, 2008, http://www.guardian.co.uk/culture/2008/jun/27/filmandmusic1.filmandmusic6.

33. Scanlon, "'Your Flag Decal Won't Get You into Heaven Anymore,'" 177.

34. Stephen King, *The Mist* (New York: Signet, 1980), 45.

35. Ibid., 144, 146, 151.

36. Fredric Jameson, "The Dialectics of Disaster," in *Dissent from the Homeland: Essays after September 11*, ed. Stanley Hauerwas and Frank Lentricchia (Durham, NC: Duke University Press, 2003), 60–61. Similarly, Baudrillard contends that the terrorists "appropriated for themselves the very weapons of the dominant power—money, stock market speculation, computer and aeronautic technologies, the specular dimensions and its media networks." "L'Esprit du Terrorisme," trans. Michel Valentin, in Hauerwas and Lentricchia, *Dissent from the Homeland*, 155.

37. Craig Bernardini, "*Auteurdämmerung*: David Cronenberg, George A. Romero, and the Twilight of the (North) American Horror Auteur," in *American Horror Film: The Genre at the Turn of the Millennium*, ed. Steffen Hantke (Jackson: University Press of Mississippi, 2010), 185. Bernardini also applies this analysis to David Cronenberg's recent films.

38. It may also betray an uneasiness about the fact that visual representation, like capital, was instrumental to the impact of the 9/11 attacks. As Stephen Prince argues, "Osama bin Laden knew that the airplane attacks of September 11 would be photo-

graphed and videotaped and that these images would be broadcast around the world, making the event into a horrifying theater of mass destruction. This symbolic value, achieved by way of modern media and the manner in which they would inevitably collude to emphasize the theatricality of the attacks, was of tremendous importance to al Qaeda." *Firestorm: American Film in the Age of Terrorism* (New York: Columbia University Press, 2009), 3.

PART 3

HORROR IN ACTION

CHAPTER EIGHT

Historicizing the Bush Years

Politics, Horror Film, and Francis Lawrence's I Am Legend

STEFFEN HANTKE

WHOSE LEGEND AM I?

Francis Lawrence's *I Am Legend* (2007), the third cinematic adaptation of Richard Matheson's 1954 novel of the same title, ends with this voice-over narration: "In 2009, a deadly virus burned through our civilization, pushing humankind to the edge of extinction. Dr. Robert Neville dedicated his life to the discovery of a cure and the restoration of humanity. On September 9, 2012, at approximately 8:49 p.m., he discovered that cure. And at 8:52, he gave his life to defend it. We are his legacy. This is his legend." The narration is delivered by Anna, a young Hispanic woman who has reached safety in the final scene of the film, and its purpose is to establish an authoritative reading of the fictional events that make up the story the film has just told. As a closing gesture, this final voice-over, placed so conspicuously at a moment that allows neither contradiction nor correction, seems strangely emphatic. Why do we, the audience, need to be told what just happened? Do the events not speak for themselves? Why this anxiety over possible misinterpretations?

In fact, the most peculiar aspect of this final clarification, in light of the film's title, is that it is not spoken by Robert Neville himself—the "I" in *I Am Legend*—but by someone else. Unlike Matheson's original conceit in the novel, important enough for the author to incorporate it into the title, Neville is not allowed to be the teller of his own tale. Perhaps this is appropriate, considering that legends are always the stories people tell about someone else, and thus are notoriously unreliable (it is hardly a coincidence that John Ford's *The Man Who Shot Liberty Valance* [1962] ends with the famous choice between printing the truth or printing the legend). But if this is so, then is there not an odd contradiction between the simultaneous acknowledgement that Robert Neville's "discovery of a cure and . . . restoration of humanity" is merely a legend—a story that, potentially, is not even true or might have been altered, amended, corrected, or modified—and the earnestness with which the voice-over asserts that this is exactly how things happened?

With two writers (Mark Protosevich and Akiva Goldsman) having worked over a screenplay by two other writers (John William and Joyce Hooper Corrington), used originally for Boris Sagal's *The Omega Man* (1971), it is hardly surprising that *I Am Legend* feels overwritten. Add to this mix of writers the star persona of Will Smith, who was at that time the highest-paid actor in Hollywood,[1] and what emerges is a complex set of interlocking or competing authorships. This is not to say that the film makes no sense; in fact, quite the opposite is true. Emerging from the multiple sources of creative input, the film has one strong and single-minded ideological thrust, which establishes and unpacks the core ideology most viewers will take away from it. Surrounding this core, however, are layers of visual details and kernels of un-, or under-, developed ideas that provide points of departure for viewers unable or unwilling to invest themselves in the film's core ideology. Though these details do not fundamentally change the film's politics, they make it more interesting than its otherwise single-minded political agenda would allow. For a viewer willing to take a closer look, they broaden the appeal of the film.[2] Instead of coming across as a simple prescriptive political statement, it has to offer a range of political imagery, disorganized yet urgently relevant to the historical conditions under which it was produced and released. The purpose of the discussion to follow will be to describe the core political meaning of *I Am Legend*, to separate from it some of the film's less structured and coherent adjunct imagery, and, finally, to place the film in its historical context as a key text of the final period of the Bush years, drawing on a comparison with the two earlier adaptations of Matheson's novel.

RIGHT-WING SOLUTIONS TO RESTORING HUMANITY

In order to describe the film's core political position, let me return to that final scene from which I quoted Anna's voice-over. As she addresses us directly, we see Anna and Ethan, a little boy she picked up somewhere along her flight from Latin America, driving up to Vermont. She has heard that there is a community—"colony" is the term used repeatedly—of survivors in New England, and she has taken to the road in pursuit of this safe haven. Her escape from a doomed New York City begins with a fade-in from the white screen to which the film faded out when, in the previous scene, Neville blew up himself and a group of the infected in order to safeguard her getaway. Out of

FIGURE 8.1. *God, guns, and gates: community in Bush's America (*I Am Legend, *Warner Bros., 2007).*

the flames of the explosion, we go from the fade to black to a helicopter shot over a seemingly endless expanse of autumnal New England forest, with the camera looking toward the far horizon. After a brief point-of-view shot that shows the country road unwinding before the driver's eyes, we cut to Anna steering the car and the boy sleeping beside her in the passenger seat. She stops in the middle of the road, and in a suspenseful medium-long shot looking back at the car, we see her and Ethan approach the camera, now shaking slightly to indicate that it is handheld. Only the delayed reverse-angle shot reveals that they are approaching a black gate so big that it fills and extends past the screen. The gate opens, and the first thing we see, over Anna's and Ethan's shoulders, is a white church steeple rising into the sky. Church bells are ringing. Flanking the gate, as well as the shot, on both sides are armed soldiers.[3] A black-and-white dog is frolicking on what looks like the beginning of Main Street in a small town. In close-up, we see Anna's hand pass on the vial containing the cure, fabricated out of Neville's own blood, to a muscular male hand. Another helicopter shot follows, this one a backward-tracking shot giving us a panoramic overhead view of the town in its peaceful pastoral setting, surrounded in its entirety by a wall.

This final panoramic shot marks not just a location but also the destination, the telos, of the entire narrative. It is to this place that all events have been leading us. The emblematic placement of the church and the soldiers demonstrates what exactly the forces are that provide this community with safety and collective identity. Anna, a Hispanic woman, is welcomed with open arms; the part of the wall around the town she faces happens to be the front gate, which opens the moment she has established that she is not one of the infected. In fact, there is a sensor in the wall that, having recognized her, opens the gates, suggesting that the wall itself is parting for her to enter. As her voice-over confirms, this town, or towns like it, are the source of the survival of humankind—utopia realized.

As the terminology used in the film suggests, this town is also paradise regained. The term "colony," as much as the film's relentless visual insistence that its location is New England, links the United States' future, as it unfolds to the survivors of the traumatic catastrophe, with its past. This future lies in small towns, in the political ideal of what Republican candidates during the 2008 presidential election incessantly referred to as "Main Street America," equating it with—an equally loaded term—"real America." Though virtually the entire film takes place in New York City, enhanced and transformed into a lush jungle with the help of spectacularly detailed CGI, and though the story explores this urban setting with a keen appreciation of the various opportunities for action and adventure it provides, the film ultimately rejects the city in favor of the small town. The city is doomed, a place of violence and fear, of uncontrollable contagion; it requires constant vigilance and yet may kill you—the urban jungle, literally. It is the place Anna and Ethan must leave in order to survive, while Neville stays and dies. Apparently, there seem to be no churches in New York; all major events take place in secular locations, which define the urban environment for the duration of the film.

Though the film must elide any thematic reference to the Puritan element in New England's early history, the role religion plays in the utopian return to the postapocalyptic small town is crucial. After all, Anna, before she even knows whether this colony exists, sets out on her journey because she has faith: "God told me," she answers when Neville, the cynic and atheist, questions her about how she knows that the colony exists. "The world is quieter now; if we listen, we can hear God's plan." The film bears out her position. Coincidences and symbolic correspondences conspire in the climax of the film so that Neville's assertion that "God did not do this, we did," appears like a less likely rationale than Anna's religious faith in a divine plan. In fact, Neville's decision to sacrifice his own life in order to secure the existence of the cure constitutes a kind of deathbed conversion; coming around to Anna's convictions, he acts in accord with them and sacrifices his life for others.

Before Neville sacrifices himself, he had already created what, in the light of the film's final ideal community, must appear as a prototype of the good, safe place—his New York brownstone on Washington Square Park where he used to live with his family before the outbreak. While in earlier stages of the film's development Arnold Schwarzenegger had been cast in the role of

Neville, the final decision to go with Will Smith shifts the character from exceptional action hero to American everyman.[4] Consequently, the film depicts Neville's home, which he controls and the location of which he keeps a secret from the infected, as a space of bourgeois normality. The scenes that show Neville moving through this space are beautifully constructed around routines and objects: he runs on a treadmill; makes a "healthy" dinner for his dog, Sam; replaces cans of food in his cupboards according to expiration date, and so forth. There is some clutter, but it is the mess we would expect from a bachelor.

In contrast, in Sagal's 1971 *The Omega Man*, Neville's apartment is a museum, a space hopelessly cluttered with art, weapons, alcohol bottles, and expensive furniture randomly assembled. The place is a testimony to Neville's unlimited access to the city, his freedom to take anything he wants, and as such, it communicates a sense of individual entitlement, class privilege, and futility. While Will Smith's character carefully accumulates paintings from the Museum of Modern Art, the earlier Neville (played in the 1971 version by Charlton Heston, and in the 1964 version by Vincent Price) randomly plunders treasures and trinkets, which casts doubt on his moral right to be the sole inheritor of humanity's accomplishments. In contrast to the family brownstone in *I Am Legend*, the apartment of Heston's Neville is not associated with family, which makes it, literally, a bachelor pad.

Another detail is worth noting here. From Matheson's novel to the first two adaptations, Neville's house is under siege for the duration of the story. Only in *I Am Legend* has Neville succeeded in keeping the location of his house a secret. The building is still secured by elaborate measures, as we discover in the final shoot-out during which hordes of the infected storm the building, but the most effective measure of survival over a period of years has been Neville's secrecy. The routines of bourgeois normality enacted by Neville within this space reflect his concern that the infected, whom he is used to fighting out there in the city, are going to follow him home. This comes true when Anna fails to follow the elaborate security rituals by which Neville routinely covers his tracks. The climactic action sequence during the storming of Neville's house enacts the dreaded scenario conjured up by George W. Bush in his repeated assertion that the war on terrorism must be fought globally, because if we don't fight them "over there," they will surely follow us home.[5] Neville's ultimate failure to defend his house against the onslaught of the infected confirms the veracity of Bush's prediction, and, at the same time, it enacts the nightmare scenario from which, we can rest assured, the "colony" up in Vermont is permanently protected by the things Neville is missing: genuine family life, a higher fence, religion, and a well-organized military.

I have mentioned the "infected" several times in passing; their morphology, the carefully designed details of their appearance and behavior, plays a crucial role in the ideological dynamic of the film. The overriding theme is their complete and utter lack of humanity, a fact established at the most fundamental level by the film not using actors but rather relying predominantly on CGI. While this allows Lawrence greater freedom and mobility in action sequences, it also sets the infected categorically apart from their human counterparts. Though the film refers to the fact or process of transformation from human to infected, there is no scene in which we see a CGI creature morph into an actual actor or vice versa; the otherness of the infected is an unalterable fact.

Further, CGI permits Lawrence to write this fact into the morphological and behavioral construct. The infected are hairless, and their skin is gray, lifeless, leathery, and yet loose. Veins are visible beneath the epidermis. Apart from the increased capacity for speed and strength, the entire body has increased flexibility: jaws gape, backs arch, arms flail in humanly impossible angles and arcs. The most pronounced feature is rapid breathing, a quick, shallow panting less akin to that of a person out of breath and more to that of a dog. This breathing animates the body even in moments of relative immobility, giving it a sense of temporarily or just barely suppressed aggression. Together with an increased heart rate and body temperature, the infected bodies are abject displays of horror, driven by constant, uncontrollable rage. They emanate menace, and their sight causes disgust. They are unambiguously not human.

As Neville dictates his medical notes, he characterizes their behavior as the result of "social de-evolution," noting that "typical human behavior is now entirely absent." Though they form groups, there is no sense of conscious social organization: at best, the groups are like packs of wild animals (though without the social order those packs display in the animal world). They have reverted to cannibalism when other food sources have been unavailable. In accord with the term "hive" Neville uses to describe their gathering into groups, which casts them as an evolutionary form of life even lower than predatory mammals, their numbers come in waves, swarming like insects, when they run after prey or attack Neville's house. In the theatrical release of the film, it remains virtually impossible to understand why they are invading Neville's house, which suggests that their aggression is largely aimless and not harnessed to any rational motivation.

How insistent this theme of complete dehumanization is becomes clear when comparing the infected in *I Am Legend* with those in *The Omega Man* and *The Last Man on Earth* (Ubaldo Ragona, 1964). In both earlier films, the infected are capable of speech and feature at least one character Neville used to know personally before the epidemic. Both films presuppose internal differentiation among the infected, with each different stage of the infection serving as a foundation for its own unique social form. In *The Omega Man*, these distinct types of social organization are each headed by a charismatic leader. While the first two adaptations preserve these aspects of Matheson's novel, *I Am Legend* erases them almost completely. The result is a clearer demarcation between Neville (as well as Anna and Ethan and those good folks up in Vermont) and the infected.

In its depiction of the infected, the film embraces Matheson's efforts in the novel to strip the horror genre of its spiritual and metaphysical rationale and to substitute a scientific rationale instead. Matheson's infected display all the symptoms of classic folkloric and literary vampirism, but "that prowling, vulpine ghost was as much a tool of the germ as the living innocents who were originally afflicted. It was the germ that was the villain."[6] Lawrence's film enriches this source material by drawing on the tradition of horror films devoted to apocalyptic or postapocalyptic scenarios, from George Romero's zombie films to their more recent successors in the action/adventure mode (*Blade* [Stephen Norrington, 1998], *Resident Evil* [Paul W. S. Anderson, 2002], *Underworld* [Len Wiseman, 2003], etc.).[7] The infected do not inspire—erroneously, as Matheson would have it—spiritual dread, as vampires would have; they tap into the affective reservoir of the zombie, inspiring physical disgust. The result is a reversal of Matheson's revisionist project; though the film retains the scientific rationale for the existence of these abject bodies, the loathing and disgust they inspire bring about a return from the mode of science fiction to horror, albeit a form of body horror linked to biological, or, more broadly speaking, biotechnological origins.

There is another manifestation of this face of absolute evil, one that is somewhat less obvious though nonetheless relevant to the film's ideology. Responsible for the virus is a scientist, Dr. Alice Krippin, who, played by Emma Thompson, appears only briefly in a televised interview in the opening of the film. She explains how, by redesigning the measles virus, she cured cancer. But her considerable accomplishment is discredited when the virus mutates and the intended cure for cancer turns into a very real pandemic with cataclysmic consequences. There is a reason her name is reminiscent of the famous murderer Dr. Hawley Harvey Crippen. The film illustrates her good intentions turning into disaster by a montage of images of New York City depopulated, decayed, and in ruins. As Krippin's voice fades out, these images speak for themselves. And if viewers have not noticed that the self-conscious pause preceding Krippin's answer that, yes, indeed, she *has* cured cancer, denotes a modesty that rings completely and utterly untrue, to the point of hypocrisy, the clash of good news in the dialogue and bad news in the images makes the point all too clearly. To some extent this is a critique of science common to the horror film, but then Krippin is not a mad scientist either. She is soft and feminine, smart and well educated, and has dedicated her work to the worthiest of humanitarian causes. Far from being evil or insane or driven by hubris, her character makes the case for the dangers of good intentions and a liberal agenda. She is not monstrous, unlike the products of the mutated virus named after her, but she is a cautionary example of the wrong person being in charge.

Given these details, I think it is fair to say that this adaptation of *I Am Legend* is a film on the right of the political spectrum. Its return to an idealized, utopian past as a solution to the problems of the present, its distrust of urbanity and confidence in the small town as a model of civic integrity, its faith in church and military as the foundations of social order and security, its validation of divine providence as a rationale of historical progression, its insistence on the absolute otherness of the enemy (and, concomitantly, on the absolute goodness and normality of the bourgeois subject), and, finally, its distrust of what it codes as a liberal humanitarian and political agenda—these elements come together in a clear sense of where the film stands politically.

REMAKING THE COLD WAR: FEARS FROM THE FIFTIES

In a grab for historical relevance that is all the more understandable for a remake of a 1954 novel, Lawrence's film deploys a number of key signals that link *I Am Legend* to post-9/11 America. While *The Last Man on Earth* used an unspecified American city (which nonetheless looks exactly like the Italian urban areas in which the film was shot), and *The Omega Man* transplanted the story, iconically so given an impressive degree of location shooting, to Los Angeles, Lawrence's film takes place in what, since 9/11, has become a commonplace: New York City. Though there is a long-standing cinematic tradition of destroying New York on-screen, *I Am Legend* (like *Cloverfield* [Matt Reeves, 2008]) is very precise in its use of apocalyptic urban imagery.[8] The flashback sequence showing the evacuation of Manhattan, for example, culminates in the military blowing up the bridges out of the city: the spectacular explosions and the slow-motion collapse of landmark structures such as these resonate with 9/11 imagery. This is further emphasized by Neville's constant references to New York as "ground zero" of the epidemic, a none-too-subtle reminder that the apocalyptic fantasy we are watching feeds off post-9/11 anxieties.

Once the film manages to establish 9/11 as a theme, other details fall into place. Watching the infected attack in a state of rage in which their bodies become weapons, damaged or destroyed in their assaults, it is difficult not to see in them the right-wing rhetoric of the so-called War on Terror: subhuman enemies, incapable of rational decision making, flinging themselves at us in a grim and never-ending attempt at destruction. An isolated Manhattan and the fortified Vermont village also resonate with the siege mentality of the United States under the Patriot Act. As mentioned above, Neville's attempts to ensure the inviolability of his brownstone by keeping its location a secret are evocative of George W. Bush's repeated assertion that the United States must fight the terrorists anywhere but at home. In short, the Bush administration's War on Terror appears to provide the one allegorical subtext that *I Am Legend* visualizes, dramatizes, and ideologically justifies.

If the film were to exhaust itself in the simple, or perhaps even simplistic, attribution of diegetic details to historical events, however, it would hardly rise above the level of two-dimensional allegory. In order to grasp the film in its full complexity, therefore, critical readings should at least give as much credit to the story's Cold War genesis as they tend to give to the ways in which its assorted teams of writers have pried the material loose from these origins, updated it, and tailored it to the specific anxieties and desires of the United States after 9/11. One might argue that, to the degree that the writers' efforts are successful, the story's origins would hardly matter: a successful adaptation overwrites all such traces.

Contrary to this argument, one might find it significant that films from the horror/science fiction cycles of the Cold War have, in recent years, provided a rich source of material for Hollywood remakes. The most recent adaptation of Jack Finney's 1955 novel, *The Body Snatchers*, has been a post-9/11 film titled, simply, *The Invasion* (Oliver Hirschbiegel, 2007). I would also count among these remakes those Cold War films that are located in the gray area between horror and science fiction: *The Day the Earth Stood Still* (Robert Wise, 1951/ Scott Derrickson, 2008), and films like *Cloverfield* or Frank Darabont's *The Mist* (2007) that revive a specific cycle of Cold War horror (in this case, the giant creature/bug-eyed monster movie).[9] Seen in this context, Lawrence's *I Am Legend* suddenly seems as interesting for its Cold War origins as for its post-9/11 release.

According to Christina Klein, most "cultural histories of the Cold War take the foreign policy and ideology of containment as their foundation." They focus on the ways in which Cold War science fiction and horror films addressed fears of the other, no matter if that other appeared in the shape of giant mutated insects, aliens from outer space, shapeless blobs of protoplasmic goo, or incredibly shrinking or expanding human beings.[10] Though this critical account is accurate in many respects, it also oversimplifies a rich and diverse field of cultural production. A canonical text of Cold War horror like Don Siegel's *Invasion of the Body Snatchers* (1956) is both a perfect representative of this "containment approach" and an example of its limitations. As critical opinion on Siegel's film broadened to include the possibility that the terrifyingly lifeless pod people could just as well be the internal forces combating the invasion as the invaders themselves—that is, that the terrors of mindless conformity might just as well be a product made in the United States as in the Soviet Union—critical discourse came to reorient itself toward domestic issues. Scholars like Mark Jancovich have helped to refocus critical attention away from the exclusively xenophobic reading of Cold War horror (which also includes a thematic preoccupation with the threat of nuclear war or contamination), and, instead, toward recognizing how films from the 1950s and 1960s address problems of corporate technocracy, civil disobedience, generational conflict, and issues of gender and race. At their best, the two schools of criticism are not mutually exclusive, but rather succeed in demonstrating the complex ways in which containment issues interacted with domestic social concerns.

The current debate also recognizes that American domestic and foreign politics were not based exclusively on the paradigm of containment either. In her examination of what she calls "Cold War Orientalism," Klein demonstrates that containment was, in fact, only one of two coexistent pillars of foreign policy, the other one calling for a strategy of "sentimental education" of Americans at home.[11] She sees this attitude articulated most clearly by Francis Wilcox, "a mid-level State Department official," in a speech "to an audience of educators in Philadelphia" in 1957, which recasts "the problem of foreign resistance to U.S. expansion into an issue of domestic pedagogy."[12] Klein calls this complementary attitude "a global imaginary of integration," emphasizing that its view was directed "to the world beyond the nation's borders" and representing "the Cold War as an opportunity to forge intellectual and emotional bonds with the people of Asia and Africa."[13] Winning the hearts and minds of those nations, rather than conquering or militarily controlling them, would not only cleanse the United States of the stigma of domestic racism, a sensitive issue in dealing with the Soviet Union, whose internationalist agenda automatically provided privileged access to this particular moral high ground. It would also exonerate the United States from the critique of imperialism, distinguishing its global political ambitions categorically from those of the Soviet Union. In short, integration could provide a positive humanist and moral agenda—unlike that of mere "anticommunism," the concept on which containment was predicated.

Although this internationalist, inclusionary ideology was forged by political elites, it depended for its efficiency on "a broad base of public support."[14] This support could be created only by an extensive educational effort within the domestic sphere. American attitudes toward foreign cultures were to be reshaped on the basis of real or perceived similarities with other cultures, which was then to produce new Americans to be accepted and embraced as formal or informal ambassadors of their nation whenever abroad. Much of American popular culture of the 1950s, Klein argues, devotes itself to the substantiation, the exploration, or, at times, the refutation of this ideology of integration. As a powerful ideology, it provided a point of discursive reference, something that provoked responses of one kind or another.

What emerges from the parallel consideration of "containment" on the one hand, and Klein's ideology of integration on the other, is a critical account immediately relevant to Cold War horror cinema. As Tom Engelhardt writes,

> In the science fiction films that prospered in the 1950s, exclusionary villains came from the other side of borders previously unimagined and unerringly headed for (or burst to life in) the United States with mayhem in mind. . . . On the other hand, in the inclusionary mode, similar beasts or robots or space aliens turned out to be, if not lovable, then far wiser than Americans. . . . The exclusionary films were apocalyptic and hysterical about them; the inclusionary ones about us. In either case, every stand in these films was potentially the last one.[15]

Engelhardt's distinction between "inclusionary" and "exclusionary" films is prefigured in Peter Biskind's seminal *Seeing Is Believing*, which presents an even more complex expression of "not one but several warring ideologies, so that it is possible to speak of radical (left- and right-wing) as well as mainstream films."[16] Depending on where a film is located on this sliding scale, the threat is either us or them; the solution to the problem is either talking or shooting; those who will save us are cops, scientists, or ordinary citizens.

In contrast to the more simplistic readings of Cold War horror, the model Biskind proposes is less constrictive and more akin to defining the paradigmatic boundaries within which the discourse can take place—that is, the possibilities for people who share basic commonalities to disagree with one another. While this view has helped to elevate the level of critical debate on the Cold War itself, it also seems a far better explanation for why Hollywood studios have started remaking Cold War horror and science fiction films in ever-increasing numbers during the last decade. If the critical assessment of a film like Lawrence's *I Am Legend* is not to fall behind the complexity of the debate that scholars have already reached in regard to Cold War culture, the analysis must adopt if not Biskind's, then at least Engelhardt's model of inclusionary/left-wing versus exclusionary/right-wing films. In other words, the affinity between Cold War culture and American culture after 9/11 is not a matter of simple analogy, but rather the result of shared paradigms in the public debate.

MARGINAL OPPOSITION: COMPLICATING *I AM LEGEND*

Given the complexity of the scholarly debate on the Cold War, the fact that the original material for Francis Lawrence's *I Am Legend* is grounded in this period seems suddenly less simple. It is within the limitations of the discursive paradigm that some of the inconsistencies—the film's less structured and coherent adjunct imagery—can be explained. Instead of having been corrected or contained by the two final writers of the script, the film retains traces of its being overdetermined.

Upon closer inspection, and taking our cue from the critical debate on Cold War culture that recognizes more than one context for American science fiction/horror cinema of the 1950s, some of the film's imagery is quite ambiguous. Though the imagery of infection appears, at first glance, to be a direct expression of fears surrounding terrorism, there are scenes in the film in which we see groups of infected dash and run in large swarms. During the storming of Neville's brownstone, they are not clever or precise, but they do outnumber him, crashing through walls and digging through ceilings. Their behavior is animalistic, insect-like, and as such, also brings to mind American fears about illegal immigration. The images of swarming infected under cover of night are eerily reminiscent of infrared footage of groups of illegal immigrants running across the border between the United States and Mexico.

A second level of significance also opens up beneath the film's imagery of post-epidemic New York City. More than buildings demolished by violent impact, the film dwells on images of what, in its lush abundance and against geographic verisimilitude, looks like subtropical vegetation reclaiming urban space. A soundtrack of jungle noises, birdcalls, and the sounds of unknown animals runs in the background. Vines grow in pockets of dirt washed out of the ground and running in streaks off buildings. While the bridges are ruins of violent action and provide images of terrorist attacks on city landmarks, downtown and midtown Manhattan are subject less to massive attack and more to abandonment, neglect, and slow decay. Viewers will readily recognize post-Katrina New Orleans in the beautifully and meticulously composed CGI cityscapes. Like the horror films of the Cold War, Lawrence's *I Am Legend*, besides revolving around the conflict between self and other as its dramatic, narrative, and thematic structuring device, also addresses domestic issues not immediately linked to the War on Terror. While official rhetoric during the Bush years often tried to contain the debate about these domestic issues by integrating them into the larger theme of terrorism, the film does not. Images of illegal immigration and post-Katrina New Orleans remain latent in the film, visible and recognizable yet unexplored and irrelevant to its dominant ideology.

Another inroad into the ideological coherence of the film occurs early on, during the television interview in which Dr. Alice Krippin explains how exactly her engineered retrovirus works: "If you can imagine your body as a highway, and you picture the virus as a very fast car driven by a very bad man, imagine the damage that that car could cause. But then if you replace that man with a cop, the picture changes." While the meaning of this metaphor is perfectly clear for Krippin and the fictional television audience standing in for us, the metaphor, in a larger sense, also equates the human body, as the site of viral infection, with geographic space: the civic body, the body of the city.

This latter meaning becomes relevant when—three years later, as an insert shot tells us—we catch the first glimpse of Neville racing a red sports car down the canyons of a New York City depopulated by the Krippin Virus. The sequence serves as an introduction to the film's main character, and of course as an adolescent power fantasy, but it also picks up Krippin's metaphor and literalizes it. To the degree that the analogy is obvious, the question arises: Is Neville the "very bad man" or the "cop" whom Krippin was talking about? In regard to Neville's past history, and to his sense of himself as the man who has, as of yet, failed to stop the epidemic from spreading, he might very well be Krippin's bad man. He might be the virus traveling, so to speak, through the bloodstream of the city, though this reading, again, leaves it unclear whether he is the virus that causes disease or the retrovirus that cures it. The story wants him to be the cop—after all, "the picture changes" because he is the man who will have discovered and sacrificed himself for the cure by the penultimate scene—but the residual meaning lingers: perhaps he is the bad man after all.

This lingering sense of an oppositional meaning may originate from the source material the two writers of the film inherited from the two writers of the original screenplay, who may in turn have inherited it from Matheson's novel. *The Last Man on Earth* and *The Omega Man* both cast Neville explicitly as a Christ figure: Vincent Price dies, literally, on the altar of a church, while the last shot of Charlton Heston shows him in a pose of crucifixion in a water fountain overflowing with his own blood. *I Am Legend* preserves this connotation, but unlike its predecessors it fails to retain a trope that is essential for counterbalancing the heavy-handed Christian allegorizing. This is how Matheson puts it in the final scene of the novel as those who will emerge as the hybrid survivors of the epidemic kill the hero:

> Robert Neville looked out over the new people of the earth. He knew he did not belong to them; he knew that, like the vampires, he was anathema and black terror to be destroyed. And, abruptly, the concept came, amusing to him even in his pain. . . . Full circle, he thought while the final lethargy crept into his limbs. Full circle. A new terror born in death, a new superstition entering the unassailable fortress of forever.
> I am legend.[17]

The point of view in this scene is Neville's, his recognition of his own abjection, of the role he is to play for future generations as the monstrous other. Monstrosity, as Matheson puts it, is not a matter of appearance or actions; it is a matter of being the only one of one's kind. Two of the central themes of fifties culture resonate in this statement—conformity and the plight of the outsider.

A product of the United States' coming to terms with its 1960s counterculture, *The Omega Man* rewrites the theme of evolutionary and cultural progress in Matheson's novel in the register of generational change. Neville belongs to neither of the two groups of survivors who are fighting for control of the postapocalyptic future: the neo-medieval Luddites, all of them rendered the same spooky white color by the epidemic, headed by a former television personality, which represent the Dionysian aspect of the sixties; or the extended and racially diverse patchwork family heading out to the countryside to start civilization afresh (like the Garden of Eden, just without the snake, as their leader puts it), as its Apollonian counterpart.

Neither the theme of evolutionary nor that of generational change enters into Robert Neville's heroic self-sacrifice at the end of Lawrence's *I Am Legend*. In fact, traces of these themes remain in the film, but since they are not systematically developed or even raised to the level of consciousness for the audience, they constitute the core of what I term its "oppositional information." The film maintains the pathos, the Christian allegory, found in its predecessors, but it reverses the original meaning of "I am legend," the closing

FIGURE 8.2. *Moses as Christ: Charlton Heston in* The Omega Man *(Warner Bros., 1971).*

words of Matheson's novel: Neville will be remembered not as the monster, the other, the nightmare creature used to frighten children, but as the savior of humanity—and not the hybrid kind either, but a humanity untouched and unaffected by the Krippin Virus. Neville's epiphany about his function in the history to be written in the last moments of his life, which grants the character a tragic dimension in all preceding versions of the text, is turned by Lawrence's film into a religious conversion. The progress of history is not driven by tragedy or, even worse, by irony; it is driven by a heroic narrative that enshrines self-sacrifice as its primary engine. It is Matheson's Christian allegory, but sanitized by being stripped of its complexity. To guarantee the simplicity of the vision, the voice-over must have a narrator other than Neville himself: Anna, speaking for a grateful posterity, the existence of which assures us that Neville was the cop and not the bad man all along.

"PEOPLE ARE ALIKE ALL OVER": THE ALTERNATE ENDING

While the film is, in some ways, less single-minded in its pursuit of a conservative agenda than its core meaning suggests, even its handling of fragmentary oppositional material falls squarely within the discursive parameters of Cold War horror and science fiction films. Case in point is the much-discussed alternate ending of *I Am Legend*, not seen in the theatrical release but included in the extras of the DVD and available online weeks before the DVD release.[18] At first glance, the vision of the story's outcome may differ in its political substance from the ending of the theatrical release. In fact, for many viewers who went to the trouble of watching and thinking about this alternate ending, it improved or even redeemed the film. What it in fact does, however, is reorganize some of the oppositional material into a narrative that, though ostensibly different, still falls squarely within the same ideological parameters.

The alternate ending cuts into the story as Neville, during the storming of his New York brownstone, has taken refuge with Anna and Ethan behind the Plexiglas partition, where they must make their last stand. As the alpha male among the infected keeps flinging himself against the partition, while Neville is shouting, "I can help you! I can save you!" the attack gradually begins to slow down. Tracking the creature's sight line, Neville realizes that the alpha male is, in fact, not attacking blindly but is trying to reach the female infected on whose body Neville's experiments have finally produced a cure. Neville puts down his gun, orders the terrified Anna to open the door, and hands over the prone body of the female infected. The scene makes it clear that the infected do, after all, have a form of social organization, as the alpha male calls back the other infected from attacking Neville, and that there is a strong emotional bond between the male and the female, demonstrated by an exchange of physical affections between them. A point-of-view shot from Neville's perspective draws attention to the wall of images he has taken of all those infected test subjects he killed in the course of his medical experiments.

Ostensibly, this scene bridges the gap between self and other. Once Neville recognizes the humanity in his enemy, he is not attacked when he puts down the gun and renders himself defenseless. There is a trace of Matheson's point that Neville is himself the legendary creature of darkness in his look at the wall of photographs: this is the moment he realizes what he must be to his enemies.[19] Retrospectively, the scene also explains some of the behavior of this alpha male: in the scene in which Neville captures the female, the alpha male exposes himself to, for him, fatal daylight in an attempt to go after her; later on, Neville himself is caught in exactly the same trap he has set to capture specimens for his operating table. Obviously, Neville and the alpha male infected are doppelgangers, and a moment of truce is struck when Neville recognizes this fact and makes the choice to trust his opponent. The alternate ending suggests that people are alike all over.

This last phrase, "people are alike all over," is the title of an episode of the first season of *The Twilight Zone*, that hallmark of American Cold War culture, broadcast originally on March 25, 1960. In it, a young scientist about to travel into outer space for the first time confesses his apprehension to his fellow astronaut about the otherness of whatever alien life they may encounter.

Not to worry, his colleague assures him, "People are alike all over." The sentiment expressed is virtually identical to that in the alternate ending of *I Am Legend*: it is the recognition of our common humanity that will preclude all conflict. Wrapped in this sentiment is also the tacit assumption that the basic nature of this common humanity is goodness. In *The Twilight Zone*, the young astronaut crashes on an alien planet and is rescued by a civilization of aliens who, by all counts, are as human as he is. Being human, they do, however, lock him up in a cage as a part of a display in a zoo where he will probably spend the rest of his life. People really are, as he realizes with some bitterness, alike all over.

Unlike the tongue-in-cheek cynicism of *The Twilight Zone* episode, *I Am Legend* proposes the denial of otherness, coupled with the assertion of essential human goodness, as a serious solution to conflict. There are two obvious problems with this toothless and simplistic misreading of the Kantian categorical imperative in which the otherness of the other is simply disavowed. For one, it does not abandon, in the strict sense, the distinction between self and other: that both are, in fact, one and the same is established on the basis of how similar to *us* "they" are, and not vice versa. Note that Neville's realization of the alpha male's essential humanity comes at the moment he recognizes his behavior as evidence of monogamous heterosexual bonding.[20] Whatever forms of sexuality the "hive" might have posed as an alternative to existing social norms are summarily dismissed. Validation remains inseparable from the dictate of bourgeois normality, which the film worked so diligently to establish as beyond all critical challenge.

There is also something appallingly self-congratulatory about the fact that, in the alternate ending, it is Neville who puts down the gun. His self-sacrifice in the theatrical ending comes as a confirmation that the infected cannot be negotiated with (if one is to understand negotiation as a process of mutual concessions during which both sides reach a viable compromise). His pleas to them, his assurances that he has the cure and that he can help them if they would only stop and listen, go unheeded.[21] The alternate ending softens this condemnation of the infected; Neville's putting down the gun signals the possibility, perhaps even the likelihood, of negotiations to come. But all negotiations are based on the fact that Neville has a cure to offer—that is, that the ultimate goal of negotiations will be the reversal of the infection and the return of the infected to the standards of humanity Neville himself represents. As in the present moment, the future does not hold any chance of recognizing the otherness of the other. The self, reconfirmed, takes absolute precedence.

One final note on the alternate ending: following the climactic scene in which Neville surrenders the infected female is a brief coda of Neville and

Anna, with Ethan in the backseat, driving out of New York City together. Neville is in the driver's seat of his own SUV, and Anna, gazing at him adoringly from the passenger's seat, narrates the voice-over that informs us that they are on their way to Vermont, hoping to find the colony of survivors they heard about. This scene makes the film's ideological position clear. Matheson's novel—as much as its previous two cinematic adaptations—is adamant about the need for Neville's removal from the passing of evolution or the turnover of generations. On the progressive end of the political spectrum of its time, Matheson's *I Am Legend*, as well as other work from the same period, "questions the historical validity of the dominance of white maleness in the 1950s."[22] Lawrence's adaptation may stay true to the questioning of whiteness, albeit ambiguously and halfheartedly at best, but it reverses Matheson's critique of masculinity. With Neville in the driver's seat, and the rest of the nuclear family restored to him, patriarchy has been redeemed in full.

When Wheeler Winston Dixon, in his book on neglected films of the 1950s, asks, "What do the 1950s mean to us now?" his answer seems to be the same that the makers of *I Am Legend* might give: "In many respects, we are living in the 1950s right now: repressed, obsessed with 'terror alerts,' eagerly seeking phantom security in ever-increasing hypersurveillance, reverting to the patriarchal order for a measure of safety and reassurance, retreating to our digital home entertainment centers to experience the world as filtered through a variety of 'news' filters rather than experiencing the joys and sorrows of the human community firsthand."[23] What better reason to remake Cold War horror films could there be than the realization that the United States after 9/11 is eerily reminiscent of the Cold War and its foreign policies and domestic social and political climate? While Dixon's list of the dystopian features of the United States during the Bush years rings true to some, it will not to everyone. Just as the limits of the discursive paradigm within the period are more significant than any individual opinion within those limits, we must not forget that horror films from the 1950s both critiqued the culture of their time *and* participated in its creation and maintenance. Nonetheless, while the analogy between the two periods is polemically oversimplified as soon as we try to align specific details for both periods with each other, the larger discursive paradigm is a good fit—containment politics on one end of the political spectrum, integrationist politics on the other; inclusionary films on one end of the political spectrum, exclusionary ones on the other; some horror films "apocalyptic and hysterical about them," others about us. Time will tell whether Francis Lawrence's *I Am Legend*, released at the tail end of George W. Bush's second and final term in office, will come to count more for its central right-wing politics or its acknowledgement of complexity in the margins. We can see what the legend is that the film has to tell; we will have to wait to find out what its own legacy is going to be.

NOTES

I would like to express my gratitude to the Research Department of Sogang University, which, by providing a Special Research Grant in 2008, made work on this essay possible.

    1. Lacey Rose, "Hollywood's Best-Paid Actors," Forbes.com, July 22, 2008, http://www.forbes.com/2008/07/22/actors-hollywood-movies-biz-media-cx_lr_0722actors.html.

    2. This might also be a symptom of the blockbuster, a cinematic format that, in order to recoup its considerable production and distribution costs, must try to court as many demographics as possible, trying to be all things to all people.

    3. During the flashback sequences that show the evacuation of New York City, we see other soldiers in action. Like their later counterparts, they are, though perhaps slightly in over their heads given the unexpected extent of the catastrophe, entirely competent and reasonable. Following the original screenplay for *The Omega Man*, Neville himself starts out as a member of the military.

    4. Gary Susman, "'Omega' Dittoes," *Entertainment Weekly*, March 20, 2002, http://www.ew.com/ew/article/0,,202975,00.html.

    5. For a more detailed discussion, see Ivan Eland, "The Terrorists-Follow-Us-Home Myth," ConsortiumNews.com, March 20, 2007, http://www.consortiumnews.com/2007/031907b.html.

    6. Richard Matheson, *I Am Legend* (New York: Tor, 1995), 77.

    7. For a more detailed genealogy of the hybridization of popular horror tropes, especially the merging of the vampire and the zombie in recent American horror film, see Steffen Hantke, "On the Acceleration of the Undead: Paradigm Change in the American Zombie Film," *Jura Gentium Cinema*, n.d., http://www.jgcinema.com/single.php?sl=Horror-Fear-Capitalism-Market.

    8. For a list of examples of such films, see "The Ten Best Movie Destructions of New York City," *New York*, December 13, 2007, http://nymag.com/daily/entertainment/2007/12/list_ten_best_movie_des.html, an article published on the occasion of the release of *I Am Legend*. Another, more extensive, source of historical precedents is Max Page, *The City's End: Two Centuries of Fantasies, Fears, and Premonitions of New York's Destruction* (New Haven, CT: Yale University Press, 2008).

    9. Among these 1950s cycles, the only one that has yet to make a comeback is that in which hapless individuals either shrink or expand in size (*The Incredible Shrinking Man* [Jack Arnold, 1957], *Attack of the 50 Foot Woman* [Nathan Juran, 1958], etc.). At the time of writing, only the Japanese film *Big Man Japan* (Hitoshi Matsumoto, 2007) seems to return to this cycle. But given Hollywood's current investment in remakes, there is no telling if new versions of any of these films are currently in development; in any event, their release would fall outside the historical period determining the political significance of the film under discussion here.

10. Christina Klein, *Cold War Orientalism: Asia in the Middlebrow Imagination, 1945–1961* (Berkeley: University of California Press, 2003), 23.

11. Ibid.

12. Ibid., 21.

13. Ibid., 22.

14. Ibid., 28.

15. Tom Engelhardt, *The End of Victory Culture: Cold War America and the Disillusioning of a Generation*, rev. and exp. ed. (Amherst: University of Massachusetts Press, 2007), 102.

16. Peter Biskind, *Seeing Is Believing: How Hollywood Taught Us to Stop Worrying and Love the Fifties* (New York: Pantheon, 1983), 4.

17. Matheson, *I Am Legend*, 159.

18. In the "Latest News" section of the website FirstShowing.net, Alex Billington embedded the alternate ending in an article posted on March 5, 2008 ("The DVD is arriving in a few weeks and Francis Lawrence's original ending that was made is included on it. Thankfully we've grabbed the new version for your viewing pleasure below."). See http://www.firstshowing.net/2008/03/05/must-watch-i-am-legends-original-ending-this-is-amazing/.

19. One of the key images in *The Last Man on Earth* is a vast pit where the military disposes of the dead; Neville (named Morgan in this film) continues this practice, dumping the bodies of those infected that he himself has tracked and killed. The image of the pit and the practice of large-scale disposal and burning of bodies are strongly reminiscent of Holocaust imagery, retrieved, presumably, as a response to Cold War anxieties about nuclear disaster. The wall of photographs plays on a similar register: to the degree that the faces in these pictures are gaunt and emaciated, they resemble concentration camp survivors, which would make Neville a figure of terror akin to a Nazi scientist like Mengele. Except for the brief visual cue in the alternate ending, earlier scenes in *I Am Legend* that presage this moment of recognition do not register with the viewer in the same way. In other words, the theatrical release of the film suppresses this latent reading.

20. The fact that both CGI creatures are also coded as white adds another troubling dimension to this significant moment—the film does not privilege whiteness but rather disavows racial difference altogether. Not by coincidence is Will Smith the African American Hollywood star with the least "black" public persona, which makes him perfect for casting Neville as an "everyman." (Note the development from his hip-hop career with DJ Jazzy Fresh and his starring role on TV's *The Fresh Prince of Bel-Air* [Andy and Susan Borowitz, 1990–1996], toward more racially neutral roles, such as *Enemy of the State* [Tony Scott, 1998] and *The Pursuit of Happyness* [Gabriele Muccino, 2006].) But it is also worth noting that there are no interracial personal relations in the film at all: Anna is Hispanic, which, within the racial logic of the film, renders her a "person of color" on a par with Smith, while Neville's late wife and child are black like him. This avoidance of race is particularly striking in contrast to *The Omega Man*, in which race is an explicit thematic concern throughout.

21. In both the theatrical and the alternate endings, the resistance of the infected to Neville's offering of a cure is seen as confirmation of his heroism and the fact they cannot be redeemed. In the context of Cold War culture and politics, this refusal of the other to consent to benevolent influence has always troubled the United States

and thus necessitated a particularly careful management of the discourse. David Ryan sees this as a crucial aspect of the ideology of containment: "Within this framework, the United States was identified as the guarantor of Western security, the regenerator of its economy, and the instigator of a period of freedom and prosperity. Precluded from this framing were alternative narratives that explained the hostilities [i.e., resistance against American interference within European politics] as a function of US economic, political, ideological and cultural expansion across the Atlantic. . . . Rather than recalling the immediate past of cooperation with the Soviets and economic engagement with the Nazis or other awkward colonial relationships, the initial and most powerful Cold War narratives called on the sacred documents of US diplomacy, providing continuity, benevolence, comprehension and closure to the unfolding story." "Mapping Containment: The Cultural Construction of the Cold War," in *American Cold War Culture*, ed. Douglas Field (Edinburgh: Edinburgh University Press, 2005), 61.

22. Gwendolyn Audrey Foster, "Monstrosity and the Bad-White-Body Film," in *Bad: Infamy, Darkness, Evil, and Slime on Screen*, ed. Murray Pomerance (Albany: State University of New York Press, 2004), 50. While Foster's argument certainly rings true for the self-sacrificing protagonist of *I Am Legend*, it is particularly relevant to other texts central to Matheson's oeuvre, such as *The Shrinking Man* (1956) and "Nightmare at 20,000 Feet" (1961), both of which trace in meticulous detail the emasculation, by way of technological or social forces, of their white middle-class protagonists. *The Shrinking Man* also provides a poignant example of Matheson's resistance to traditional forms of "re-masculation" as part of the novel's resolution.

23. Wheeler Winston Dixon, *Lost in the Fifties: Recovering Phantom Hollywood* (Carbondale: Southern Illinois University Press, 2005), 184.

CHAPTER NINE

"I Am the Devil and I'm Here to Do the Devil's Work"

Rob Zombie, George W. Bush, and the Limits of American Freedom

LINNIE BLAKE

On September 11, 2001, as the entire world now knows, two hijacked aircraft were flown into the Twin Towers of the World Trade Center, a third into the Pentagon building, while a fourth, seemingly headed for the Capitol building in Washington, crashed in rural Pennsylvania. Self-evidently, as commentators such as Noam Chomsky have argued, this was a massive symbolic attack on the Western world—most specifically, on the military-industrial complex of American corporate capitalism.[1] But while the sheer ambition of al-Qaeda's assault was entirely without precedent, the seismic media event of 9/11 was, in fact, the culmination of a number of attacks on American interests that throughout the previous decade had indicated a growing disparity between American self-image and the ways in which certain elements of the international community perceived the United States.[2]

One might imagine that having been assailed by a foreign threat from within its own national boundaries for the first time since 1812, and in a manner so utterly spectacular as to appear logically impossible, the United States, a nation now locked in the posttraumatic loop of endlessly recycled images of the falling towers, would enter into a period of national self-examination—as a means not only of bearing witness to the events of September 11, but also of understanding why they had occurred in the first place. But such an examination was not forthcoming from the U.S. political establishment. Instead, in a manner decidedly reminiscent of Nixon's wholesale demonization of antigovernment elements, and Reagan's revisionist perspective on the events of the 1970s, the Right opted to exacerbate domestic paranoia and thereby avoid a detached and nonpartisan examination of the situation.

Repeatedly, it was said that forces antithetical to expansionist American "interests" abroad were at work within the nation's borders, threatening the very foundations of both social cooperation and democratic individualism.

Thus, fostering a climate of introspective paranoia highly evocative of the 1970s, the Bush administration insistently emphasized the unconventional nature of the enemy, which, being divorced from an individual state or an ideology of nationhood, became, in Slavoj Žižek's words, "an illegal, secret, almost virtual worldwide network"[3] that invidiously and invisibly challenged everything an exceptionalist United States stood for. As President Bush so bombastically put it in his January 2002 State of the Union address, what the United States stood for was "freedom": "Our enemies send other people's children on missions of suicide and murder. They embrace tyranny and death as a cause and a creed. We stand for a different choice, made long ago, on the day of our founding. We choose freedom and the dignity of every life. . . . We have known freedom's price. We have shown freedom's power. And in this great conflict, my fellow Americans, we will see freedom's victory."[4] Notable here is the way in which the president conceives of the terrorist threat in ways that adopt the repressive, retrograde, and primitive image of the Orient constructed by colonialist Europe as a means of justifying its own economic interests and territorial ambitions in the East.[5] Thus Bush's attempts to "control, manipulate, even to incorporate [the] manifestly different . . . world"[6] that had attacked the United States can be seen to rest on that old Orientalist binarism that counterposed the post-Enlightenment rationality of the West (in this case, evoking the concertedly American ideology of democratic individualism) and the older, darker, more primitive, and fundamentally inferior religious culture of the undemocratic and anti-individualistic East. It was, of course, a reductive, simplistic, and fundamentally misleading opposition, but it offered a highly attractive assertion of national cohesion and political supremacy at a time of great confusion. In short, it was an extremely effective piece of political rhetoric, feeding, as it did, into a number of potent American myths of national origins and national identity, myths that would find their contemporary embodiment in a range of popular cultural texts, most notably the cinematic subgenre of hillbilly horror.

The United States has a very long history of representing the inhabitants of its own isolated rural places or backwoods communities as monstrous, grotesque, diseased, and polluted. Emerging as it did from the trauma of the Revolutionary War, the foundational study of colonial period self-image—J. Hector St. John de Crèvecoeur's 1782 *Letters from an American Farmer*—participates enthusiastically in this trend. Here, Crèvecoeur stresses the enormous disjunction between the backwoodsmen and those good country people whose adherence to the Protestant virtues of sobriety, thrift, Christian morality, and hard work was transforming the ancient, hostile, and potentially unknowable American wilderness into a utopian land of

"happiness and prosperity . . . [with] hospitality, kindness, and plenty everywhere."[7] But far "beyond the reach of government" and closely aligned with
the dark irrationality of his habitat, warned Crèvecoeur, were the backwoodsmen. These individuals had turned from peaceful and exhausting agriculture
to a life of hunting in the game-rich forests, a practice that led not only to
"drunkenness and idleness . . . contention, inactivity, and wretchedness,"[8] but
also to a kind of sociobiological degeneration—a falling away not only from
the ideals of the new republic but also from humanity itself. So, for all the
hopeful, forward-looking qualities of the age, the backwoods community became, in Crèvecoeur's words, "a mongrel breed, half civilized, half savage."[9]

In their deviant hybridity, it is nonetheless possible to see how the backwoodsmen proffered a radical challenge to exceptionalist models of American identity. Further, this challenge continues to resurface in the popular
imagination when historic trauma encourages the citizenry, if not their rulers,
to engage in a national self-examination. For the backwoodsman was most
certainly not an American Adam, building a democratic Eden in the amply
legislated garden of the New World; instead, he was one who inhabited the
physical and conceptual margins of the nation, the abject territory of "out-
casts, outlaws, and paupers."[10] Resisting cultural assimilation by dominant expansionist ideologies, and thus illustrating how those who had settled down
to a life of hard work on the farm or in the emergent city had tacitly acqui-
esced to the limits placed on their freedoms, the backwoodsman thus established his own vision and version of the United States. His freedom was not
mediated by its conceptual embodiment in a constitution. His independence
was asserted not by its declaration or by its validation in law, but in his refusal
to be subject to that law.

With his monstrous physicality, all rotten teeth and rapacious sexuality,
the backwoodsman thus repudiated any subordination of his material body
to his cognitive self. And, in turn, he was cast off and disavowed by the civilized mainstream that itself was simultaneously attracted to and terrified of
his unspeakable desires and unimaginably grotesque acts. As Jack Nichol-
son's portrayal of an alcoholic lawyer, George, puts it shortly before being
beaten to death by angry small-town conformists in Dennis Hopper's *Easy
Rider* (1969): "Talking about [freedom] and being it—that's two different
things. . . . I mean, it's real hard to be free when you're bought and sold in the
marketplace. 'Course, don't ever tell anybody . . . that they're not free, cause
they're gonna get real busy killin' and maimin' to prove that they are." And so,
it was entirely appropriate that in the 1970s—as the United States sought to
bring the light of freedom to the misguided "Orientals" of North Vietnam, as

the battle for civil rights raged across the nation, and as a host of countercultural philosophies of Eastern origin challenged American capitalism's white Anglo-Saxon Protestant hegemony—the hitherto-repressed figure of the backwoodsman made a spectacular cinematic return. He functioned, I would argue, as a means of negotiating the increasingly traumatic disjunction between the aspirations of a "civilized" society and the acts of savagery perpetrated in its name. In films such as Herschell Gordon Lewis's *Two Thousand Maniacs!* (1964), Tobe Hooper's *The Texas Chain Saw Massacre* (1974), and Wes Craven's *The Hills Have Eyes* (1977)—all recently remade—as well as John Boorman's *Deliverance* (1972) and Walter Hill's *Southern Comfort* (1981), the monstrous alterity of the historically embedded backwoodsman enabled filmmakers to address not only American foreign policy in South Asia, but also the ongoing desecration of American ecology (*Deliverance*), the paranoid militarism of American life (*Southern Comfort*), the degeneration of the frontier ethos at the hands of consumer culture (*Southern Comfort*), and the ramifications for workers of the decay of America's industrial base (*The Texas Chain Saw Massacre*).

With his congenital abnormalities, bizarre sexuality, appalling dentistry, and in the case of the Cajun backwoodsman, perverse insistence on speaking French, the horror hillbilly broke free of the mechanisms of social, cultural, and psychological repression that attempted to contain his deviant repudiation of dominant norms and values. In so doing, of course, he not only enabled audiences to share in his vicarious pleasures, but also provided horror cinema with an iconic means of peeling back ideologically expedient dressings that other branches of the culture industry had applied to the wounds of the period—specifically, the damage done to the national self-image as the war in Vietnam raged abroad and protests against it at home informed all aspects of U.S. social life.

In light of all this, it is entirely unsurprising that the subgenre of hillbilly horror has experienced a renaissance since the bombing of the World Trade Center and George W. Bush's subsequent "War on Terror," which, for all its recent rebranding as a "struggle against violent extremists," has had major implications for civil liberties within the United States and human rights around the world. Establishing a Department of Homeland Security beyond the scrutiny of Congress and introducing legislation that has had major implications for Americans' freedom of association, information, and speech, and the right to legal representation and to trial by jury, the Patriot Act brought about a radical transformation to the relationship between the American people, their police forces, and the U.S. military. It is, of course, one that is itself highly reminiscent of President Nixon's wholesale surveillance of potentially damaging oppositional groups in the name of freedom, though in Nixon's case this meant freedom from the evils of communism.

And as in the Nixon period, such developments have been reflected in film culture in general and in the subgenre of hillbilly horror in particular. For a new generation subject to oppressively normative conceptions of what it means to call oneself a citizen of the United States, hillbilly horror thus offers its audience a means of critically engaging with the nation's territorial ambitions, allowing for both an interrogation of the implications of President Bush's Orientalist demonization of the terrorist as deviant other, and the ability to ask the most shocking of questions: whether, in the age of the propagandistically named Patriot Act, the concentration camp that is Guantanamo Bay, and the judicially sanctioned form of kidnap and torture that is "extraordinary rendition," Americans retain the right to speak of liberty at all.

As the 1970s and the opening years of the new millennium coalesce—as Iraq becomes Bush's Vietnam and a new generation of civil rights campaigners emerge—a whole new generation of filmmakers have set out to pay homage to their 1970s predecessors in their exploration of the will to social and cultural heterogeneity currently demanded by the War on Terror, as it was earlier demanded by the Vietnam conflict. They include Eli Roth's *Cabin Fever* (2002), Rob Schmidt's *Wrong Turn* (2003) and Joe Lynch's *Wrong Turn 2: Dead End* (2007), Marcus Nispel's *The Texas Chainsaw Massacre* (2003), and Alexandre Aja's *The Hills Have Eyes* (2006) along with its 2007 sequel by Martin Weisz, *The Hills Have Eyes II*.[11] So, for all the president's protests nine days after the fall of the Twin Towers, that "what is at stake is not just America's freedom. This is not just America's fight. This is the fight of all those who believe in progress and pluralism, tolerance and freedom,"[12] it seems to have become the self-proclaimed mission of a new generation of horror directors to remind the nation of some rather unpleasant home truths, specifically that the repetition of the word "freedom" (however reinforced by "killin' and maimin'") is no substitute for liberty itself.

The rest of this essay will argue, therefore, that this new generation of hillbilly horror films possesses a distinctive cultural function, providing audiences with a "process of acting out, working over, and to some extent working through" recent events, "giving voice to the past,"[13] and in so doing, throwing light on an unsettling and disorienting present. Nobody, I contend, gives voice quite like Rob Zombie—erstwhile singer with the metal band White Zombie, more recently solo recording artist and filmmaker, and the director of the two really significant works of recent hillbilly horror to which I will now turn, *House of 1000 Corpses* (2003) and *The Devil's Rejects* (2005). For, in

FIGURE 9.1. *Rob Zombie's backwoods Uncle Sam as spirit of radical independence (*House of 1000 Corpses, *Lionsgate, 2003).*

the grotesque excesses of these stylistically playful and technically inventive films, I will argue, we see a radical challenge proffered to the post-9/11 ideology of identity promulgated by the neoconservative right. As neoconservatives wage war on the moral, theological, and ideological deviance of the intrinsically foreign terrorist threat, as well as the putatively un-American defiance of liberal challenges to such policies in the mass media and elsewhere, Zombie brings the hillbillies down once more from the hills. And in their repudiation of the models of national identity promulgated by both the neocons and their liberal opponents, his monstrous backwoodsmen show themselves to be no more accessible to cultural assimilation or homogenization than they were in the historic past, this being a highly political critique of the nation-state and its modes of political organization and representation in times of national crisis.

House of 1000 Corpses opens in rural Texas on October 30, 1977 (Halloween weekend), with four young "white-breads"—Bill and his girlfriend, Mary; Jerry and his girlfriend, Denise—who are driving across this parched and sparsely inhabited region in order to write a book on the peculiarly American phenomenon of the roadside attraction. To this end (in time-honored tradition) they stop at Captain Spaulding's Museum of Monsters and Madmen, a gas station-cum-roadside commemoration of serial killers everywhere, but one that pays specific tribute to the local boy, Dr. Satan, allegedly executed for his crimes nearby. Traveling to the supposed site of his alleged execution, our ill-fated young folk (again, in time-honored tradition) pick up a hitchhiker—an unfortunate choice in most genres but invariably cataclysmic in hillbilly horror. She is the lovely Baby Firefly, whose house they head to when the tire of their car is mysteriously shot out. There, they are introduced to the entire family: Mother Firefly, Tiny, Otis, Grandpa Hugo, and the slightly less rococo Rufus; among them, they cover just about every hillbilly stereotype in circulation since the eighteenth century. When a fight breaks out over Baby's slutty flirtation with Bill, the young people are taken hostage (a bit of a family hobby, it seems, as Otis has, until now, been busy out in the barn, torturing seven recently kidnapped cheerleaders). Needless to say, over Halloween weekend things go from bad to worse, as our unlucky protagonists are tortured, buried alive, and experimented on by the "not really dead" Dr. Satan, who has taken up his work in the cavernous cellars beneath the Firefly house. It's a gloriously grizzly festival of gore, unrelenting in pace and inexhaustible in its conceptual and technical inventiveness.

In each of his films, Rob Zombie is keen to intersperse the action with sequences that simultaneously highlight the constructed status of the artifact while giving the present narrative a more complex sweep and scope. Here, he interjects a series of montages, including home interviews with the family and both clips and stills from numerous horror films. He also indulges in the use of color filters and various baroque transitions, all of which destabilize our notion of narrative "truth" and call into question any easy assumptions we may be inclined to make about ourselves, the world we inhabit, and the ways in which that world may be accurately represented. In interpolating a range of sepia flashbacks, for example (a practice he reprises in color in *The Devil's Rejects*), Zombie evokes a vanished photographic, cinematic, and familial past. This technique loans an elegiac feel to the present moment that, in its awareness of all that has passed, mourns not only the "mortality, vulnerability, mutability" of people but testifies, in Susan Sontag's words, to "time's relentless melt."[14] The past, for Rob Zombie and his terrifying protagonists, is never truly past, for like the Firefly clan, it endlessly erupts into the present, repudiating its own abjection and returning, all guns blazing, to challenge the ostensible rationality of the here and now. The homogenized grand narrative of national cohesion and shared communal endeavor evoked by presidents such as George W. Bush as a means of demonizing the alien "other" are here denied by the terrifying savagery that lies at the heart of America itself.

The tale of the Firefly clan, in other words, is told in the form of a series of disjunctive micro-narratives—television advertisements, interviews with characters, grainy monochrome pornography—that not only undercut the binarisms on which dominant identity discourse rests (civilization versus savagery, self versus other, rationality versus irrationality), but also illustrate, as does the consistent use of color filters, that we have no transparent or unmediated access to "truth" at all. "I love famous people," Baby will remark in the sequel, "they're so much better than the real thing." Running beneath the post-Enlightenment narrative of progress and perfectibility on which dominant formulations of national identity rest, we can see an alternative and far darker story. And, unsurprisingly, given the political context from which this film emerged, it is the selfsame story of dispossession, degeneration, and unimaginable savagery that films such as *The Texas Chain Saw Massacre*, *Deliverance*, *The Hills Have Eyes*, and *Southern Comfort* had told some thirty years before. For, as is the case with just about all the hillbilly horrors of the post-9/11 period, *House of 1000 Corpses* and *The Devil's Rejects* pay self-conscious tribute to their generic precursors—Otis Firefly's penchant for wearing the faces of his victims, his brother Tiny's deformity, their charnel house of a homestead, the implication of incest and inbreeding, their insatiable taste for blood, and their penchant for hunting their prey down to the last woman—all echoing Hooper's and Craven's films of the 1970s. More significantly, of course, such generic self-reflexivity has the effect of purposefully deconstructing the straightforward, transparent, universally acknowledged linear narratives of American freedom that so insistently informed the rhetoric of the Vietnam era in which the film is set, which have been insistently resurrected by the expansionist Right since 9/11.

Needless to say, *House of 1000 Corpses* was critically eviscerated. James Brundage of FilmCritic.com sums up the general opinion in his claim that the film was simply "hick after hick, cheap scary image after cheap scary image, lots of southern accents and psychotic murders. . . . It's too highbrow to be a good cheap horror movie, it's too lowbrow to be satire, and it's too boring to bear the value of the ticket."[15] But, as I would argue, Brundage and others who condemned the sickening immorality of the film rather missed the point. In this film's absorbing take on the conflict between the forward-looking urban self (Bill and Jerry, Mary and Denise) and the savage vitality of the traditional rural community (the Firefly clan and their associates), we actually see a set of significant concerns emerging: the Fireflys come to encapsulate all the anarchic potentiality of the irrational other while allowing for ideological reflection on simultaneously repressive and oppressive qualities of everyday (civilized) life. In their familial war against society, their utter disregard for consensual morality, their passionate contempt for the strictures of the law, and their utter freedom to do and be whatever they goddamn please, Tiny and Rufus, Otis and Baby, Mother and Spaulding, and Dr. Satan himself offer Americans a timely reminder of the limits they have consensually allowed to be placed on their liberty. The film reminds them, in other words, that for all the president's proclamations, they are not "free" at all.

This position is unequivocally reaffirmed in *The Devil's Rejects*, the opening montage of which (Polaroid stills of *House of 1000 Corpses'* victims) once again brings the past into the present while reaffirming the existence of a savage American heart beating beneath the conformist breasts of its civilized citizenry. This time out, the sheriff is John Quincy Wydell (the brother of the previously murdered George), and he and his posse of state troopers kick off the action by mounting a retributive attack on the Firefly residence, which, for all its necrophiliac inhabitants and corpse-strewn decor, takes on the resonance of the besieged American homestead. In a breathtakingly relentless shoot-out scene, Rufus is killed, Tiny runs off, and Mother Firefly is arrested while Baby and Otis escape (to the strains of the Allman Brothers' "Midnight Rider"). Murdering a passing maid for her car, the two take refuge in a small motel where they kidnap, and then torture and murder, a traveling country band, in a symbolic murder of the down-home, corncob coziness it espouses. Seeking refuge at Charlie's Frontier Fun Town, a low-rent whorehouse owned by Spaulding's adoptive brother, they are captured by Wydell (who has already murdered their matriarch) and returned to the family farm. It is there that the dividing line between civilization and savagery, between the moral authority of the state and the amoral excrescence that is the Firefly clan, collapses as Wydell (avenging the death of his brother and some seventy other posited victims) tortures his victims with the enthusiasm of a madman. He nails Otis's hands to his chair, staples a crime scene photograph of a victim to Baby's chest, and beats Captain Spaulding around the head with a cattle prod, which he uses to electrocute all three before transmuting into the ax-wielding stalker of 1970s slasher fame to chase Baby into the night.

Here, we can see Zombie bringing into play a range of long-standing cultural contradictions. Up until this point, of course, he has pitted the highly individualistic and distinctly transgressive Firefly clan against the common good, the degenerate criminal against the lawman, the psychopath against the machinery of urban-industrial life under capitalism (specifically, the judicio-moral imperatives of the state). But now he graphically shows that the opposition might not be as clear-cut as we have been led to believe. In Wydell's retributive insanity, and in his assertion that he comes from a long line of violent men prone to "vigilante justice," we see the distinction between outlaw and sheriff, gunslinger and cavalryman, black hat and white hat, slip away in an orgy of violence. Here, on the frontier of human experi-

FIGURE 9.2. *What is an American?* (*The Devil's Rejects, Lionsgate, 2005*).

ence, that "meeting point between savagery and civilization,"[16] we see some foundational myths of American history challenged, specifically the thesis espoused in Frederick Jackson Turner's seminal 1893 essay, "The Significance of the Frontier in American History." This work effectively erased the mass slaughter that had facilitated the birth of the nation in favor of a sentimental pastoralism that championed the farmer over the gunslinger while attempting to conceal the nation's origins in violence and expansion through chattel slavery, industrial exploitation, genocide, and ecological decimation. With Turner, the figure of the murderer-as-frontier-hero was officially erased from the official account of the nation's coming-into-being, an erasure that would be replicated in the classic Western's insistent sanitizing of the history of the frontier. In hillbilly horror, however, a counter-memory is recovered. As Wydell goes crazy, actively enjoying his acts of bloody torture and sadistic terror, Zombie seems to ask a range of questions concerning American social life: Who can be said to define or constitute a nation? Who really owns the land? On whose dreams was that land founded? Who decides what it is to be an American? And what rights and responsibilities may that entail?

As in the previous film, the action is intercut with grainy, pixilated news reports, while the insistent editorial use of the wipe and Super 16 film stock further evokes the past—in this case, the stylistic practices of the era in which the film is set. This is echoed by this highly self-reflexive film's inventive cinematography and idiosyncratic characterization: beginning with an evocation of the recently remade *Ned Kelly* (Tony Richardson, 1970), ending with a slow-motion tribute to *Bonnie and Clyde* (Arthur Penn, 1967), and quoting the Manson Family's Tex Watson along the way. And so, I would argue, the Fireflys amply illustrate the long-standing, problematic positioning of the redneck, the backwoodsman, the hillbilly at the heart of the United States' formulation of its own national identity.

The figure of the backwoodsman has long been central to America's dissemination of idealized and exceptionalist models of its own national identity. On the one hand was a wholesale cultural valorization of the backwoodsman as the epitome of republicanism (visible in tales of Kit Carson, Davy Crockett, Daniel Boone, and later mass-cultural renderings, such as *The Beverly Hillbillies* [Paul Henning, 1962–1971]).[17] This was the "real American" of pithy sayings and medicinal, astronomical, and meteorological knowledge, whose uncomplicated integrity was guaranteed by the purifying forces of nature itself (that being a realm entirely antithetical to the cunning political machinations of the civilized urban world). On the other hand, we can see an innate distrust of those who occupied the hinterland, portraying them as the fugitives and outlaws that populate the backwoods of American nightmares (clearly visible in the immediate post–Revolutionary War texts of Hector de Crèvecoeur and in the post–Civil War writings of local colorists like Joel Chandler Harris).

For, like the cowboy hero and his successor, the serial killer, the hillbilly amply illustrates the limits placed on liberty by an increasingly organized and urbanized society.[18] But unlike the cowboy or the serial killer—who, I would argue, are frequently reappropriated by mass culture to serve dominant ideologies of nationhood—the hillbilly is less suited to cultural assimilation, being tied firmly to a sense of place and an extended kinship structure (Spaulding's "one big happy family"). This is a distinct cultural milieu with its own sense of history, tradition, and class. Being less an individual than a member of an entire social group that challenges the totalizing claims for national identity embodied in the Declaration of Independence and other foundational texts, the hillbilly of American horror cinema is a dangerous figure indeed.[19] And so, the Firefly clan and the rest of the hillbilly horror subgenre come to encapsulate all the archaic disorder, medieval darkness, anticlassical savagery, and pantheistic paganism of the American other and the terrorist threat alike—while making amply apparent that Americans are not now, and indeed have never been, "free" in the sense that self-serving ideologues such as George W. Bush affirm.

NOTES

Parts of this essay originally appeared in Linnie Blake's *The Wounds of Nations: Horror Cinema, Historical Trauma and National Identity* (Manchester, UK: Manchester University Press, 2008).

1. Noam Chomsky, *9-11* (New York: Seven Stories Press, 2001).

2. These were the 1993 attack on U.S. Marines in Mogadishu, the truck bombing of a U.S. military location in Riyadh in 1995, the bombing of the Khobar Towers (which was housing foreign military personal) in Dhahran in 1996, the bombing of U.S. embassies in East Africa in 1998, and the attack on the USS *Cole* in 2000.

3. Slavoj Žižek, "Are We in a War? Do We Have an Enemy?," *London Review of Books*, May 23, 2002, http://www.lrb.co.uk/v24/n10/slavoj-zizek/are-we-in-a-war-do-we-have-an-enemy.

4. George W. Bush, "State of the Union Address," *Washington Post*, January 29, 2002, http://www.washingtonpost.com/wp-srv/onpolitics/transcripts/sou012902 .htm.

5. Edward Said, *Orientalism: Western Conceptions of the Orient* (London: Penguin, 1991).

6. Ibid., 12.

7. J. Hector St. John de Crèvecoeur, *Letters from an American Farmer* (London: Penguin, 1982), 80.

8. Ibid., 72.

9. Ibid., 77.

10. William Byrd quoted in James R. Masterson, "William Byrd in Lubberland," *American Literature* 9 (May 1937): 167.

11. The same can also be said of films that reached considerably smaller audiences. *Undertow* (David Gordon Green, 2004) depicts the discovery of a small rural town's guilty secret in the form of "the boy"—a mutant giant who stalks them through the woods before killing them off in a variety of predictably graphic ways. Christopher Burgard's *The Ruining*, reedited and released in 2004 (though written and partly shot a decade earlier), sees two couples going to the California backwoods, where they discover a remote community poisoned by the government thirty years ago and now dead, insane, or degenerated into doglike mutants. *Shallow Ground* (Sheldon Wilson, 2004), winner of Edinburgh's Dead by Dawn film festival's Best Feature prize, brings a great deal of gallows humor to the proceedings as the staff of a soon-to-close sheriff's station is confronted with a blood-soaked and naked teenager who emerges from the woods. The considerably less inventive *The Attendant* (Corbin Timbrook, 2004) is also set in the present day but wears its 1970s credentials fairly heavily; for example, the opening title sequence evokes that of *The Texas Chain Saw Massacre*, with its tale of "six campers who planned to spend a relaxing weekend in those mountains [but] had no idea of the horrible fate that awaited them." The supernatural infusion of the genre is similarly clear in *The Fanglys* (Christopher Abram, 2004), which amply illustrates just how truly unpleasant camping can be if one is accosted by the soul-gobbling matriarch of a family of cannibalistic hillbillies!

12. George W. Bush, "Address to a Joint Session of Congress and the American People," September 20, 2001, http://georgewbush-whitehouse.archives.gov/news/ releases/2001/09/20010920-8.html.

13. Dominick LaCapra, *Writing History, Writing Trauma* (Baltimore: Johns Hopkins University Press, 2001), 186.

14. Susan Sontag, *On Photography* (New York: Farrar, Straus and Giroux, 1977), 15.

15. James Brundage, review of *House of 1000 Corpses*, FilmCritic.com, April 14, 2003, http://www.filmcritic.com/reviews/2003/house-of-1000-corpses/.

16. Frederick Jackson Turner, "The Significance of the Frontier in American History," in *The Early Writings of Frederick Jackson Turner*, ed. Everett E. Edwards (Madison: University of Wisconsin Press, 1938), 187.

17. The image of the hillbilly is not invariably negative, in other words, for at times it has become necessary to deploy this iconic figure in mass-cultural service of the United States' dominant myths. For example, as the Great Depression dispossessed a third of the country's farming families of their land and forced many into the role of internal refugees, John Ford's 1940 film *The Grapes of Wrath* (from John Steinbeck's 1939 novel) not only established the iconicity of the truck piled high with familial effects and elderly relatives, but deployed the star status of the unthreatening good guy Henry Fonda to affirm the validity of the New Deal, thereby rejecting in the process any less American (i.e., communistic) solutions. Moreover, as the mass migration of some three million Appalachian people to the mid-Atlantic and midwestern cities of the 1950s threatened to undermine Cold War pretensions to cultural homogeneity and national stability, television stepped into the breach with programs like *The Real McCoys* (Irving Pincus, 1957–1963), Americanizing the Appalachian in its tale of West Virginia farmers seeking a new life in California. It was a strategy echoed throughout the 1960s, as the subject of Appalachian poverty (or the "plight of the hill people") became not only a campaign issue for the young John F. Kennedy in the West Virginia primaries, but also the subject of a 1964 CBS television special (*Christmas in Appalachia*, illustrating the failure of Kennedy's New Deal–style Area Development Administration). As if to counter such a deeply subversive impression, American mass culture kicked into action. *The Andy Griffith Show* (Sheldon Leonard, 1960–1968), based on Griffith's own hometown of Mount Airy, North Carolina, was eclipsed in popularity only by the massively successful *Beverly Hillbillies*. This tale of Jed Clampett—an Ozark farmer whose oil-rich land is bought for twenty-five million dollars, thereby enabling him to relocate his entire family to Beverly Hills—not only underscored preexisting regional, class, and ethnic stereotypes, but also refashioned them in the context of both Cold War and Vietnam-era reaffirmations of a unified national identity.

18. The rural population may have doubled between the end of the Civil War and the beginning of World War I, but the urban population multiplied sevenfold, so that by 1914 only a third of the American population was involved in agriculture. See Arthur M. Schlesinger and Dixon Ryan Fox, eds., *A History of American Life*, vol. 10, *The Rise of the City, 1878–1898* (New York: Macmillan, 1933), 57.

19. And, as such, he was repeatedly the victim of sociological, literary, and pseudo-scientific calumny. Thus by 1891, in the climate of social Darwinism, an investigator from the Department of Labor could credibly claim that "the mind of the poor white is feral, fatalistic, bordering on bitterness, unable to improve, and unwilling to relent." Quoted in Sylvia Jenkins Cook, *From Tobacco Road to Route 66: The Southern Poor White in Fiction* (Chapel Hill: University of North Carolina Press, 1976), 4. Into the twentieth century, moreover, the Eugenics Records Office would conduct some fif-

teen "Eugenic Family Studies," setting out to expose the genetic defects of the poor white, which were caused, it was argued, by miscegenation, incest, and alcoholism. See Nicole Hahn Rafter, ed., *White Trash: The Eugenic Family Studies, 1877–1919* (Boston: Northeastern University Press, 1988). In literature, such a perspective was echoed in William Faulkner's picture of the rural South and in Ellen Glasgow's Southern Gothic school of writing. Clearly, by the mid-twentieth century, dualistic conceptions of urban progress and rural regression, good country people and the savagery of poor white communities, traceable to the eighteenth century, had solidified into a lexicon of essentializing prejudice most commonly applied by whites to blacks. And if, during the eighteenth century, the binarism had functioned as a vindication of the continued existence of social hegemonies, class distinctions, and slavery within this ostensibly egalitarian nation, then it continued to operate to the advantage of dominant interest groups here.

CHAPTER TEN

"Forever Family" Values

Twilight *and the Modern Mormon Vampire*

TRAVIS SUTTON AND HARRY M. BENSHOFF

"I dream about being with you forever," Bella confesses to Edward as they dance together in a gazebo at the end of *Twilight* (Catherine Hardwicke, 2008). The desire for a long-lasting relationship in a romantic narrative is fairly conventional; however, in a romantic vampire narrative propelled by Mormon metaphors, this desire for a long-lasting—indeed, everlasting—relationship is doubly intriguing. The author of the original 2005 novel, Stephenie Meyer, describes herself as a believing member of the Church of Jesus Christ of Latter-day Saints, popularly known as the Mormon or LDS Church.[1] For believing Mormons, marriage and the family unit are eternal concepts; indeed, Mormon discourse often uses the term "forever family" to acknowledge this idea.[2] Being part of a forever family is critical for receiving the highest blessings of heaven after death. To do so requires baptism, heterosexual marriage in an LDS temple, and lifelong adherence to the Mormon Church's commandments and policies. These rituals and beliefs encourage and enforce heteronormative assumptions, including the ideas (1) that gender is a distinct and eternal characteristic of human identity, (2) that gender includes divinely mandated roles wherein men "provide and preside" over families while women "nurture" children, (3) that God ordains marriage to be between "man and woman" in order to "multiply and replenish the earth," and (4) that sex acts are to be understood as "powers of procreation" to be used with "complete fidelity" between a lawfully married heterosexual couple.[3] But all these heteronormative Christian ideals are somewhat complicated throughout *Twilight*, because Edward's "forever family" is a vampiric one, and the classical mythology of Western vampires has always figured them as antithetical to Christ and Christian teachings.[4] *Twilight*, then, is part of a decades-old trend in vampire fiction that bends classical vampire mythology to new ends, rewriting its thematic myths in new and often surprising ways.

Mormon creed. Since vampires have been used in recent decades to dramatize outsider status, particularly through sexual difference, the good vampires in *Twilight*—the Cullen family—seem to situate fundamentalist identity in the role of sympathetic outsider. *Twilight* is a narrative that depends on clear distinctions between good and evil as defined by Mormon ideologies, which serve to sustain the energy of (Christian) fundamentalist thought in a post-9/11 culture.

Fans and critics of *Twilight* alike have discerned that many elements of Mormon culture—including forever families—permeate both Stephenie Meyer's novel and the director Catherine Hardwicke's film adaptation. Hardwicke was perhaps the ideal director for *Twilight*, having effectively dramatized modern teen angst in her films *Thirteen* (2003) and *Lords of Dogtown* (2005), as well as overt religious themes in *The Nativity Story* (2006). In *Twilight*, which centers on the chaste romance between the human teen Bella and the vampire "teen" Edward Cullen, Meyer and Hardwicke have reworked Mormonism within the contexts of contemporary teen culture and gothic horror. As noted above, Meyer has been open in interviews about her identity as a believing Mormon and alumnus of Brigham Young University, and she claims that the most influential book in her life is *The Book of Mormon*.[9] Meyer admits to exploring theological principles such as "free agency" and "sacrifice" in her writing,[10] while readers of her books and fans of the movie, particularly those familiar with Mormon culture, discuss more overt forms of Mormon content, such as the dietary code of the texts' vampire family. Some Mormons resent Meyer's use of Mormonism in a story with elements they perceive to be dark and sinful, namely, gothic horror and sexual titillation.[11] At the same time, critics of Mormon doctrine, whether atheist or evangelical, often think of *Twilight* as part of a strategy to indoctrinate unsuspecting readers with Mormon beliefs.[12]

In some ways, the reworking of classical vampire mythology from a Mormon perspective is to be expected. Historically, the vampire has been a protean figure adapted by various cultures to fit their needs. Since the publication of Bram Stoker's *Dracula* in 1897, the vampire has been especially prominent in Christian cultures as the embodiment of all that is unholy. But more recent decades have seen the rise of the "new vampire," a figure used to reflect social more than theological difference.[13] Films such as *Blacula* (William Crain, 1972) and *Deafula* (Peter Wolf, 1975) use vampirism as a metaphor to express aspects of the black and deaf experiences, respectively. Many other texts, from Anne Rice's *The Vampire Chronicles* series (1976–2003) to HBO's *True Blood* (Alan Ball, 2008–), figure their vampires as more or less coded expressions of sexual others, most obviously homosexuals. Now, with the popularity of the

As post-9/11 texts, the novel and film *Twilight* reformulate
a unique and metaphorically religious context, and the popula
these texts seems to reveal this era's ongoing cultural interest in r
ters. "When death becomes the center, then religion begins," v
erary critic Harold Bloom in his study of the United States' "rel
culture."[5] Bloom asserts that religion develops because human
that they are going to die, and they fear death. Thus, for Bloom
stitutionalizes strategies that individuals use to obscure the rea
and provides a context for human existence and meaning. The ter
of September 11, 2001, forcefully brought Bloom's configuration
and religion into the American consciousness. The mass murder
soil reminded onlookers of their own mortality, and this, accordin
theory, would cultivate a need for religion. At the same time, th
of 9/11 was interpreted widely as a religiously motivated act, give
extremists involved, and revealed religion's capacity for cruelty
These ideas introduced a potential tension in the aftermath of S
people became attracted to religion as they recognized their mo
at the same time they feared religion and its potential for destru

Arguably, it has been this simultaneous attraction and repulsi
after 9/11 that has contributed to the continued growth of Chr
mentalism in the United States, even as less fundamentalist r
reported decreasing membership trends.[6] Fundamentalist logi
somewhat oxymoronic concept—might affirm it was not religic
motivated the terrorists; rather, it was a false or misguided rel
therefore important to practice the true and inerrant religion,
fundamentalist might believe that religion to be. Former presiden
Bush, a particularly religious national leader, along with othe
echo this kind of response when they shaped the conflict as a
tween good Christians and evil Muslims. Such a response fuel
create paradigms of "us" and "them," the projection of an othe
wait to destroy the one true church, the one true god, and the
gious ideology. (Of course, an atheist might view *all* religions a
state apparatuses designed to manipulate the thoughts and beha
subjects.)[7]

One writer, recalling his childhood experience in a fundamen
reminds his readers that such religious groups often disbelieve t
"moral majority" and understand themselves to be an oppress
constantly battling dominant worldliness.[8] As a fundamental
LDS Church not only reports rising numbers in membership bu
ally asserts an oppressed status against anything or anyone that

Twilight franchise (including four books, each with its own film adaptation), the Mormon vampire has arrived on the pop-culture stage. This essay examines the ways the novel and film versions of *Twilight* integrate Mormon culture and beliefs into vampire mythology, and how that connection changes some aspects of the vampire myth while nonetheless retaining reactionary messages about gender and sexuality. Instead of depicting the vampire as a repressed other who must be annihilated in order to maintain dominant (Western Christian) culture and ideology, *Twilight*'s Mormon vampires—the Cullen family—are angelic, godlike figures who restore repression to an ideologically confused culture, and in the process reinforce heteronormative "forever family" values.

RELIGION, REPRESSION, AND THE VAMPIRE

As various critics have pointed out, the classical Western vampire myth is in many ways an inversion of (and simultaneous reinforcement of) Christian theology. Some critics argue that the rise of Christianity and the cultural circulation of the vampire myth are deeply intertwined, primarily through the vampire myth being a "ghastly parody of the Eucharist."[14] As the vampire scholar James B. Twitchell puts it, "What the medieval church found in the vampire legend was not just an apt mythologem for evil, but an elaborate allegory for the transubstantiation of evil. The reason this was so important was that the vampire myth explained the most difficult concept in the last of the sacraments to be introduced—the Eucharist."[15] Thus, just as Christians partake of the flesh and blood of Christ in order to receive eternal life (becoming godlike in the process), so, too, does the vampire partake of the flesh and blood of his or her victims in order to live forever (becoming monstrous rather than heavenly). Bram Stoker's *Dracula*, certainly one of the most important texts of Western vampire mythology, deliberately figures the vampire as an Antichrist, an unholy creature who can be opposed through Christian symbols such as holy water, the cross, and the Communion wafer. Blood is the transformative element in both Christian and vampire mythologies, and scholars have noted that many of the Methodist hymns that circulated in Victorian England during Stoker's era emphasized "the mystique of blood, and particularly . . . the avid drinking of the blood of Christ."[16] Considering such hymns, Christopher Herbert observes that "sometimes this craving transposes itself into an unmistakably sexualized register marked by the strongest possible insistence on the fantasy of gulping warm blood directly from Christ's wound—or of actually entering that wound."[17]

Such observations underscore the cultural links between Christianity and gothic horror, blood and other bodily fluids, penetration and sexuality. The conflation of those various tropes arguably constitutes the appeal of all gothic literature, which tends to displace aspects of sex and sexuality onto monstrous signifiers, inviting readers to experience the thrill of the sexually deviant within the safe or "innocent" zone of a fictional, make-believe generic construct. As George E. Haggerty suggests in *Queer Gothic*, gothic "terror is almost always sexual terror, and fear, and flight, and incarceration, and escape are almost always colored by the exoticism of transgressive sexual aggression."[18] But whereas sophisticated critics may understand the gothic as about little else but sex, many of its consumers value it precisely for its manifest denial or repression of sexual content (as in Christianity). One perceptive review of the novel *Twilight* seems to allude to that dual/repressive approach: "It's never quite clear whether Edward wants to sleep with Bella or rip her throat out or both, but he wants something. . . . That's the power of the *Twilight* books: they're squeaky, geeky clean on the surface, but right below it, they are absolutely, deliciously filthy."[19]

Robin Wood's famous figuration of horror as a collective "American nightmare" suggests that the genre works as a gigantic repression-displacement defense mechanism for an entire culture.[20] Wood draws on psychoanalysis to distinguish between basic repression, which is inescapable and part of the human development of self-control, and surplus repression, which is culturally specific.[21] In white heteronormative cultures, surplus repression entails the repression of various forms of sexual energy that do not serve to maintain the dominance of white patriarchal capitalism—the sexualities of women, children, queers, and racial, ethnic, and ideological others. It is those sexualities that are displaced onto monstrous signifiers in the horror film, and therefore seemingly disowned from the patriarchal self. Wood writes, "Otherness represents that which bourgeois ideology cannot recognize or accept but must deal with (as Barthes suggests in *Mythologies*) in one of two ways: either by rejecting and if possible annihilating it, or by rendering it safe and assimilating it, converting it as far as possible into a replica of itself."[22] Classical horror films (and the classical vampire myth) usually dramatize the first option: rejecting and destroying the monstrous other. The novel and film of *Twilight*, on the other hand, seem to work in the latter mode, rendering the other safe by attempting to assimilate it to dominant values. Indeed, these two options are directly schematized in *Twilight*. Its "bad" vampires—represented by the nomadic vampires Laurent, James, and Victoria—are the figures the text must eradicate in order to restore "normality." But *Twilight*'s more prominent

FIGURE 10.1. *Nomadic vampires versus the Cullens in* Twilight *(Summit Entertainment, 2008).*

vampires—the Cullen family—are "good" vampires because they work to assimilate to dominant notions of white heteronormativity.

The (classical) vampire in Western culture functions as a valuable metaphoric other, since he or she is a notably queer figure that transcends cultural boundaries of gender, sexuality, nation, race, and even mortality. At the center of the vampire's queerness is his or her capability to merge feeding with reproduction; a vampire can feed on a human victim while allowing that victim to become a new vampire. The penetration of the vampire's fangs into the victim alludes to sexual penetration, especially since it often takes place on the neck, an erotically charged zone of the body. The collapse between feeding and reproduction further enables a collapse between identity categories such as heterosexual/homosexual and masculine/feminine. Vampires are often "bisexual": the satisfaction of penetrating a victim occurs regardless of the victim's gender. Further, the vampire enacts the masculine/active role of penetration regardless of whether the vampire is a man or a woman, while simultaneously engaging in the more feminine role of reception—receiving fluid from the victim. Still other critics see the vampire as a metaphoric expression of interracial sexualities. Thus, in *Dracula*, the count is evil because he feeds on men and women and is a foreigner. He "is the ultimate social adulterer, whose purpose is nothing if it is not to turn good Englishwomen like Lucy and Mina away from their own kind and customs."[23]

In *Twilight*, the three nomadic vampires are similarly evil for the ways they prey on both men and women and refuse to conform to the heterosexual matrix. (In the film, an African American actor plays Laurent, thus adding race to the equation.) The Cullens, on the other hand, successfully repress their desire to feed on humans (male or female), are paired up in strict male/female binaries, and are associated with a blinding whiteness both through their visual design and their cultural attitudes. In this respect, the nomadic vampires are the terrifying others who cannot be assimilated into the white heteronormative community that is perversely embodied and exemplified by the repressed and repressing Cullen family. In *Twilight*, the Cullens have replaced Professor Van Helsing from the classical myth, becoming both (bad) vampire killers and the voice of white patriarchal capitalism.

THE VAMPIRE AND THE MORMON

The idea of a Mormon vampire is not entirely new. During the Victorian era, when Mormons were practicing polygamy in Utah settlements, popular fiction represented them as cultish and potentially monstrous, and this cultural demonization continued into the twentieth century. In his study of Mormon representation during this period, James V. D'Arc identifies similarities between the depiction of Mormon characters and the depiction of vampires, specifically Count Dracula, who can also be understood as polygamous because of his many brides. Anti-Mormon literature and film would present the Mormon male with a "sexual magnetism" not unlike Dracula's, which allowed him to prey on the "hypnotized passivity of his innocent victim."[24] While Dracula might use such hypnosis to suck the blood of his victims and thus enact a transfer of identity, the victims of Mormon males in these stories similarly experience a change of identity after sexual conquest and initiation into a polygamous harem. But in the end, just as symbols of Christianity can repel Dracula, so too can "'letting in the daylight' of knowledge and orthodox Christianity" triumph over the Mormon infidel.[25] Much of this Mormon-as-vampire imagery, at least in film, disappeared upon implementation of the Hollywood Production Code. It was during the ensuing decades that mainstream Mormonism also underwent a radical cultural shift, moving away from polygamy, no longer gathering in a single area called Zion, and no longer being quite so excluded from more conservative notions of American identity and Christian belief systems.

It was after this cultural shift that first-time author Stephenie Meyer reformed and reintroduced the Mormon vampire. Mormon iconography and allusions to Mormon culture appear throughout the *Twilight* texts. First, to learn the truth about Edward's identity, Bella turns to Native American history. For Mormons, the key to discovering the truth of Christ's ministry and Mormon identity can be located in the history of Native Americans, as found in the stories of *The Book of Mormon*. Additionally, the generational animosity between the Cullens and the local Indian tribe further echoes the framework of *The Book of Mormon*, wherein two civilizations separated by skin color (the Nephites and the Lamanites) are constantly at war with each other. Second, in the film version, after a night of searching vampire lore and history, Bella leaves the grounds of the schoolyard for the seclusion of a grove of trees, whereupon Edward follows her. There she recognizes his metaphysical identity and for the first time verbally confirms it to herself. Similarly, the foundational Mormon narrative includes a moment when the young Joseph Smith sought the seclusion of the "Sacred Grove" of trees, whereupon he was visited by God the Father and Jesus Christ, who revealed truth to him. Third, the language and tone surrounding Edward's rescue of Bella from getting hit by a sliding car echoes tales in Mormon legends about angels rescuing faithful members from danger. Specifically, Mormon culture circulates stories about the "three Nephites" who were blessed to remain alive until Christ's millennial return. Many Mormons believe they roam the land today, and stories that involve three strangers providing a benevolent action reinforce their mystery and appeal. (*Twilight*'s three nomadic vampires also suggest this symbolic system, albeit in an inverted way.) Fourth, another curious parallel with Christian/Mormon mythology occurs when Edward takes Bella into the mountains to reveal himself to her. In the Bible, God's prophets often enter the mountains to commune with the deity, as Moses did on Mount Sinai. *The Book of Mormon* foregrounds a similar setting when the prophet Nephi is "caught away in the Spirit of the Lord, yea, into an exceedingly high mountain" (1 Nephi 11:1).

Other Mormon metaphors in *Twilight* associate the Cullens with a religious identity. First, each member of the Cullen family appears to have a special talent, such as Edward's ability to read minds, father Carlisle's to heal, and daughter Alice's to see the future. These traits suggest what Mormons accept to be the spiritual gifts of discernment, healing, visions, and prophecy. Such spiritual gifts can be understood as special abilities that "are essentially endowments of power and authority [from God through the Holy Spirit] . . . sometimes with accompanying conditions that may appear to be supernatural."[26] Second, quite unlike classical vampires, the Cullens have a Christian cross in their home. Though Mormons typically shun representations of the cross in their homes and churches, it is important here as a mechanism for separating the Cullens from traditional assumptions about vampires.[27] The Cullens apparently do not fear Christ and perhaps might even revere or worship him. Additionally, their home itself comes across as a sacred space since the book describes the inside as being dominated by various shades of white, suggesting not only a heavenly atmosphere but also a Mormon temple, where white is a pronounced color in many rituals.[28] Finally, the Cullens live by a restricted diet, as do Mormons (called the Word of Wisdom). Mormon doctrine forbids the consumption of alcohol, tobacco, coffee, and tea; the Cullens restrict their diet by forsaking human blood, using the word "vegetarian" to describe their dietary lifestyle (apparently, they only feed on the blood of animals). Intriguingly, the movie includes a cameo appearance by Stephenie Meyer in which a waitress in a diner brings Meyer her order and says, "Here's your veggie plate." On one level it works as an in-joke for fans who recognize Meyer, but on another level it connects her Mormon identity with the "vegetarian" lifestyle of the Cullens. Likewise, Bella is also a vegetarian, which—along with her paleness and a name that recalls Bela Lugosi—foreshadows her eventual alignment with the Cullens.

Though vampiric, the Cullens present themselves as an ideal nuclear family. While they might be considered incestuously queer in the sense that foster siblings pair up as heterosexual couples, the texts work hard to defuse that reading, making the connection between said couples spiritual rather than sexual. Further, the texts repeatedly emphasize the gendered roles of the nuclear family, as when (motherly) Esme commands (daughterly) Rosalie to clean up a broken bowl, or when Carlisle asserts his fatherly role to convince the others to help Bella. And just as Mormons are commanded to set aside time each week to spend with family members, the Cullens (rather improbably) enjoy playing baseball—what Edward refers to as the "American pastime"—in the middle of a thunder storm (which they must do to cover the noise of their superhuman base hits). The baseball game specifically links the Cullens to mainstream American culture, particularly a nostalgic and conservative one. The Cullens also look like an ideal nuclear family when compared to the rest of the community. Bella's family is obviously "broken": her parents are divorced, her father is distant, and her mother treats her more as a peer than a parent. Bella is attracted to Edward, but also to his ideal forever family. The texts imply that she is drawn to their conservative family values precisely because her family lacks them.

The clannish and superior quality of the Cullens within the human society of Forks, Washington, also suggests that they are a group of chosen people, an allusion to the biblical separation between Israelites and Gentiles, which shapes Mormon identity. Mormons, too, perceive themselves to be a chosen people, literal descendants of Abraham and heirs to the biblical blessings God promised to Abraham's posterity.[29] This particular similarity is once again anchored in a blood metaphor, the idea of "believing blood": "The Mormon prophet himself is quoted as saying that some people have the blood of Abraham running in their veins while, in other instances, if individuals wished to become Latter-day Saints, their Gentile blood had to be replaced by the blood of Abraham. . . . The occasion of the transfer was the descent of the Holy Ghost which, according to LDS belief, follows baptism."[30] In *Twilight*, the Cullens appear to be a favored people, as they are more beautiful, more powerful, more intelligent, more wise, and more affluent than the rest of the community. It is their literal bloodline (anchored by the patriarch Carlisle, who has supposedly created them all) that infuses them with power and immortality.[31] Just as replacing the blood in a human changes his or her identity into a vampire and grants immortality, so, too, does baptism and receiving the Holy Ghost, in Mormon doctrine, literally change the blood of the convert into that of an Abrahamic descent and heir to eternal life. And if the Cullens are a chosen people who have successfully transcended death, then a Mormon perspective on their immortal condition might suggest that they are on a level with angels or gods. As one LDS leader "simplified Joseph's radical theology: 'As man now is, God once was. As God now is, man may become'"; divine and angelic beings are simply humans who have completed a mortal experience and now enjoy a more advanced condition.[32]

In *Twilight*, Edward confirms his advanced metaphysical identity to Bella when he steps into the sunlight and shimmers with a diamond-like quality. This moment significantly alters previous vampire mythology in two important ways. First, while *Twilight* maintains the mythic assumption that vampires must avoid sunlight, it changes the reason why. Instead of burning to death when exposed to the sun, as is dramatically depicted in any number of vampire movies, in *Twilight* sunlight exposes and draws attention to the vampire through his or her shimmering body. Thus, if vampires wish to conceal their identity among humans, as the Cullens do, then avoiding sunlight becomes imperative. Second, by using the glittering body as confirmation of vampiric identity, the usual moment of the vampire exposing his or her fangs to reveal identity is no longer necessary. The vampires in *Twilight* do not have fangs (which are associated with predatory violence and animal-like hungers); instead, they gloriously shimmer in heavenly sunlight. Angels have a prominent place in Mormon stories, as it was the angel Moroni who directed Joseph Smith to *The Book of Mormon*. Edward's angelic quality is also suggested when Bella first sits with him in science class and the stuffed owl behind him gives him the appearance of having white wings. Further, Edward's angelic quality (in conjunction with his chosen lineage and immortality) might even suggest that he is a god in the Mormon sense, in that he is in an advanced human state. But for Mormons, godhood and eternal progression require one further step: heterosexual coupling and the creation of a forever family; otherwise,

FIGURE 10.2. *The vampire as angel (*Twilight, *Summit Entertainment, 2008).*

those who do not marry "are appointed angels" to serve those who do marry and enjoy the blessings of godhood.[33] It is this need that the *Twilight* texts dramatize: whether Bella will become Edward's eternal vampire bride.

FOREVER FAMILY VALUES AND THE "EROTICS OF ABSTINENCE"

Twilight can thus be read as Edward's progression from an angelic (single) Mormon vampire toward a godlike (heterosexually coupled) Mormon vampire. At the beginning of the text, Edward resents his existence as a vampire and does not quite fit in with the rest of his family. He is the stereotypical problem "teenager," even though we eventually find out he is more than one hundred years old. (This fact introduces an element of intergenerational intimacy—some might even say pedophilia—that the texts work hard to contain.) Like many teenage boys—or at least, the myth of teenage boys—Edward has trouble controlling his desires, in this case his urge to drink the blood of humans. This trope directly links vampiric urges with sexual ones, figuring desire as violent and dangerous, yet another aspect of the texts' conservative views of sexuality. Edward's difference from his foster siblings is underlined during his first entrance into the school cafeteria. His four (hetero-paired) siblings are all wearing the color white, which is culturally associated with purity, goodness, and heaven, while Edward is wearing dark colors, which emphasize his inner conflict and perhaps exclusion from the highest reaches of heaven. When the five Cullens are seated at the table in the cafeteria, the two couples are noticeably paired together while Edward remains unmistakably single. As their white clothes convey, none of the other Cullens appear to be racked with guilt about their vampiric status or perceive themselves to be monstrous. They seem to have achieved more advanced states of maturity, wisdom, and self-control than Edward. It will only be through his pairing with Bella that he can finally be transformed and made complete in his Mormon identity and be given equal status with his siblings.

But that pairing is fraught with danger, supposedly because Edward's vampiric urges may cause him to harm Bella. After their first kiss in Bella's bedroom, Edward forcefully launches himself from her bed, smashing his back into the bedroom wall, a sequence of events that suggests both the power of his vampiric sexuality and the willpower needed to overcome it. It becomes Bella's responsibility to change her expectations for dating and intimacy and ensure that Edward's desire for her does not get out of control. This again echoes the cultural construction of gender and sexuality in some Mormon communities. As the Mormon writer Carol Lynn Pearson notes about her own adolescence, "Whether or not I would follow the Church's moral code was never questioned. . . . Keeping myself clean for my temple marriage made perfect sense to me. . . . But boys were weaker. We had always been taught that. Boys were more easily tempted, so it was up to girls to help them resist."[34] *Twilight* sounds the same note when Bella first visits the Cullens at their home: "newest vegetarian" Jasper looks at Bella with bloodlust until his sister/wife Alice reassures him, "It's OK, Jasper—you won't hurt her." Aside from its essentialism about gender, these beliefs further posit sexuality as a monstrous force that must be repressed. Edward describes his desire for Bella as his "own personal brand of heroin," again linking desire to an unhealthy physical addiction rather than a natural aspect of human existence. Similarly, the texts allow Edward to conclude that the sexual thoughts of teenage boys are "vile, repulsive things," as when he overhears other boys thinking about Bella.

In fact, Bella *is* willing to give in to Edward's desires—to die for love—as the opening voice-over of the film asserts: "I'd never given much thought to how I would die, but dying in the place of someone I love seems like a good way to go." (The emphasis on Bella dying for love also suggests that she does not care about her own welfare or sexual desire, as long as Edward's male desire is met.) Her willingness to sacrifice herself for Edward obviously echoes Christian mythology: Jesus Christ said that there was no greater love than for "a man to lay down his life for his friends" (John 15:13). But Christ is not the only one who sacrificed himself for humankind in Mormon scripture. Some Mormons interpret Eve's partaking of the forbidden fruit in the Garden of Eden as a deliberate sacrifice on her part to beget humanity.[35] Mormon scripture cites Eve's retrospection of her transgression with rejoicing that she could not have had children or obtained knowledge without it.[36] Perhaps unsurprisingly, allusions to Adam and Eve also permeate *Twilight*. Bella remarks in jest with her friends that she moved to Forks because she had been kicked out of Phoenix, suggesting the idea of expulsion from Eden—or as Bella explains it in the novel, "I exiled myself."[37] At another point in the story, Bella's class takes a field trip to a garden center, where they learn how compost will produce abundant crops. There are even several moments in the film when Bella is presented as handling a piece of "fruit," flirting with the idea of biting into that which is forbidden (in yet another homology of the vampire myth). When Bella drops an apple in the cafeteria, Edward skillfully catches it and offers it back to her. Bella also handles an apple during the first day of sunshine in Forks while searching for Edward. Perhaps the most notable moment of foodie foreplay occurs in the science classroom when Bella and Edward win an award for working together on an assignment. The award is a golden onion, and the assignment for which they were given this metonym is significant because it centered on their knowledge of cellular reproduction.

If the story of Adam and Eve is sexual and the vampire myth is sexual, where is the sex in *Twilight*? On one level, the atmosphere of teenage life depicted in the texts appears to capture the potent sexuality of adolescent life. When trying on prom dresses, one of Bella's friends draws attention to her breasts. In the cafeteria, Bella's friends discuss penis size, joking about "Speedo padding" and the "Olympic size" of a male student. Significantly, it is during this interchange that the Cullens first appear, almost literally representing the repression of sexuality. (Paradoxically, the scene also associates the Cullens with a sense of sexual potency and superiority, perhaps a historical holdover from the images of Mormon sexual magnetism in the early twentieth century.) Bella's friends and mother live in an environment where sexual interest and activity are assumed and enjoyed; her mother asks her about boyfriends and whether Bella is "being safe." But the novel also posits Bella's mother as "erratic" and "hare-brained," a divorced woman who has abandoned her sacred marriage vows.[38] It is the entrance of Edward and the rest of the Cullens into this environment that changes more open sexual dynamics into abstinence and repression, what at least one critic has identified as the texts' "erotics of abstinence," where everything is titillation that never comes to consummation.[39]

This potential for varying interpretations of *Twilight*'s eroticism—from the banal to the intense—accounts for the story's appeal to both young readers with little sexual comprehension as well as adults with wider sexual knowledge. There are moments in the novel where the language has the potential

FIGURE 10.3. *Bella and Edward, breathless (*Twilight, *Summit Entertainment, 2008).*

for multiple levels of interpretation, as when Bella narrates her own desire for Edward: "His white shirt was sleeveless, and he wore it unbuttoned, so that the smooth white skin of his throat flowed uninterrupted over the marble contours of his chest, his perfect musculature no longer merely hinted at behind concealing clothes. He was too perfect, I realized with a piercing stab of despair. There was no way this godlike creature could be meant for me."[40] This slow, very slow, progression of erotic desire magnifies each step in anticipation for the moment of sexual connection (which must be saved for after marriage, when Bella becomes part of Edward's forever family). Under the erotics of abstinence, each new part of the body and each new moment of physical contact, however minimal, prolong the sexual and dramatic curiosity of the reader and viewer. But this strategy also risks becoming overdue and uninteresting, as some critics of the novel have made clear—not much happens for the bulk of the book except for Bella's prolonged mooning over Edward.

As we have been arguing, and true to its roots in gothic literature, *Twilight* displaces its sexuality onto vampiric signifiers.[41] One of the sequences most pregnant with displaced sexuality is Edward's magical run through the forest with Bella on his back. Edward pulls Bella onto his body, she wraps her legs around his waist, the music swells, and they breathe heavily in the exhilaration of the moment. The wording of the novel is even more sexually suggestive: "He threw me across his back as he had before, and I could see the extra effort it took for him to be as gentle as he was. I locked my legs around his waist and secured my arms in a choke hold around his neck. . . . And I could hardly tell we were moving. I could feel him gliding along beneath me, but he could have been strolling down the sidewalk, the movement was so smooth."[42] Additionally, Bella's entrance into the woods not only echoes imagery of Joseph Smith in the Sacred Grove, it also suggests an entrance into the wild, a metaphoric id space separated from the constraints of cultural expectations. This space appropriately prepares her for the sexually displaced run through the forest. The scene in the meadow also displaces sexuality, as Bella slowly lays her body on the grass in a medium close-up. The music and framing suggest that she is submitting herself to Edward, yet he enters the frame to lie next to her without touching her. A reading of this scene as displaced sexual intercourse between Bella and Edward is further supported when they return to the school and the other students notice something new and curiously different about the couple. Like a teenage boy announcing his conquest, Edward chooses to revel in the attention by placing his arm around Bella. But his conquest has been chastely spiritual, neither sexual nor vampiric.

Since the Cullens successfully repress their vampiric desires and pair together in eternal male-female spiritual bonds, *Twilight*'s true others can be found in the nomadic vampires who have no desire for assimilation, repression, coming together as a family unit, or exclusive relationships. Whereas much of the suspense of the first part of *Twilight* is fueled by Bella's learning about the Cullens, once she learns of them, trusts them, and is trusted by them, the story shifts to the threat posed to Bella by James, Laurent, and Victoria. The film depicts James and Victoria as monstrous vampires who take pleasure in the hunt for and consumption of humans; they also lack respect for the boundaries and interests of other vampires, including the Cullens. The pleasures James and Victoria find in the hunt easily translate into sexual pleasures, making them apt foils for the Cullens' Mormon worldview of eternal gender roles, abstinence before marriage, and monogamous heterosexual couplings. James himself is among the film's most overtly sexualized characters—he wears tight jeans, a ponytail, a scruffy beard, and is bare-chested in his initial appearance. James, Victoria, and Laurent are not divine or angelic vampires, as are the Cullens; they inhabit an opposing realm of (more traditional) sexualized, demonic vampires, and this is where the text locates its cosmic battle between good and evil.

The vampire James becomes the most dangerous of all, partly because he sees Bella as a desirable "snack," but also because he uses Bella as bait in a sort of extended homosocial cat-and-mouse game with Edward. This James-Bella-Edward homoerotic triangle is not that different from similar formulations in gothic literature and classical Hollywood horror films.[43] The woman in such a structure is used both to mask and facilitate the desire between the men, in this case James's desire for Edward, which is hinted at when he stares provocatively at Edward at the baseball game even before realizing that Bella is human. This triangulation continues as James kidnaps Bella and imprisons her at the dance studio, where he sets up a video system to record his actions so that Edward might watch. "Edward has nothing to do with this!" Bella exclaims, although she is wrong. Rather than simply killing Bella, James sadistically uses her to taunt and inflame Edward, the real object of his desire. "Tell Edward how much it hurts," James commands while crushing Bella's leg and shoving the camera in her face. To James's great satisfaction, Edward does arrive, whereupon James penetrates Bella's flesh with his teeth while staring at Edward. The two vampires fight with much grunting, swirling, grimacing, and groaning until Edward's jealousy and rage lead him to bite into James's flesh, perhaps the displaced sexual response James has had in mind all along.

But the moment does not last long for James, because Carlisle arrives to stop Edward from feeding on his victim. The rest of the siblings rip James apart, a symbolic castration of this queer character. Carlisle's statement to Edward, "Son . . . remember who you are," seems odd at this particular moment. Were Edward simply defending Bella from James, his work as protector would appear to comply with eternal notions of masculinity and require nothing to remember. But this statement circulates almost as a cliché between parents and teenagers in Mormon cultures, as it is used to emphasize religious identity in order to prevent sinful behavior. Carlisle sees Edward's homoerotic activity with James as transgressive or outside his conservative expectations; thus, after Edward does remember his assimilated identity, he returns to his exclusive heterosexual partner, Bella, to suck *her* blood. He must do so to retrieve the "venom" injected into her bloodstream by James. This is another trope that *Twilight* alters from classical vampire mythology. Rather than the creation of a new vampire occurring via an exchange of blood (e.g., as between Count Dracula and Mina Harker), *Twilight* posits that one becomes a vampire because of "venom," a term that seems to allude to the snake that tempted Eve in the Garden of Eden. Edward must suck James's venom out of Bella while finding the will not to drain her altogether (and thus kill her). Torn between consummating his lust and repressing it, Edward—urged on by the patriarch Carlisle—removes James's venom but then stops himself from finishing off Bella. Whether approaching "real" sex or its vampiric displacement, Meyer's and Hardwicke's Mormon vampires know when to stop.

CONCLUSION

Just as Bella searches the Internet and discovers vampires in a variety of cultures and eras, so, too, has the cinematic vampire been continually reinvented in different times and contexts. In the aftermath of 9/11, as many people seek solace within traditional or fundamentalist religions, perhaps it is not surprising that the Mormon vampire has made his millennial debut. (Intriguingly, *Twilight* might be seen as part of a post-9/11 moment of Mormon chic, alongside the HBO serial *Big Love* [Mark V. Olsen and Will Scheffer, 2006–2011]; the prominence of Mormon personalities in reality television; and the appearance of the first serious Mormon candidate for president of the United Sates, Mitt Romney.) Although it might be an overstatement to suggest that the texts proselytize for Mormonism, both versions of *Twilight* do interweave vampire mythology and Mormon doctrine into texts that present certain characteristics of Mormon religious identity—such as the erotics of abstinence and forever families—in a favorable, supernatural, even heavenly light. This could be good news for an institution that expends a great deal of its resources on a missionary workforce to introduce its doctrines to the world. On the other hand, those same characteristics of Mormon culture continue to be critiqued for the ways in which they uphold dominant notions of white heteronormativity, marginalizing and even demonizing everyone else—queers, people of color, women, and children. One should not forget that the Mormon Church has a long history of overt-to-covert racism and has forcefully opposed equal-rights legislation for women and queers.[44] *Twilight*'s Mormon vampires might be perceived as the other by some, but they are others who are rendered safe, assimilating within the dominant repressed culture and capable of withstanding the true others—those who challenge forever family values and resist heteronormative assumptions about gender and sexuality.

Ultimately, *Twilight* concludes with the return to a repressed culture and an abstinent existence—no sex and no bloodsucking. Bella's girlfriends, who had previously been part of an environment of sexual dialogue and intrigue, are now settled in exclusive relationships with boys. Bella and Edward are also paired together in heteronormative bliss as they participate in one socially acceptable outlet for repressed sexual desire: dancing at the prom. Indeed, Mormons are big on dancing, or at least they used to be. The LDS scholar Terryl Givens cites one commentator on nineteenth-century Mormon culture as saying, "The Mormons love dancing. . . . Their children *ought* to learn to read, but they *must* learn to dance."[45] This love of dancing could be the product of a culture that values kinship and sociality, or one that needs a social outlet to displace sexual energy. Bella and Edward appear content in such an environment, wherein Bella climactically repeats the forever family principle: "I dream about being with you forever." Perhaps she forgot Rosalie's concern from earlier in the story, which also applies to families that last forever: "The entire family will be implicated if this ends badly!" According to the horror formula, things end badly only for those who do not conform to the surplus repression in a heteronormative culture, so as long as Bella conforms to the assumptions of the Mormon vampires and their forever family values, she should be fine.

NOTES

1. Lev Grossman, "Stephenie Meyer: A New J. K. Rowling?," *Time*, April 24, 2008, http://www.time.com/time/magazine/article/0,9171,1734838,00.html.

2. Thomas S. Monson, "First Presidency Message: The Prayer of Faith," *Ensign*, August 1995, 2. While there are many religious groups that can trace their origins to Joseph Smith and his 1830 publication of *The Book of Mormon*, the largest and most prominent of these groups is the Church of Jesus Christ of Latter-day Saints, now based in Salt Lake City, Utah. The use of the terms "Mormon" and "Mormonism" in this essay is intended to refer to active members of this church along with its body of doctrines and cultural influence.

3. Gordon B. Hinckley, "Standing Strong against the Wiles of the World," *Ensign*, November 1995, 100.

4. The term "Christian" is used here in a broad sense to describe various religious groups, including the Church of Jesus Christ of Latter-day Saints, that claim to follow the teachings of Jesus Christ as found in the New Testament, and that value conservative notions of sex and gender. While many Christian groups would oppose the inclusion of Mormons and their doctrine under the "Christian" label, the broad use of the term here focuses not on the theological differences between Christians and Mormons, but rather on the cultural similarities that have enabled them to function as allies in socially conservative movements.

5. Harold Bloom, *The American Religion: The Emergence of the Post-Christian Nation* (New York: Simon & Schuster, 1992), 29.

6. Barry A. Kosmin and Ariela Keysar, "American Religious Identification Survey (ARIS 2008): Summary Report" (Trinity College, Hartford, CT, March 2009), http://www.americanreligionsurvey-aris.org/reports/ARIS_Report_2008.pdf.

7. Louis Althusser, "Ideology and Ideological State Apparatuses," in *Lenin and Philosophy, and Other Essays*, trans. Ben Brewster (New York: Monthly Review Press, 2001), 85–126.

8. Michael Warner, "Tongues Untied: Memoirs of a Pentecostal Boyhood," in *Curiouser: On the Queerness of Children*, ed. Steven Bruhm and Natasha Hurley (Minneapolis: University of Minnesota Press, 2004), 222.

9. Rose Green, review of *Twilight*, by Stephenie Meyer, Association for Mormon Letters, December 1, 2005, http://www.aml-online.org/Reviews/Review.aspx?id=3849.

10. William Morris, "Interview: *Twilight* Author Stephanie [*sic*] Meyer," *A Motley Vision: Mormon Arts and Culture*, October 26, 2005, http://www.motleyvision.org/2005/interview-twilight-author-stephanie-meyer/.

11. Hawkgrrrl, "*Twilight* and 'The Great Mormon Novel,'" *Mormon Matters*, November 24, 2008, http://mormonmatters.org/2008/11/24/twilight-and-the-great-mormon-novel/.

12. Bruce F. Webster, "Finally: Some Evangelical Criticism of *Twilight*," *Adventures*

in Mormonism, January 23, 2009, http://adventures-in-mormonism.com/2009/01/23/finally-some-evangelical-criticism-of-twilight/.

13. Jules Zanger, "Metaphor into Metonymy: The Vampire Next Door," in *Blood Read: The Vampire as Metaphor in Contemporary Culture*, ed. Joan Gordon and Veronica Hollinger (Philadelphia: University of Pennsylvania Press, 1997), 17–26.

14. John Allen Stevenson, "A Vampire in the Mirror: The Sexuality of Dracula," *PMLA* 103 (March 1988): 144.

15. James B. Twitchell, *Dreadful Pleasures: An Anatomy of Modern Horror* (New York: Oxford University Press, 1985), 108.

16. Christopher Herbert, "Vampire Religion," *Representations* 79 (Summer 2002): 116.

17. Ibid.

18. George E. Haggerty, *Queer Gothic* (Urbana: University of Illinois Press, 2006), 2.

19. Grossman, "Stephenie Meyer."

20. Interestingly, Meyer is open with the public that she developed the idea for *Twilight* from a dream she had. James Blasingame, "Books for Adolescents: *Twilight*, by Stephenie Meyer," *Journal of Adolescent & Adult Literacy* 49 (April 2006): 631. Not only are dreams the forum where psychoanalysts believe they can access the repressed unconscious, but also, Wood observes, "according to the testimony of their creators, all three of the archetypal works to which virtually all our horror literature and cinema can be traced back—*Frankenstein* (1818), *Dr. Jekyll and Mr. Hyde* (1886), and *Dracula* itself—had their origins in nightmares. . . . The monstrous figures from our dreams are our images of our repressed selves . . . our culture's sexual dreads." "Burying the Undead: The Use and Obsolescence of Count Dracula," in *The Dread of Difference: Gender and the Horror Film*, ed. Barry Keith Grant (Austin: University of Texas Press, 1996), 369.

21. Robin Wood, *Hollywood from Vietnam to Reagan . . . and Beyond*, rev. and exp. ed. (New York: Columbia University Press, 2008), 70–71.

22. Ibid., 65–66.

23. Stevenson, "Vampire in the Mirror," 140.

24. Craig L. Foster, quoted in James V. D'Arc, "The Mormon as Vampire: A Comparative Study of Winifred Graham's *The Love Story of a Mormon*, the Film *Trapped by Mormons*, and Bram Stoker's *Dracula*," *Brigham Young University Studies* 46, no. 2 (2007): 177.

25. D'Arc, "Mormon as Vampire," 179.

26. James E. Talmage, *The Articles of Faith* (Salt Lake City: Deseret, 1990), 197.

27. Terryl L. Givens, *People of Paradox: A History of Mormon Culture* (Oxford: Oxford University Press, 2007), 114.

28. Stephenie Meyer, *Twilight* (New York: Little, Brown, 2008), 322.

29. Givens, *People of Paradox*, 56.

30. Jan Shipps, "From Peoplehood to Church Membership: Mormonism's Trajectory since World War II," *Church History* 76 (June 2007): 255.

31. Edward explains in the novel that no one knows who transformed Alice into a vampire, and she has no memory of her human life; the movie adaptation ignores this plot point. Nevertheless, describing the creation of the Cullen family as a male-only

enterprise further alludes to the divine status of Carlisle in the sense that God the Father needed no woman to create Adam and Eve in the Old Testament.

32. Givens, *People of Paradox*, 42.

33. *The Doctrine and Covenants of the Church of Jesus Christ of Latter-day Saints* (Salt Lake City: Church of Jesus Christ of Latter-day Saints, 1981), 132:16.

34. Carol Lynn Pearson, *Good-Bye, I Love You* (Springville, UT: CFI, 2006), 23–24.

35. Margaret Toscano and Paul Toscano, *Strangers in Paradox: Explorations in Mormon Theology* (Salt Lake City: Signature Books, 1990), 159.

36. *The Pearl of Great Price* (Salt Lake City: Church of Jesus Christ of Latter-day Saints, 1981), Moses 5:11.

37. Meyer, *Twilight*, 4.

38. Ibid.

39. Grossman, "Stephenie Meyer."

40. Meyer, *Twilight*, 256.

41. There is another amusing instance of sexual displacement, not having to do with vampires, that occurs during the beach scene. As the Native American Jacob Black relates the story of his tribe's previous encounters with the Cullens, a teenage boy wielding a dead eel (or slimy rope—it is hard to see in the long shot) chases after a shrieking girl. Regardless of whether this background action was intentional on the part of the director, it hardly seems out of place in a text filled with so much delayed and displaced sexual desire.

42. Meyer, *Twilight*, 363–364.

43. See Harry M. Benshoff, *Monsters in the Closet: Homosexuality and the Horror Film* (Manchester, UK: Manchester University Press, 1997); and Eve Kosofsky Sedgwick, *Between Men: English Literature and Male Homosocial Desire* (New York: Columbia University Press, 1985).

44. For nearly 150 years after the establishment of the LDS Church, members throughout the world with black African ancestry were banned from ordination to the priesthood, the governing authority of the institution. These members were also excluded from participating in many temple rituals. Race-based policies such as these originated from Mormon scriptures, including *The Book of Mormon* and *The Pearl of Great Price*, which described dark skin tones as signs of a cursed bloodline. Early church presidents, including Brigham Young, violently condemned mixed-race marriages. These racial bans ended for the most part in the late 1970s. But women in general continue to be denied ordination to the priesthood, which prevents them from many positions of leadership. Church leaders value traditional ideas about gender and sexuality, and leaders have a history of mobilizing members to influence political causes that address these issues, from defeating the Equal Rights Amendment in 1982 to supporting California's Proposition 8 in 2008, which overturned the state's Supreme Court ruling to legalize same-sex marriage.

45. Quoted in Givens, *People of Paradox*, 137.

CHAPTER ELEVEN

Assimilation and the Queer Monster

SAM J. MILLER

Monsters are riddles to be solved. Horror movie heroes spend most of their time hunting down the answer to the question Ripley asks the evil robot in *Alien* (Ridley Scott, 1979): "How do we kill it?" This search can take up most of the movie, since horror film heroes are always dealing with limited re-sources. *I can't just call the cops, because my cell phone gets no reception way out here. I can't just call the cops, because the cops are in cahoots with the cannibalistic hill folk. I can't just shoot the monster, because bullets don't kill it.* And even when you've got a platoon of heavily armed marines on your side, it's no easy matter to kill a monster. You've got to find its weak spot.

In the same way, patriarchal power is constantly on the lookout for ways to neutralize new threats. "How do we kill it?" asks big business and white supremacy, when faced with organized labor or the Black Power movement or environmental activism. Every one of these bogeymen is a riddle to be solved, a monster to be killed. Organized labor's role as a major political force for social justice was curtailed by a combination of sustained corporate attacks and the decline of the most heavily unionized industries. For the Black Power movement, the status quo relied on the imprisonment or the outright assas-sination of key figures. And the American response to the terrorist attacks of September 11, 2001, is another example of the way that authority exploits threats to expand and intensify its own operations. Despite the evidence that neoliberal U.S. interventions — such as the funding and arming of the Afghan mujahideen against the Soviets — had ultimately set the stage for the attacks, the events of the day were used as justification for the expansion of those same neoliberal principles.

The threat caused by queer liberation activists, on the other hand, was nullified through assimilation. Scholarship such as Harry M. Benshoff's *Monsters in the Closet* has highlighted the deep relevance of the horror film

FIGURE 11.1. *Norman Bates as Mother (*Psycho, *Paramount, 1960).*

to queer audiences and queer scholars.[1] Charting the predominance of queer artists in behind-the-scenes Hollywood, from directors like James Whale to screenwriters like Arthur Laurents, reveals an elaborate history of hidden narratives and subversive messaging lurking in some of the most iconic of American films. Since queer desire was implicitly coded as monstrous in patriarchal cinematic convention — and explicitly under the Hays Code — filmmakers like Alfred Hitchcock could invoke queerness to deepen a character's monstrosity (without, of course, ever saying so), as seen in the characters of Mrs. Danvers in *Rebecca* (1940), Norman Bates in *Psycho* (1960), or all three of the main characters in *Rope* (1948). David Skal, among others, has studied the connections between the rise of HIV/AIDS and the cinematic resurgence of the vampire.[2]

Much of this scholarship is celebratory. For myself and many other LGBT viewers, the queer monster not only provides an opportunity to identify with someone on-screen, it also allows us to vicariously live out our rage against a social order that oppresses us. Which one of us doesn't feel a thrill of horrified euphoria when Norman Bates comes charging into the basement room, knife held high, wearing a wig and a dress? Who doesn't dream, like the queer psychopath in *The Old Dark House* (James Whale, 1932), of burning the whole building down?

But there are no more queer monsters. The post-9/11 horror renaissance has filled our multiplexes with vampires and werewolves and zombies and killer aliens again, but the queer monster has been killed off with an efficiency and finality that the heroes of many a monster franchise would envy. Why have these threats to the sexual and social order fled from movie screens? It is my contention in this essay that the death of the queer monster provides an analogy for the normalization of queer identity, at the same time as queer activism and queer culture evolved from militant movements against fundamentalism and ignorance into assimilation-minded and professionalized forums for gaining access to two of patriarchy's most cherished institutions: marriage and the military. The backdrop of 9/11, and the subsequent resurgences of oppression and horror movies, provides an additional level of narrativity, as it also allows us to observe the means by which power neutralizes difference.

For the queer subspecies of the American horror film, 1980's *Cruising* (William Friedkin) represents the beginning of the end. With its lurid exploration of a miserable gay underworld, and its murderous gay psychopath, the film casts aside all the subtlety and artfulness that filmmakers had historically used to hint at homosexuality and equate it with monstrosity. Yet *Cruising* also represents the first time the queer community fought back against a movie's homophobic assumptions. With filming taking place in Greenwich Village, protests of *Cruising* disrupted shooting repeatedly, which brought the production around 60 percent over budget and ultimately (and paradoxically, perhaps) empowered the gay community. As Alexander Wilson wrote in 1981, "The riots themselves demonstrate our ability to organize mass militant action to challenge hegemonic social and sexual relations."[3]

Cruising did not change everything overnight, but American films after 1980 are nowhere near as problematic in their representation of the queer community. Invisibility, tokenism, and stereotypes (the "Magical Negro," the Bravely Suffering, Chaste AIDS Patient) have proved far more sustainable and effective strategies than hate speech in preventing real dialogue and analysis concerning race and gender oppression in contemporary American society. By this same mechanism, the queer figure in horror films shrank almost into invisibility, surfacing only rarely, usually as the harmless friend who tends to get murdered in the early stages of the film (e.g., *Warlock* [Steve Miner, 1989], *Single White Female* [Barbet Schroeder, 1992]).

Eleven years later, another A-list horror/thriller would feature a sexually twisted monster. "Buffalo Bill," the serial-killer kidnapper at the heart of *The Silence of the Lambs* (Jonathan Demme, 1991), is ostensibly a transgender man who wishes to become a woman but is too disturbed to qualify for sex-reassignment surgery, and as a consequence must resort to skinning overweight women and making clothing out of their skin. The character of Buffalo

FIGURE 11.2. *Buffalo Bill as queer monster (*The Silence of the Lambs, *Orion Pictures, 1991).*

Bill follows old conventions of the queer psychopath whose deviant sexuality (and its attendant violence) derives from childhood trauma—he was abandoned by an alcoholic mother, raised in foster care, and murdered his grandparents at the age of twelve. In addition, the film betrays a familiar failure to grasp the realities of the transgender experience, with the male who wishes to divest himself of phallic privilege reduced to stark monstrosity.

The Silence of the Lambs, and the queer response to it, shows the extent to which the LGBT community had transformed. There were no notable street protests or attempts to sabotage production. GLAAD (the Gay and Lesbian Alliance Against Defamation) issued a press release ("What makes this film's extremely negative portrayal so damaging . . . is that the film industry has shown itself . . . incapable of depicting positive gay or lesbian characters"),[4] and many gay rights groups called for a boycott. For the first time, representatives of the LGBT community made an argument for normalization based not on any political analysis or critique of oppression, but rather on the LGBT community's function as consumers.

This strategy seems to have been far more successful. It would be the last time, to date, that such an explicitly queer monster would haunt a horror movie—with the possible exception of *Basic Instinct* (Paul Verhoeven, 1992), which followed so closely on *The Silence of the Lambs* that its script and shooting schedule had probably been finalized when the public outcry around Buffalo Bill began.[5] Some of the "credit" for this development might be left at

GLAAD's doorstep, although it is also important to look at the cumulative effect of the complex struggle for HIV/AIDS justice that had pushed gay people and their anger into every American home. The boycott of *The Silence of the Lambs* represented a massive tactical shift from the ACT UP (AIDS Coalition to Unleash Power) protests, but it would never have had any impact without the hard, long, bloody street fighting of the AIDS activists.

The "gay struggle for equal rights" is, at best, an oversimplification. At worst, it's outright revisionism. The attempt to impose a retroactive narrative of gays fighting for acceptance in mainstream society overlooks the multitude of distinct voices and demands that characterized the queer community well into the 1990s, as well as its connections to the Black Power movement and other struggles by marginalized communities to radically restructure the societies that oppress them. The instrumental Gay Liberation Front (GLF) stated, in its 1971 introductory manifesto, "We are a revolutionary group of men and women formed with the realization that complete sexual liberation for all people cannot come about unless existing social institutions are abolished." "It's not a question of getting our piece of the pie," said GLF. "The pie is rotten."[6]

In the 1980s, the AIDS crisis—and the response to it by the government and the media—served as the catalyst for a whole new world of queer anger and resistance in art, literature, and film. David Wojnarowicz used government-funded art exhibits to talk about his desire to "douse [Senator Jesse] Helms with a bucket of gasoline and set his putrid ass on fire"; he also referred to Catholic Cardinal O'Connor as a "fat cannibal from that house of walking swastikas up on Fifth Avenue."[7] ACT UP New York famously disrupted services in St. Patrick's Cathedral. And in the early 1990s, filmmakers like Derek Jarman, Todd Haynes, and Gregg Araki ushered in the vibrant and exciting "new queer cinema" movement. These films, targeted at queer audiences and taking for granted a fundamental rage against the status quo, were remarkable for their in-your-face flouting of conventional morality.

Yet by the mid-1990s the new queer cinema had succumbed to "commodification and assimilation," according to the *Village Voice* critic B. Ruby Rich (who had coined the term in the first place).[8] The 1990s also saw the landscape of queer activism move away from the radical activist model. Magazines like the *Advocate* sold themselves to advertisers based on a pars pro toto argument—that educated, upper-middle-class professionals represented the entire gay community—and grew to mainstream prominence in the process. GLAAD positioned itself as the arbiter of gay opposition and approval, and many other 501(c)(3) "advocacy" organizations sprouted up to fight for gay access to the most emblematic sites of white power and entitlement: corporate boardrooms, government agencies, and prime-time television shows. This branch of the nonprofit-industrial complex, with its reliance on foundation and corporate funding and the saber-rattling press releases favored by the Catholic League, had no need of democratic participation or direct action. GLAAD was perfectly happy with the kind of pie that patriarchy offered. They just wanted their piece.

A look at the most commonly cited indicators of gay "acceptance" into mainstream popular culture—and, the implication goes, into real-world tolerance—exposes the fraud that the gay community has arrived at the threshold of full equality: television shows like *Ellen* (Carol Black, Neal Marlens, and David S. Rosenthal, 1994–1998), *Will & Grace* (David Kohan and Max Mutchnick, 1998–2006), and *Queer Eye for the Straight Guy* (David Collins, 2003–2007); and movies like *Philadelphia* (Jonathan Demme, 1993) and *Brokeback Mountain* (Ang Lee, 2005). All focused on white queers, almost exclusively male, in whom difference has either been completely eradicated or is grounded in the sort of exaggerated material privilege that conforms to an old and comfortable understanding of the effete aesthete (as in *Queer Eye's* upscale tastemakers). Queer youth of color do not see themselves in *Will & Grace*, particularly if they are homeless, as they are disproportionately likely to be.

Contrary to predictions that came in the weeks following the terrorist attacks, 9/11 has reinvigorated the horror film. Aside from the familiar folklore-derived monsters (vampires, werewolves, zombies), several distinct trends dominate post-9/11 horror. Marauding giant monsters are back (*Cloverfield* [Matt Reeves, 2008], *The Host* [Bong Joon-ho, 2006]), as are home-invasion films (*The Strangers* [Bryan Bertino, 2008], *Them* [David Moreau and Xavier Palud, 2006], *High Tension* [Alexandre Aja, 2003], *Funny Games* [Michael Haneke, 2007]). We get remakes galore, most of them focusing on xenophobia and revenge—as in *The Hills Have Eyes* (Alexandre Aja, 2006), *The Texas Chainsaw Massacre* (Marcus Nispel, 2003), and *The Last House on the Left* (Dennis Iliadis, 2009)—where wholesome, handsome young people are attacked by savage isolated lunatics, killed off in horrible ways, and those who survive then fight back and inflict some satisfactory collateral damage. New genres have cropped up, too, such as "torture porn," like the *Hostel* and *Saw* series, in which graphic and unflinching representations of torture constitute the "meat" of the film.

How do queer characters fit into the current horror movie explosion? The short answer is, they don't. In *Jeepers Creepers II* (Victor Salva, 2003), one of the imperiled high-school kids is gay, and he gets to be a tiny bit smarter than the rest of them, right up until he gets killed. The film *2001 Maniacs*

(Tim Sullivan, 2005) features a bisexual character who actually gets to have sex with a guy before he gets strapped down and anally speared to death. Of course, the fact that gay characters always get killed is not itself a very meaningful point, since everybody tends to die in horror movies.[9]

Yet the language and iconography of the queer monster is alive and well, which is explored in great detail in Eli Roth's *Hostel* (2005). This film crystallized the current trend of horror films structured around explicit depictions of bodily harm inflicted on attractive young people; in fact, it was in a review of this film that the term "torture porn" was first used.[10] *Hostel* draws a clear line of descent from the queer monsters exemplified in *Psycho* and *The Old Dark House*—human men whose deviant desires make them monstrous—to the monsters of torture porn. The villains in movies like *Saw* (James Wan, 2004) and *Turistas* (John Stockwell, 2006) are men with desires so socially proscribed that they can only be accessed through money. But now, instead of furtive extramarital intercourse or gay affairs, sexual release is achieved by subjecting starlets to prolonged and violent death. Normalized gay desire is no longer frightening.

The analogy between these torture aficionados and the queer monster—and, by extension, closeted gay men in general—is made explicit in the *Hostel* character referred to as the "Dutch Businessman." When Josh, one of our handsome young male heroes, meets him on a train, the businessman expresses a leering interest in him, putting his hand on the boy's leg and asking, "What is your nature?," all of which the audience interprets as conventional gay sexual desire. "I had a family because it was important to me," the businessman says. "But you do what you need to do"—familiar rhetoric from closeted gay men who pursue random sexual encounters with strangers. Josh is coded as sexually confused; when the two buddies bring women back to their hotel room, his attention is divided between his friend's backside and the woman he's with. But, as we find out when we get to the titular hostel, the Dutch businessman's dangerous desire is not queer at all. His love that dare not speak its name is a love of torture, violence, and murder. He is willing to pay lots of money to get Josh alone, but only so he can inflict unthinkable pain on him. So, while *Hostel* does revive the conventional tropes of gay desire and the queer monster, it does so only to catch the audience in its own assumptions and then introduce something far more monstrous.

This plotline offers another look at why the queer monster got killed off: queerness just isn't scary anymore. Assimilation has taken us a long way from *The Children's Hour* (William Wyler, 1961—the year after *Psycho*), when the whisper of homosexuality could destroy lives and careers. So, if a horror movie really wants to shock us, the closeted queer just isn't going to get the job done.

We need stronger stuff, like a closeted torture-phile. Or maybe a pedophile, like in 2008's *Doubt* (John Patrick Shanley), a recapitulation of the same story as *The Children's Hour*.

The dominant horror discourse of the 1980s and 1990s focuses on home-grown horror—often the threats posed by women and the working class—and their reactionary politics are indicative of "the era of hysterical masculinity that countered the radical feminism of the 1970s."[11] Of course, there are many exceptions, but the era's biggest horror successes focus on banal and local monsters, derived from our everyday American surroundings—as in the *A Nightmare on Elm Street* (Wes Craven, 1984), *Friday the 13th* (Sean Cunningham, 1980), and *Halloween* (John Carpenter, 1978) franchises, whose monsters are, respectively, a janitor, the son of a cook, and a disturbed, privileged, suburban white boy. Horror films of the pre-9/11 period are about hegemony threatened and privilege imperiled. Being haunted, being afraid, becomes its own sort of privilege: "Fear [is] somehow endowed with the status of an inalienable right or property, conferring dignity or legitimacy to the individuals who experience it."[12] In addition, these films speak from the perspective of a consumer culture attempting to destroy its increasingly marginalized discontents: "The genre of the horror film presents owning a house in particular as a form of proprietorship which automatically entitles the buyer to the experience of fear, as if fear itself were a commodity included with the total package."[13]

As one facet of a collective response to profound national trauma, the post-9/11 horror film is obsessed with neutralizing difference. Instead of internal threats, filmmakers focus on those posed by foreign or corrupting influences. Handsome American travelers venture into eastern European or Latin American backwaters and are met with astonishing torture-porn violence. Giant monsters crawl out of the ocean to stomp New York City à la Japanese *kaiju*. Asian horror films are transplanted to the Pacific Northwest or New York City, their protagonists replaced by white Americans.

This shift away from our own racial, economic, and sexual diversity being a source of monstrosity has only accelerated the death of the queer monster. While this might not exactly constitute a clear causal connection between 9/11 and that death, it does help to show how thoroughly the "queer monster"—the mythological "radical homosexual agenda," an understanding of queer identity as an assault on racist-patriarchal society—has been neutralized. As an example, many aspects of the unconstitutional and repressive agenda pushed through by the executive branch in the aftermath of 9/11 explicitly targeted immigrants of color or, in the case of increased regulation and control of public space, disproportionately affected homeless people (whose entire lives are lived in public space). While both of these communities include LGBT people, the mainstream queer advocacy groups mounted no significant resistance to these policies—nor would such action even have made sense within the scope of their work. A complete shake-up of the whole social order is no longer desirable. The pie isn't rotten anymore—the pie is just fine, as long as I can get my slice. In times of trouble, power will target people who are perceived to be unable to fight back. Those who cannot "pass," or hide their otherness, will be the ones who suffer. And the ones who *can* pass, who have clawed their way into mainstream acceptance or bought their way into the country club, are no longer willing to fight in solidarity with those who can't. The "success" of gay assimilation can be measured by the extent to which the gay community's critique of a patriarchal status quo has evaporated. The queer voice against racism and xenophobia has been silent for a long time, and this is only very slowly being reclaimed by grassroots organizing within low-income queer communities of color.

The simplistic response to critiques of assimilation is that gays and lesbians have achieved the equality they fought for, and therefore they have no further need of militancy or activism. "We've come so far" is the perspective of groups like GLAAD. The situation is no longer the same. Yet assimilation has primarily benefited white people who conform to a mainstream understanding of masculinity or femininity. Massive numbers of queer youth of color are homeless. Trans people of color are routinely the targets of violent attacks. These realities rarely flicker on the radar of the predominately white and male decision makers at the nonprofit gay groups that present themselves as the voice of the "LGBT community." A brutal illustration of this disconnect was provided in the wake of the recent passage of Proposition 8, with many gays blaming African American voters (70 percent of whom, according to initial reports that were later proved false, voted for the referendum banning gay marriage).[14]

In speaking about the death of the queer monster, I don't mean to discount the few thriving strains of truly independent gay cinema, such as the gay slasher flick *HellBent* (Paul Etheredge, 2004). Another example is Bruce LaBruce's *Otto; or, Up with Dead People* (2008), which blends gore, politics, and pornography to detail the plight of a gay zombie. "Zombies are the ultimate conformists," LaBruce has said, citing one of the most commonly referenced reasons for the explosion of zombies-take-over-the-world movies. "They come in masses and they're the ultimate consumers. Part of the thesis of the movie is that gays are now model consumers. Gay culture has become extremely conformist; gays are getting married and having children and they're very upwardly mobile and bourgeois."[15]

LaBruce's work has always mixed porn with politics, in the cinematic tra-

FIGURE 11.3. *Jey Crisfar as Otto (*Otto; or, Up with Dead People, *Existential Crisis Production, 2008; image courtesy of Bruce LaBruce).*

dition of Pasolini and even Eisenstein; propaganda is prioritized over plot or character, violence and exploitation are explored as the flip side of sexual desire. In 1991's *No Skin off My Ass*, a gay hairdresser is obsessed with a skinhead, while his sister directs a film about the Symbionese Liberation Army. In 2004's *The Raspberry Reich*, a queer terrorist cell kidnaps the son of a wealthy industrialist, urges people to "join the homosexual intifada," and argues that "heterosexuality is the opiate of the masses." It's worth noting that LaBruce is also a former student of the aforementioned queer film critic Robin Wood, whose seminal "Responsibilities of a Gay Film Critic" urged queer folks to participate in an all-out attack on the old and oppressive modes of making and reading film: "The attack, for instance, could—indeed, should—be directed at the economic structures of capitalism that support the [dominant ideological] norms, as they are embodied in the structure of the film industry itself as well as in its products."[16]

As such, Bruce LaBruce and other fringe filmmakers seem like the perfect point of contact for a potential cinematic shake-up. The entire post-9/11 period, in which so much more seems to be at stake, is ripe for this kind of polemic approach. The independent movement that so thoroughly transformed mainstream American filmmaking in the early 1990s has been corporatized and has lost its edge; movies sorely need the next big, gorgeous, messy step forward.

A common refrain in the immediate post-9/11 period, cited in several of the essays in this book, held that 9/11 was itself a (horror) movie. What other frame of reference did a sheltered and privileged nation have for such profound violence, inflicted, for the first time, *on us* and within our own borders, instead of *by us* and in distant corners of the world? The events of that day transformed the entire nation into one big movie audience, watching horrific events unfold from the edges of its seats—except that these events were real, and from the very first moments they were clearly understood as a devastating assault on the American way of life and national identity. The trauma of this experience cannot be overstated. Ample scholarship within the medical community has documented the literal trauma suffered by people who were at no point even remotely close to physical danger on September 11: "It is, however, possible that, in some persons, the belief that their personal safety was threatened, coupled with weeks of reinforcement of this danger from media coverage, may have produced a subjective response to 9/11 sufficient to produce PTSD symptoms."[17]

Two wars and a ballooning Pentagon budget that has negatively affected all other government functions; the Patriot Act; warrantless wiretapping; near-consensus within mainstream politics and media approving the use of torture; an overall massive political shift to the right—our collective national response to this trauma has been profoundly repressive. Increasing mainstream acceptance of the LGBT community within the same period must not be understood as an exception to this repressive response, but rather as a consequence. Some threats get destroyed; others get assimilated.

Many of the most popular and emblematic horror films of the post-9/11 period have exceedingly bleak endings, even by horror film standards. In many of the films discussed in this book, the hope that the monster is definitively dead, and that the happy world our heroes inhabit is safe, has become extremely rare. In this regard, the contemporary horror moment is analogous to another blossoming of the genre—the late 1960s and early 1970s work of filmmakers like George Romero, Tobe Hooper, and Roman Polanski—which was itself a response to a period of national trauma and problematized identity related to the Vietnam War, the civic unrest of the 1960s, and the challenge to white supremacy. Discussing the horror films of the 1970s, Robin Wood references Andrew Britton in pointing out that they "have one premise disturbingly in common: annihilation is inevitable, humanity is now completely powerless, no one can do anything to arrest the process. Ideology, that is, can encompass despair, but not the imagining of constructive radical alternatives."[18]

But against a backdrop of financial collapse and massive governmental disinvestment in social services, radical alternatives are becoming not only necessary but inevitable. The military theorist John Robb, author of *Brave New War: The Next Stage of Terrorism and the End of Globalization*, has posited that, as the global economic crisis continues, "the legitimacy of the developed democracies will fade and the sense of betrayal will be pervasive (think of the collapse of the Soviet Union). People will begin to shift their loyalties to any local group that can provide for their daily needs. Many of these groups will be crime fueled local insurgencies and militias. In short, the developed democracies will hollow out."[19]

New directions are as certain in horror movies as in the social sphere. Monsters have a way of surprising us. The horror movie character who smugly celebrates the monster's death tends to get killed moments later, when the alien/psychopath/werewolf bursts out of the shadows and severs his head. So, as I mourn the death of the queer monster, I do so in the hopes that it will jerk its eyes open the second I turn my back on it. And just like the queer monster might come strutting into the multiplex at any moment, I know that a truly radical anti-assimilation queer movement is in the making. Many queer voices are refusing access to mainstream culture in glamorous and radical ways, as evidenced in work like Mattilda Bernstein Sycamore's 2008 anthology *That's Revolting! Queer Strategies for Resisting Assimilation.*[20] If the queer monster returns to stalk the cinema, it will come from all the pissed-off, eloquent, subversive faggots lurking in the shadows, the ones that mainstream society really should be afraid of.

NOTES

1. Harry M. Benshoff, *Monsters in the Closet: Homosexuality and the Horror Film* (Manchester, UK: Manchester University Press, 1997).

2. David J. Skal, *The Monster Show: A Cultural History of Horror*, rev. ed. (New York: Faber and Faber, 2001). For another fascinating discussion of gay monsters, see Michael William Saunders, *Imps of the Perverse: Gay Monsters in Film* (Westport, CT: Praeger, 1998).

3. Alexander Wilson, "Friedkin's *Cruising*, Ghetto Politics, and Gay Sexuality," *Social Text* 4 (Autumn 1981): 98.

4. Jessica Grose, "From Borat to Mammy: The Top Ten Stereotypes in Cinema History," quoted by Carmen Van Kerckhove, in "Radar Online's List of Racial Stereotypes in the Movies," *Racialicious*, January 31, 2007, http://www.racialicious.com/2007/01/31/radar-onlines-list-of-racial-stereotypes-in-the-movies/.

5. For a discussion — and critique — of queer protests against this film, see Judith Halberstam, "Imagined Violence/Queer Violence: Representations of Rage and Resistance," in *Reel Knockouts: Violent Women in the Movies*, ed. Martha McCaughey and Neal King (Austin: University of Texas Press, 2001), 252–256.

6. Quoted in Jason Victor Serinus, "The Legacy of the Gay Liberation Front," *Bay Area Reporter*, June 6, 2009, http://www.ebar.com/pride/article.php?sec=pride&article=95; and Fleur Taylor, "What Happened to Sexual Liberation?," *Socialist Alternative*, May 11, 2007, http://www.sa.org.au/mag-archive-from-old-website/144-edition-38/1182-what-happened-to-sexual-liberation.

7. Quoted in Britta B. Wheeler, "Negotiating Deviance and Normativity: Performance Art, Boundary Transgressions, and Social Change," in *Performance: Critical Concepts in Literary and Cultural Studies*, vol. 4, ed. Philip Auslander (London: Routledge, 2005), 273.

8. Quoted in Jennifer McNulty, "Films Can Make a Difference, Says Critic B. Ruby Rich," *UC Santa Cruz Currents*, March 7, 2005, http://currents.ucsc.edu/04-05/03-07/film.asp.

9. Detailed analysis of gay men in post-9/11 horror films is taken in part from http://campblood.org/campbloodblog.html.

10. David Edelstein, "Now Playing at Your Local Multiplex: Torture Porn," *New York*, January 28, 2006, http://nymag.com/movies/features/15622.

11. Robin Wood, "Foreword: What Lies Beneath," in *Horror Film and Psychoanalysis: Freud's Worst Nightmare*, ed. Steven Jay Schneider (Cambridge: Cambridge University Press, 2004), xvi.

12. Aviva Briefel and Sianne Ngai, "'How Much Did You Pay for This Place?': Fear, Entitlement, and Urban Space in Bernard Rose's *Candyman*," in *Horror Film Reader*, ed. Alain Silver and James Ursini (New York: Limelight, 2000), 281.

13. Ibid.

14. Shelby Grad, "70% of African Americans Backed Prop. 8, Exit Poll Finds," *L.A. Now*, November 5, 2008, http://latimesblogs.latimes.com/lanow/2008/11/70-of-african-a.html.

15. Josh, "Undead Pride," *Myths & Monsters*, September 8, 2010, http://monsters.milkboys.org/article/undead-pride/.

16. Robin Wood, "Responsibilities of a Gay Film Critic," in *Personal Views: Explorations in Film*, rev. ed. (Detroit: Wayne State University Press, 2006), 392.

17. Randall D. Marshall and Sandro Galea, "Science for the Community: Assessing Mental Health after 9/11," *Journal of Clinical Psychiatry* 65, no. S1 (2004): S41.

18. Robin Wood, *Hollywood from Vietnam to Reagan . . . and Beyond*, rev. and exp. ed. (New York: Columbia University Press, 2003), 80.

19. Chris Arkenberg, "John Robb Interview: Open Source Warfare and Resilience," *Boing Boing*, June 15, 2010, http://www.boingboing.net/2010/06/15/john-robb-interview.html.

20. Mattilda Bernstein Sycamore, ed., *That's Revolting! Queer Strategies for Resisting Assimilation*, 2nd ed. (Brooklyn: Soft Skull Press, 2008).

Selected Bibliography

Agamben, Giorgio. *Homo Sacer: Sovereign Power and Bare Life*. Translated by Daniel Heller-Roazen. Stanford, CA: Stanford University Press, 1998.

———. *Means without End: Notes on Politics*. Translated by Vincenzo Binetti and Cesare Casarino. Minneapolis: University of Minnesota Press, 2000.

Althusser, Louis. "Ideology and Ideological State Apparatuses." In *Lenin and Philosophy, and Other Essays*, translated by Ben Brewster, 85-126. New York: Monthly Review Press, 2001.

Appadurai, Arjun. *Modernity at Large: Cultural Dimensions of Globalization*. Minneapolis: University of Minnesota Press, 1996.

Basinger, Jeanine. *A Woman's View: How Hollywood Spoke to Women, 1930–1960*. New York: Knopf, 1993.

Baudrillard, Jean. "Consumer Society." In *Consumer Society in American History: A Reader*, edited by Lawrence B. Glickman, 33-56. Ithaca, NY: Cornell University Press, 1999.

———. *Simulacra and Simulation*. Translated by Sheila Faria Glaser. Ann Arbor: University of Michigan Press, 1994.

Beard, William. *The Artist as Monster: The Cinema of David Cronenberg*. Rev. ed. Toronto: University of Toronto Press, 2006.

Beaty, Bart. *David Cronenberg's* A History of Violence. Toronto: University of Toronto Press, 2008.

Benshoff, Harry M. *Monsters in the Closet: Homosexuality and the Horror Film*. Manchester, UK: Manchester University Press, 1997.

Bhaba, Homi. "A Narrative of Divided Civilizations." *Chronicle of Higher Education*, September 28, 2001: B12.

Bishop, Kyle William. "The Idle Proletariat: *Dawn of the Dead*, Consumer Ideology, and the Loss of Productive Labor." *Journal of Popular Culture* 43 (April 2010): 234–248.

Biskind, Peter. *Seeing Is Believing: How Hollywood Taught Us to Stop Worrying and Love the Fifties*. New York: Pantheon, 1983.

Blake, Linnie. *The Wounds of Nations: Horror Cinema, Historical Trauma and National Identity*. Manchester, UK: Manchester University Press, 2008.

Blasingame, James. "Books for Adolescents: *Twilight*, by Stephenie Meyer." *Journal of Adolescent & Adult Literacy* 49 (April 2006): 628+.

Bloom, Harold. *The American Religion: The Emergence of the Post-Christian Nation*. New York: Simon & Schuster, 1992.

Breuer, Josef, and Sigmund Freud. *Studies on Hysteria*. Translated by James Strachey. New York: Basic Books, 1957.

Brooker, Will. "Camera-Eye, CG-Eye: Videogames and the 'Cinematic.'" *Cinema Journal* 48 (Spring 2009): 122–128.

Carroll, Noël. *The Philosophy of Horror; or, Paradoxes of the Heart*. New York: Routledge, 1990.

Caruth, Cathy, ed. *Trauma: Explorations in Memory*. Baltimore: Johns Hopkins University Press, 1995.

———. *Unclaimed Experience: Trauma, Narrative, and History*. Baltimore: Johns Hopkins University Press, 1996.

Cavarero, Adriana. *Horrorism: Naming Contemporary Violence*. Translated by William McCuaig. New York: Columbia University Press, 2009.

CBS News. *What We Saw: The Events of September 11, 2001, in Words, Pictures, and Video*. New York: Simon & Schuster, 2002.

Chermak, Steven, Frankie Y. Bailey, and Michelle Brown, eds. *Media Representations of September 11*. Westport, CT: Praeger, 2003.

Cherry, Brigid. *Horror*. London: Routledge, 2009.

Chomsky, Noam. *9-11*. New York: Seven Stories Press, 2001.

Chung, Hye Jean. "*The Host* and *D-War*: Complex Intersections of National Imaginings and Transnational Aspirations." *Spectator* 29 (Fall 2009): 48–56.

Clover, Carol. *Men, Women, and Chain Saws: Gender in the Modern Horror Film*. Princeton, NJ: Princeton University Press, 1992.

Clover, Joshua. "All That Is Solid Melts into War." *Film Quarterly* 61 (Fall 2007): 6–7.

Colavito, Jason. *Knowing Fear: Science, Knowledge, and the Development of the Horror Genre*. Jefferson, NC: McFarland, 2008.

Conrich, Ian, ed. *Horror Zone: The Cultural Experience of Contemporary Horror Cinema*. London: I. B. Tauris, 2010.

Cook, Sylvia Jenkins. *From Tobacco Road to Route 66: The Southern Poor White in Fiction*. Chapel Hill: University of North Carolina Press, 1976.

Crane, Jonathan Lake. *Terror and Everyday Life: Singular Moments in the History of the Horror Film*. Thousand Oaks, CA: Sage, 1994.

Cranny-Francis, Anne, and John Tulloch. "Vaster Than Empire(s), and More Slow: The Politics and Economics of Embodiment in *Doctor Who*." In *Third Person: Authoring and Exploring Vast Narratives*, edited by Pat Harrigan and Noah Wardrip-Fruin, 343–355. Cambridge, MA: MIT Press, 2009.

Creed, Barbara. *The Monstrous-Feminine: Film, Feminism, Psychoanalysis*. London: Routledge, 1993.

D'Arc, James V. "The Mormon as Vampire: A Comparative Study of Winifred Graham's *The Love Story of a Mormon*, the Film *Trapped by Mormons*, and Bram Stoker's *Dracula*." *Brigham Young University Studies* 46, no. 2 (2007): 165–187.

Dargis, Manohla. "Once Disaster Hits, It Seems Never to End." In *American Movie Critics: An Anthology from the Silents until Now*, rev. ed., edited by Phillip Lopate, 711–713. New York: Library of America, 2006.

Derry, Charles. *Dark Dreams 2.0: A Psychological History of the Modern Horror Film from the 1950s to the 21st Century*. Jefferson, NC: McFarland, 2009.

Dixon, Wheeler Winston, ed. *Film and Television after 9/11*. Carbondale: Southern Illinois University Press, 2004.

———. *Lost in the Fifties: Recovering Phantom Hollywood*. Carbondale: Southern Illinois University Press, 2005.

Drew, Wayne, ed. *David Cronenberg*. London: BFI, 1984.

Edelstein, David. "Now Playing at Your Local Multiplex: Torture Porn." *New York*, January 28, 2006. http://nymag.com/movies/features/15622.

Engelhardt, Tom. *The End of Victory Culture: Cold War America and the Disillusioning of a Generation*. Rev. and exp. ed. Amherst: University of Massachusetts Press, 2007.

Fanon, Frantz. *Black Skin, White Masks*. Translated by Charles Lam Markmann. New York: Grove Press, 1967.

Fiske, John. "Shopping for Pleasure: Malls, Power, and Resistance." In *The Consumer Society Reader*, edited by Juliet B. Schor and Douglas B. Holt, 306–328. New York: New Press, 2000.

Foster, Gwendolyn Audrey. "Monstrosity and the Bad-White-Body Film." In *Bad: Infamy, Darkness, Evil, and Slime on Screen*, edited by Murray Pomerance, 39–54. Albany: State University of New York Press, 2004.

Foucault, Michel. *Discipline and Punish: The Birth of the Prison*. Translated by Alan Sheridan. New York: Vintage, 1977.

Freeland, Cynthia A. *The Naked and the Undead: Evil and the Appeal of Horror*. Boulder, CO: Westview Press, 2000.

Freud, Sigmund. *The Interpretation of Dreams*. Translated by James Strachey. New York: Avon Books, 1965.

Fuller, Graham. "Good Guy Bad Guy." *Sight & Sound* 15 (October 2005): 12–16.

Gagne, Paul R. *The Zombies That Ate Pittsburgh: The Films of George A. Romero*. New York: Dodd, Mead, 1987.

Galea, Sandro, Heidi Resnick, Jennifer Ahern, Joel Gold, Michael Bucuvalas, Dean Kilpatrick, Jennifer Stuber, and David Vlahov. "Posttraumatic Stress Disorder in Manhattan, New York City, after the September 11th Terrorist Attacks." *Journal of Urban Health* 79 (September 2002): 340–353.

Galloway, Alexander R. *Gaming: Essays on Algorithmic Culture*. Minneapolis: University of Minnesota Press, 2006.

Gelder, Ken, ed. *The Horror Reader*. London: Routledge, 2000.

Givens, Terryl L. *People of Paradox: A History of Mormon Culture*. Oxford: Oxford University Press, 2007.

Grant, Barry Keith, ed. *The Dread of Difference: Gender and the Horror Film*. Austin: University of Texas Press, 1996.

Grant, Barry Keith, and Christopher Sharrett, eds. *Planks of Reason: Essays on the Horror Film*. Rev. ed. Lanham, MD: Scarecrow Press, 2004.

Grossvogel, D. I. "Haneke: The Coercing of Vision." *Film Quarterly* 60 (Summer 2007): 36–43.

Haggerty, George E. *Queer Gothic*. Urbana: University of Illinois Press, 2006.

Halberstam, Judith. "Imagined Violence/Queer Violence: Representations of Rage and Resistance." In *Reel Knockouts: Violent Women in the Movies*, edited by Martha McCaughey and Neal King, 244–266. Austin: University of Texas Press, 2001.

————. *Skin Shows: Gothic Horror and the Technology of Monsters.* Durham, NC: Duke University Press, 1995.

Handling, Piers, ed. *The Shape of Rage: The Films of David Cronenberg.* Toronto: General Publishing, 1983.

Hantke, Steffen, ed. *American Horror Film: The Genre at the Turn of the Millennium.* Jackson: University Press of Mississippi, 2010.

————. "On the Acceleration of the Undead: Paradigm Change in the American Zombie Film." *Jura Gentium Cinema,* n.d. http://www.jgcinema.com/single .php?sl=Horror-Fear-Capitalism-Market.

Harper, Stephen. "Zombies, Malls, and the Consumerism Debate: George Romero's *Dawn of the Dead.*" *Americana* 1 (Fall 2002): http://www.americanpopularculture .com/journal/articles/fall_2002/harper.htm.

Harpham, Geoffrey Galt. "Symbolic Terror." *Critical Inquiry* 28 (Winter 2002): 573–579.

Hauerwas, Stanley, and Frank Lentricchia, eds. *Dissent from the Homeland: Essays after September 11.* Durham, NC: Duke University Press, 2003.

Heller, Dana, ed. *The Selling of 9/11: How a National Tragedy Became a Commodity.* New York: Palgrave Macmillan, 2005.

Herbert, Christopher. "Vampire Religion." *Representations* 79 (Summer 2002): 100–121.

Higson, Andrew. "The Concept of National Cinema." *Screen* 30 (Autumn 1989): 36–47.

Hills, Matt. *The Pleasures of Horror.* New York: Continuum, 2005.

Hoberman, J. "Unquiet Americans." *Sight & Sound* 16 (October 2006): 20–23.

Horne, Philip. "I Shopped with a Zombie." *Critical Quarterly* 34 (Winter 1992): 97–110.

Hsu, Hsuan L. "The Dangers of Biosecurity: *The Host* and the Geopolitics of Outbreak." *Jump Cut* 51 (Spring 2009): http://www.ejumpcut.org/archive/jc51.2009/ Host/index.html.

Ignatieff, Michael. "The Terrorist as Auteur." *New York Times,* November 14, 2004. http://nytimes.com/2004/11/14/movies/14TERROR.html.

Jancovich, Mark, ed. *Horror, the Film Reader.* New York: Routledge, 2002.

————. *Rational Fears: American Horror in the 1950s.* Manchester, UK: Manchester University Press, 1996.

Junod, Tom. "The Falling Man." *Esquire,* September 2003. http://www.esquire.com/ features/ESQ0903-SEP_FALLINGMAN.

Kalfus, Ken. *A Disorder Peculiar to the Country.* New York: Ecco, 2006.

Kammerer, Dietmar. "Video Surveillance in Hollywood Movies." *Surveillance and Society* 2, nos. 2/3 (2004): 464–473.

Kendrick, James. "Representing the Unrepresentable: 9/11 on Film and Television." In *Why We Fought: America's Wars in Film and History,* edited by Peter C. Rollins and John E. O'Connor, 511–528. Lexington: University Press of Kentucky, 2008.

Keniston, Ann, and Jeanne Follansbee Quinn, eds. *Literature after 9/11.* New York: Routledge, 2008.

King, Stephen. *The Mist.* New York: Signet, 1980.

Klein, Christina. *Cold War Orientalism: Asia in the Middlebrow Imagination, 1945–1961.* Berkeley: University of California Press, 2003.

———. "Why American Studies Needs to Think about Korean Cinema, or, Transnational Genres in the Films of Bong Joon-ho." *American Quarterly* 60 (December 2008): 871–898.

LaBute, Neil. *The Mercy Seat*. New York: Faber and Faber, 2003.

LaCapra, Dominick. *Writing History, Writing Trauma*. Baltimore: Johns Hopkins University Press, 2001.

Lane, Anthony. "This Is Not a Movie." *New Yorker*, September 24, 2001. http://www .newyorker.com/archive/2001/09/24/010924crci_cinema.

Levin, Thomas Y. "Rhetoric of the Temporal Index: Surveillant Narration and the Cinema of 'Real Time.'" In *CTRL [SPACE]: Rhetorics of Surveillance from Bentham to Big Brother*, edited by Thomas Y. Levin, Ursula Frohne, and Peter Weibel, 578–593. Cambridge, MA: MIT Press, 2002.

Lockwood, Dean. "All Stripped Down: The Spectacle of 'Torture Porn.'" *Popular Communication* 7 (January 2009): 40–48.

Loudermilk, A. "Eating 'Dawn' in the Dark: Zombie Desire and Commodified Identity in George A. Romero's 'Dawn of the Dead.'" *Journal of Consumer Culture* 3 (March 2003): 83–108.

Lowenstein, Adam. "Interactive Art Cinema: Between 'Old' and 'New' Media with *Un Chien andalou* and *eXistenZ*." In *Global Art Cinema: New Theories and Histories*, edited by Rosalind Galt and Karl Schoonover, 92–105. New York: Oxford University Press, 2010.

———. "Living Dead: Fearful Attractions of Film." *Representations* 110 (Spring 2010): 105–128.

———. *Shocking Representation: Historical Trauma, National Cinema, and the Modern Horror Film*. New York: Columbia University Press, 2005.

———. "Spectacle Horror and *Hostel*: Why 'Torture Porn' Does Not Exist." *Critical Quarterly* 53.1 (April 2011): 42–60.

Lyman, Rick. "Horrors! Time for an Attack of the Metaphors?; From Bug Movies to Bioterrorism." *New York Times*, October 23, 2001. http://www.nytimes.com/ 2001/10/23/movies/horrors-time-for-an-attack-of-the-metaphors-from-bug-movies-to-bioterrorism.html.

Lyon, David, ed. *Theorizing Surveillance: The Panopticon and Beyond*. Cullompton, UK: Willan Publishing, 2006.

Matheson, Richard. *I Am Legend*. New York: Tor, 1995.

Mathijs, Ernest. *The Cinema of David Cronenberg: From Baron of Blood to Cultural Hero*. London: Wallflower Press, 2008.

McLuhan, Marshall. *Understanding Media: The Extensions of Man*. New York: McGraw-Hill, 1964.

Meyer, Stephenie. *Twilight*. New York: Little, Brown, 2008.

Miller, Nancy K. "'Portraits of Grief': Telling Details and the Testimony of Trauma." *differences* 14 (Fall 2003): 112–135.

Moretti, Franco. *Signs Taken for Wonders: Essays in the Sociology of Literary Forms*. Translated by Susan Fischer, David Forgacs, and David Miller. London: Verso, 1983.

Murray, Gabrielle. "*Hostel II*: Representations of the Body in Pain and the Cinema Experience in Torture-Porn." *Jump Cut* 50 (Spring 2008): http://www.ejumpcut .org/archive/jc50.2008/TortureHostel2/index.html.

Newman, Kim. "Horror Will Eat Itself." *Sight & Sound* 19 (May 2009): 36–38.

Noriega, Chon. "Godzilla and the Japanese Nightmare: When 'Them!' Is U.S." *Cinema Journal* 27 (Autumn 1987): 63–77.

Norris, Clive, and Gary Armstrong. *The Maximum Surveillance Society: The Rise of CCTV.* Oxford: Berg, 1999.

North, Daniel. "Evidence of Things Not Quite Seen: *Cloverfield*'s Obstructed Spectacle." *Film & History* 40 (Spring 2010): 75–92.

Osterweil, Ara. Review of *Caché. Film Quarterly* 59 (Summer 2006): 35–39.

Page, Max. *The City's End: Two Centuries of Fantasies, Fears, and Premonitions of New York's Destruction.* New Haven, CT: Yale University Press, 2008.

Paul, William. *Laughing Screaming: Modern Hollywood Horror and Comedy.* New York: Columbia University Press, 1994.

Phillips, Kendall R. *Projected Fears: Horror Films and American Culture.* Westport, CT: Praeger, 2005.

Pinedo, Isabel. "Playing with Fire without Getting Burned: Blowback Re-imagined." In Battlestar Galactica *and Philosophy*, edited by Josef Steiff and Tristan D. Tamplin, 173–183. Chicago: Open Court, 2008.

———. *Recreational Terror: Women and the Pleasures of Horror Film Viewing.* Albany: State University of New York Press, 1997.

Prince, Stephen. *Firestorm: American Film in the Age of Terrorism.* New York: Columbia University Press, 2009.

Puar, Jasbir K. "On Torture: Abu Ghraib." *Radical History Review* 93 (Fall 2005): 13–38.

Redfield, Marc. "Virtual Trauma: The Idiom of 9/11." *diacritics* 37 (Spring 2007): 55–80.

Rodley, Chris, ed. *Cronenberg on Cronenberg.* Rev. ed. London: Faber and Faber, 1997.

Russell, Jamie. Review of *The Host. Sight & Sound* 16 (November 2006): 60–62.

Ryan, David. "Mapping Containment: The Cultural Construction of the Cold War." In *American Cold War Culture*, edited by Douglas Field, 50–68. Edinburgh: Edinburgh University Press, 2005.

Said, Edward. *Orientalism: Western Conceptions of the Orient.* London: Penguin, 1991.

Saunders, Michael William. *Imps of the Perverse: Gay Monsters in Film.* Westport, CT: Praeger, 1998.

Scarry, Elaine. *The Body in Pain: The Making and Unmaking of the World.* New York: Oxford University Press, 1985.

———. "Citizenship in Emergency." *Boston Review* 27 (October–November 2002): http://bostonreview.net/BR27.5/scarry.html.

Schechner, Richard. "9/11 as Avant-Garde Art?" *PMLA* 124 (October 2009): 1820–1829.

Schneider, Steven Jay, ed. *101 Horror Movies You Must See before You Die.* London: Quintessence, 2009.

———, ed. *Horror Film and Psychoanalysis: Freud's Worst Nightmare.* Cambridge: Cambridge University Press, 2004.

Schneider, Steven Jay, and Daniel Shaw, eds. *Dark Thoughts: Philosophic Reflections on Cinematic Horror.* Lanham, MD: Scarecrow Press, 2003.

Sedgwick, Eve Kosofsky. *Between Men: English Literature and Male Homosocial Desire.* New York: Columbia University Press, 1985.

Shaviro, Steven. *The Cinematic Body*. Minneapolis: University of Minnesota Press, 1993.

Shin, Chi-Yun, and Julian Stringer, eds. *New Korean Cinema*. Edinburgh: Edinburgh University Press, 2005.

Silver, Alain, and James Ursini, eds. *Horror Film Reader*. New York: Limelight, 2000.

Skal, David J. *The Monster Show: A Cultural History of Horror*. Rev. ed. New York: Faber and Faber, 2001.

Smith, Richard Harland. "The Battle Inside: Infection and the Modern Horror Film." *Cineaste* 35 (Winter 2009): 42–45.

Sobchack, Vivian. *Carnal Thoughts: Embodiment and Moving Image Culture*. Berkeley: University of California Press, 2004.

Sontag, Susan. *On Photography*. New York: Farrar, Straus and Giroux, 1977.

———. *Regarding the Pain of Others*. New York: Picador, 2003.

Spiegelman, Art. *In the Shadow of No Towers*. New York: Pantheon, 2004.

Stevenson, John Allen. "A Vampire in the Mirror: The Sexuality of Dracula." *PMLA* 103 (March 1988): 139–149.

Sutherland, Meghan. "Rigor/Mortis: The Industrial Life of Style in American Zombie Cinema." *Framework* 48 (Spring 2007): 64–78.

Sycamore, Mattilda Bernstein, ed. *That's Revolting! Queer Strategies for Resisting Assimilation*. 2nd ed. Brooklyn: Soft Skull Press, 2008.

Taubin, Amy. "Model Citizens." *Film Comment* 41 (September–October 2005): 24–28.

"The Ten Best Movie Destructions of New York City." *New York*, December 13, 2007. http://nymag.com/daily/entertainment/2007/12/list_ten_best_movie_des.html.

Todorov, Tzvetan. *The Fantastic: A Structural Approach to a Literary Genre*. Translated by Richard Howard. Ithaca, NY: Cornell University Press, 1975.

Tristram, Claire. *After*. New York: Farrar, Straus and Giroux, 2004.

Tudor, Andrew. "From Paranoia to Postmodernism? The Horror Movie in Late Modern Society." In *Genre and Contemporary Hollywood*, edited by Steve Neale, 105–116. London: BFI, 2002.

———. *Monsters and Mad Scientists: A Cultural History of the Horror Movie*. Oxford: Blackwell, 1989.

Turner, John S. "Collapsing the Interior/Exterior Distinction: Surveillance, Spectacle, and Suspense in Popular Cinema." *Wide Angle* 20 (October 1998): 93–123.

Twitchell, James B. *Dreadful Pleasures: An Anatomy of Modern Horror*. New York: Oxford University Press, 1985.

Waldon, David. *Snakes on a Plane: The Guide to the Internet Sssssensation*. New York: Thunder's Mouth Press, 2006.

Walker, Janet. *Trauma Cinema: Documenting Incest and the Holocaust*. Berkeley: University of California Press, 2005.

Waller, Gregory A. *The Living and the Undead: From Stoker's* Dracula *to Romero's* Dawn of the Dead. Urbana: University of Illinois Press, 1986.

Walter, Jess. *The Zero*. New York: Regan Books, 2006.

Warner, Michael. "Tongues Untied: Memoirs of a Pentecostal Boyhood." In *Curiouser: On the Queerness of Children*, edited by Steven Bruhm and Natasha Hurley, 215–224. Minneapolis: University of Minnesota Press, 2004.

Wheatley, Catherine. "Secrets, Lies, and Videotape." *Sight & Sound* 16 (February 2006): 32–36.

Williams, Linda. "Film Bodies: Gender, Genre, and Excess." *Film Quarterly* 44 (Summer 1991): 2–13.

Williams, Tony. *The Cinema of George A. Romero: Knight of the Living Dead.* London: Wallflower Press, 2003.

———. *Hearths of Darkness: The Family in the American Horror Film.* Madison, NJ: Fairleigh Dickinson University Press, 1996.

Willis, Susan. *Portents of the Real: A Primer for Post-9/11 America.* London: Verso, 2005.

Wilson, Alexander. "Friedkin's *Cruising*, Ghetto Politics, and Gay Sexuality." *Social Text* 4 (Autumn 1981): 98–109.

Wood, Robin. *Hollywood from Vietnam to Reagan . . . and Beyond.* Rev. and exp. ed. New York: Columbia University Press, 2003.

———. "Responsibilities of a Gay Film Critic." In *Personal Views: Explorations in Film,* rev. ed., 387–405. Detroit: Wayne State University Press, 2006.

Worland, Rick. *The Horror Film: An Introduction.* Malden, MA: Blackwell, 2007.

Wright, Edgar. "The Church of George." *Virginia Quarterly Review* 81 (Winter 2005): 40–43.

Zanger, Jules. "Metaphor into Metonymy: The Vampire Next Door." In *Blood Read: The Vampire as Metaphor in Contemporary Culture,* edited by Joan Gordon and Veronica Hollinger, 17–26. Philadelphia: University of Pennsylvania Press, 1997.

Zelizer, Barbie, and Stuart Allan, eds. *Journalism after September 11.* London: Routledge, 2002.

Zimmer, Catherine. "The Camera's Eye: *Peeping Tom* and Technological Perversion." In *Horror Film: Creating and Marketing Fear,* edited by Steffen Hantke, 35–51. Jackson: University Press of Mississippi, 2004.

Žižek, Slavoj. "Are We in a War? Do We Have an Enemy?" *London Review of Books,* May 23, 2002. http://www.lrb.co.uk/v24/n10/slavoj-zizek/are-we-in-a-war-do-we-have-an-enemy.

———. *Welcome to the Desert of the Real! Five Essays on September 11 and Related Dates.* London: Verso, 2002.

Selected Filmography

HORROR (AND RELATED) FILMS AFTER 9/11

American Experience: New York: Center of the World (2003), Ric Burns.
The Attendant (2004), Corbin Timbrook.
Big Man Japan (2007), Hitoshi Matsumoto.
Cabin Fever (2002), Eli Roth.
Caché (2005), Michael Haneke.
Captivity (2007), Roland Joffé.
Cloverfield (2008), Matt Reeves.
Dawn of the Dead (2004), Zack Snyder.
The Day the Earth Stood Still (2008), Scott Derrickson.
Déjà Vu (2006), Tony Scott.
The Devil's Rejects (2005), Rob Zombie.
Diary of the Dead (2007), George Romero.
Dirty Pretty Things (2002), Stephen Frears.
Eagle Eye (2008), D. J. Caruso.
Eastern Promises (2007), David Cronenberg.
11'09"01: September 11 (2002), various directors.
Fahrenheit 9/11 (2004), Michael Moore.
The Fanglys (2004), Christopher Abram.
Flight 93 (2006), Peter Markle.
Funny Games (2007), Michael Haneke.
The Great New Wonderful (2005), Danny Leiner.
The Happening (2008), M. Night Shyamalan.
HellBent (2004), Paul Etheredge.
High Tension (2003), Alexandre Aja.
The Hills Have Eyes (2006), Alexandre Aja.
The Hills Have Eyes II (2007), Martin Weisz.
A History of Violence (2005), David Cronenberg.
The Host (2006), Bong Joon-ho.
Hostel (2005), Eli Roth.

House of 1000 Corpses (2003), Rob Zombie.

The Hurt Locker (2008), Kathryn Bigelow.

I Am Legend (2007), Francis Lawrence.

In Memoriam: New York City, 9/11/01 (2002), Brad Grey.

Inside Man (2006), Spike Lee.

The Invasion (2007), Oliver Hirschbiegel.

Jeepers Creepers II (2003), Victor Salva.

Land of the Dead (2005), George Romero.

The Last House on the Left (2009), Dennis Iliadis.

Lions for Lambs (2007), Robert Redford.

Look (2007), Adam Rifkin.

Love Actually (2003), Richard Curtis.

The Mist (2007), Frank Darabont.

Mulberry Street (2006), Jim Mickle.

9/11 (2002), Gédéon Naudet and Jules Naudet.

The Omen (2006), John Moore.

Otto; or, Up with Dead People (2008), Bruce LaBruce.

Paranormal Activity (2007), Oren Peli.

Postal (2007), Uwe Boll.

Quarantine (2008), John Erick Dowdle.

The Raspberry Reich (2004), Bruce LaBruce.

[Rec] (2007), Jaume Balagueró and Paco Plaza.

Reign over Me (2007), Mike Binder.

Rendition (2007), Gavin Hood.

Resident Evil (2002), Paul W. S. Anderson.

The Ruining (2004), Christopher Burgard.

Saint of 9/11 (2006), Glenn Holsten.

Sarah Silverman: Jesus Is Magic (2005), Liam Lynch.

Saw (2004), James Wan.

Saw II (2005), Darren Lynn Bousman.

Saw III (2006), Darren Lynn Bousman.

Saw IV (2007), Darren Lynn Bousman.

Saw V (2008), David Hackl.

Saw VI (2009), Kevin Greutert.

Saw 3D (2010), Kevin Greutert.

Shallow Ground (2004), Sheldon Wilson.

Shaun of the Dead (2004), Edgar Wright.

Snakes on a Plane (2006), David R. Ellis and Lex Halaby.

The Strangers (2008), Bryan Bertino.

Sympathy for Mr. Vengeance (2002), Park Chan-wook.

The Texas Chainsaw Massacre (2003), Marcus Nispel.

Them (2006), David Moreau and Xavier Palud.

Turistas (2006), John Stockwell.

28 Days Later (2002), Danny Boyle.

25th Hour (2002), Spike Lee.

Twilight (2008), Catherine Hardwicke.

2001 Maniacs (2005), Tim Sullivan.

Undertow (2004), David Gordon Green.
Underworld (2003), Len Wiseman.
United 93 (2006), Paul Greengrass.
Untraceable (2008), Gregory Hoblit.
Vacancy (2007), Nimród Antal.
Vantage Point (2008), Pete Travis.
War of the Worlds (2005), Steven Spielberg.
World Trade Center (2006), Oliver Stone.
Wrong Turn (2003), Rob Schmidt.
Wrong Turn 2: Dead End (2007), Joe Lynch.

PRE-9/11 HORROR (AND RELATED) FILMS

Alien (1979), Ridley Scott.
The American Nightmare (2000), Adam Simon.
Armageddon (1998), Michael Bay.
Attack of the 50 Foot Woman (1958), Nathan Juran.
Attack of the Killer Tomatoes! (1978), John De Bello.
Basic Instinct (1992), Paul Verhoeven.
Benny's Video (1992), Michael Haneke.
Blacula (1972), William Crain.
Blade (1998), Stephen Norrington.
The Blair Witch Project (1999), Daniel Myrick and Eduardo Sánchez.
The Brood (1979), David Cronenberg.
Cruising (1980), William Friedkin.
Dawn of the Dead (1979), George Romero.
The Day the Earth Stood Still (1951), Robert Wise.
Dead Ringers (1988), David Cronenberg.
Deafula (1975), Peter Wolf.
Deliverance (1972), John Boorman.
Die Hard (1988), John McTiernan.
Easy Rider (1969), Dennis Hopper.
Escape from New York (1981), John Carpenter.
The Fly (1986), David Cronenberg.
Friday the 13th (1980), Sean Cunningham.
Funny Games (1997), Michael Haneke.
Godzilla (1954), Ishirō Honda.
Halloween (1978), John Carpenter.
Hellraiser (1987), Clive Barker.
The Hills Have Eyes (1977), Wes Craven.
The Incredible Shrinking Man (1957), Jack Arnold.
Independence Day (1996), Roland Emmerich.
Invasion of the Body Snatchers (1956), Don Siegel.
King Kong (1933), Merian C. Cooper and Ernest B. Schoedsack.
The Last House on the Left (1972), Wes Craven.
The Last Man on Earth (1964), Ubaldo Ragona.

M. Butterfly (1993), David Cronenberg.
Night and Fog in Japan (1960), Nagisa Ōshima.
Night of the Living Dead (1968), George Romero.
No Skin off My Ass (1991), Bruce LaBruce.
The Old Dark House (1932), James Whale.
The Omega Man (1971), Boris Sagal.
Peeping Tom (1960), Michael Powell.
"People Are Alike All Over," *The Twilight Zone* (1960), Mitchell Leisen.
Psycho (1960), Alfred Hitchcock.
Rebecca (1940), Alfred Hitchcock.
Rope (1948), Alfred Hitchcock.
Scream (1996), Wes Craven.
Se7en (1995), David Fincher.
Shivers (1975), David Cronenberg.
The Silence of the Lambs (1991), Jonathan Demme.
The Sixth Sense (1999), M. Night Shyamalan.
Southern Comfort (1981), Walter Hill.
Tell Me Something (1999), Chang Yoon-hyun.
The Texas Chain Saw Massacre (1974), Tobe Hooper.
The Towering Inferno (1974), John Guillermin.
Two Thousand Maniacs! (1964), Herschell Gordon Lewis.
Videodrome (1983), David Cronenberg.

Contributors

Harry M. Benshoff is Associate Professor of Radio, Television, and Film at the University of North Texas. His research interests include topics in film genres, film history, film theory, and multiculturalism. He has published essays on blaxploitation horror films, Hollywood LSD films, *The Talented Mr. Ripley*, and *Brokeback Mountain*. He is the author of *Monsters in the Closet: Homosexuality and the Horror Film*. With Sean Griffin he coauthored *America on Film: Representing Race, Class, Gender, and Sexuality at the Movies* and *Queer Images: A History of Gay and Lesbian Film in America*.

Linnie Blake is Principal Lecturer in Film at Manchester Metropolitan University. She has published widely on international horror cinema and American literary and cultural studies. Her most recent book is *The Wounds of Nations: Horror Cinema, Historical Trauma and National Identity*.

Aviva Briefel is Associate Professor of English at Bowdoin College and author of *The Deceivers: Art Forgery and Identity in the Nineteenth Century*. Her essays have been published in many scholarly journals, including *Camera Obscura*, *Film Quarterly*, *Narrative*, *Novel*, and *Victorian Studies*. She appeared on the television specials *100 Scariest Movie Moments* and *30 Even Scarier Movie Moments* and has been interviewed by a number of major newspapers and magazines. She is currently writing a book titled *Amputations: Race and the Hand at the Fin de Siècle*.

Elisabeth Ford is Assistant Professor in the English Department at Wellesley College, where she teaches courses on American literature, African American literature, and film. Her work has been published in *Callaloo*, and she has recently completed a book manuscript titled *X: Intersections of Race and Place in African American Urban Literature.*

Laura Frost is Associate Professor of Literature at the New School. The author of *Sex Drives: Fantasies of Fascism in Literary Modernism*, she has published articles on James Joyce, Virginia Woolf, D. H. Lawrence, and Aldous Huxley, as well as articles on contemporary literature and visual culture, including "Still Life: 9/11's Falling Bodies" (in *Literature after 9/11*) and "Photography/Pornography/Torture: The Politics of Seeing Abu Ghraib" (in *One of the Guys: Women as Aggressors and Torturers*). She is at work on a book about modernism and pleasure.

Steffen Hantke has written on contemporary literature, film, and culture. He is author of *Conspiracy and Paranoia in Contemporary American Fiction* and editor of the following works: *Horror*; a special topics issue of *Paradoxa*; *Horror Film: Creating and Marketing Fear*; *Caligari's Heirs: The German Cinema of Fear after 1945*; *Gypsy Scholars, Migrant Teachers, and the Global Academic Proletariat: Adjunct Labour in Higher Education* (with Rudolphus Teeuwen); and *American Horror Film: The Genre at the Turn of the Millennium*. He teaches in the American Culture Program at Sogang University in Seoul, South Korea.

Matt Hills is a Reader in Media and Cultural Studies at Cardiff University. He has published widely on cult film and television, including books such as *Fan Cultures*, *The Pleasures of Horror*, and *Triumph of a Time Lord: Regenerating* Doctor Who *in the Twenty-First Century*. He has also contributed to collections such as *Dark Thoughts: Philosophic Reflections on Cinematic Horror*; *Sleaze Artists: Cinema at the Margins of Taste, Style, and Politics*; and *101 Horror Movies You Must See before You Die.*

Homay King is Associate Professor in the Department of History of Art and Director of the Program in Film Studies at Bryn Mawr College. She is the author of *Lost in Translation: Orientalism, Cinema, and the Enigmatic Signifier*. Her essays have appeared in *Camera Obscura*, *Discourse*, *Film Quarterly*, the *Quarterly Review of Film and Video*, and other journals and anthologies.

Adam Lowenstein is Associate Professor of English and Film Studies at the University of Pittsburgh. He is the author of *Shocking Representation: Historical Trauma, National Cinema, and the Modern Horror Film*, as well as essays that have appeared in *Cinema Journal*, *Representations*, *Critical Quarterly*, *boundary 2*, *Post Script*, and numerous anthologies. An interviewed scholar in the horror film documentary *The American Nightmare* and in articles for the *New York Times* and the *Village Voice*, his current projects include a book concerning cinematic spectatorship, surrealism, and the age of new media.

Sam J. Miller is a writer and community organizer. His work has been published in journals like the *Minnesota Review*, *Fiction International*, *Washington Square*, *Gargoyle*, *Alter/Net*, and the *Rumpus*. In his day job, he has organized homeless people to fight for and win concrete changes in city policy, and he has coordinated the writing of a major policy report that is now required reading in urban planning courses at Columbia University . . . and has been banned in New York state prisons.

Travis Sutton received his Master of Arts degree from the University of North Texas and is currently a PhD student at Texas A&M. His research interests include topics in film history, film theory, Mormon studies, and deaf studies. His graduate thesis, "'According to Their Wills and Pleasures': The Sexual Stereotyping of Mormon Men in American Film and Television," explores Mormon representation since the early days of cinema. He is also the producer and director of the feature-length documentary *Extraordinary Measures*, which premiered at the San Francisco Documentary Festival.

Catherine Zimmer is Assistant Professor of English and of Film and Screen Studies at Pace University. Her work has appeared in the journals *Camera Obscura*, *GLQ*, *Film and History*, and *Projections*, as well as the anthology *Horror Film: Creating and Marketing Fear*, and the textbook *The World Is a Text*. Her current research focuses on the intersections between surveillance practices and narrative formations in cinema.

Index